PROVOKING THE PRESS

Provoking the Press

[MORE] Magazine and the
Crisis of Confidence in American Journalism

Kevin M. Lerner

UNIVERSITY OF MISSOURI PRESS
Columbia

The volumes of this series are published through the generous support of the University of Missouri School of Journalism.

Copyright © 2019 by
The Curators of the University of Missouri
University of Missouri Press, Columbia, Missouri 65211
Printed and bound in the United States of America
All rights reserved. First paperback printing, 2023.

Library of Congress Cataloging-in-Publication Data

Names: Lerner, Kevin M., 1977- author.
Title: Provoking the press : (MORE) magazine and the crisis of confidence in American journalism / by Kevin M. Lerner.
Description: Columbia : University of Missouri Press, [2019] | Series: Journalism in perspective : continuities and disruptions | Revised and expanded version of the author's thesis (doctoral)--Rutgers University, 2014, titled Gadfly to the watchdogs : how the journalism review (MORE) goaded the mainstream press toward self-criticism in the 1970s. | Includes bibliographical references and index. |
Identifiers: LCCN 2018056786 (print) | LCCN 2019005560 (ebook) | ISBN 9780826274281 (e-book) | ISBN 9780826221865 (hardcover : alk. paper) | ISBN 9780826222886 (paperback : alk. paper)
Subjects: LCSH: More (N.Y.) | American periodicals--New York (State)--New York--History. | Journalism--Periodicals--History. | Press--United States--History--20th century.
Classification: LCC PN4900.M67 (ebook) | LCC PN4900.M67 L47 2019 (print) | DDC 051--dc23
LC record available at https://lccn.loc.gov/2018056786

∞™ This paper meets the requirements of the American National Standard for Permanence of Paper for Printed Library Materials, Z39.48, 1984.

Typefaces: Goudy and New Caledonia

Journalism in Perspective: Continuities and Disruptions

Tim P. Vos and Yong Z. Volz, Series Editors

❖

Journalism is a central institution in the social, cultural, and political life of communities, nations, and the world. Citizens and leaders rely on the news, information, and analysis that journalists produce, curate, and distribute each day. Their work must be understood in the context of journalism's institutional features, including its roles, ethics, operations, and boundaries. These features are themselves the product of a history emerging through periods of stability and change. The volumes in this series span the history of journalism, and advance thoughtful and theoretically-driven arguments for how journalism can best negotiate the currents of change.

Contents

Contents

Acknowledgments

This book would not have been possible without the contributions of a number of people who have helped and supported me along the way. *Provoking the Press* began its life as a dissertation in the Rutgers University School of Communication and Information, and grew out of my thinking about journalism as an intellectual practice. My dissertation adviser, David Greenberg, helped me to carve a manageable chunk out of my original proposal and has served since then as a model, mentor, editor, sounding board, and—perhaps most importantly—as a perpetual online Scrabble opponent. He lets me win about a third of the time, and I appreciate him for that almost as much as for the help he has given me in the very long project of writing this book.

Susan Keith, also at Rutgers, has been a constant friend and academic mentor as well. Her work on the journalism review movement guided my early thinking about *(MORE)*, and if I'm remembering correctly, she was actually the person who turned me on to the idea of using (MORE) as a way of looking at the role of press criticism in managing the performance of the professional press. She's also a terrific pub quiz partner.

Linda Steiner was my first adviser at Rutgers before she moved away to the University of Maryland, and I consider myself lucky that she agreed to stay on my dissertation committee even after she moved on. I considered myself lucky to be able to work with her in the first place. Thank you also to T. J. Jackson Lears, who added to David's historical perspective, and was also a perceptive and thorough editor of the earliest versions of this book.

Victor Navasky, who was a teacher and mentor of mine at the Columbia University Graduate School of Journalism, connected me to Richard Pollak, *(MORE)*'s first editor, and consistently reminded me of the importance of this book and of *(MORE)* generally. Michael Shapiro, also at Columbia Journalism, also helped me to develop ideas that are reflected in this book.

Acknowledgments

Richard Pollak opened his home to me on several occasions to sit for extended interviews about *(MORE)*. He was also gracious to trust me with his personal bound volumes of *(MORE)*, which were my primary source for reading those issues. He also opened his phone book for me, and connected me with many of the other people who were interviewed for this book. I thank all of them for their time and for sharing their memories with me. Special thanks to Martin Norman, who also trusted me with original artwork for the cartoons he drew for *(MORE)*, including the iconic "Hello, Sweetheart!" poster, which decorated the newsroom set of the *Lou Grant* show, and which is reproduced in this book.

Thank you to Kyle Pope, the editor and publisher of the *Columbia Journalism Review*, who worked with me, Richard Pollak, and *Politico*'s press critic, Jack Shafer on a project that looked into the viability of reviving *(MORE)*'s A. J. Liebling Counter-Conventions. While that has not yet come to fruition, I thank Kyle for recognizing *(MORE)*'s resonance today and for publishing my essay about it in CJR. Thank you also to the editors of *Journalism History* and *American Journalism*, each of which published different versions of shorter pieces of this book.

Many of the documents that told the history of *(MORE)* are archived at the New York Public Library, particularly in the Manuscripts and Archives Division. Historians depend on archivists, and there are none finer, more helpful, or friendlier than those at NYPL. Thanks also to the Dorot Jewish Division, which holds an oral history interview of J. Anthony Lukas. The archivists at Pacifica Radio were also amazing, helping me to track down audio recordings of the counter-conventions.

Tim Vos approached me at a convention several years ago and invited me to submit the manuscript that would become this book to a new series he was editing at the University of Missouri Press. Tim is a journalism scholar of the first rank, and his suggestions on successive versions of this manuscript have helped me to refine my arguments and to explain why *(MORE)* should be important to a broader swath of scholars and journalists than I was able to see on my own. His questions and comments were incisive and spot-on.

Gary Kass has been everything I could have asked for in an editor. He came into this project with the kind of cosmopolitanism that has allowed him both to understand how I intended this book to be read and how readers would perceive it. He has been a strong advocate for me too. Thank you to him and to the rest of the staff of the University of Missouri Press for guiding this book toward publication. Thank you also to the two anonymous reviewers who provided thorough and extremely helpful feedback.

Marist College has given me a wonderful home base for my scholarship, as well as both time and financial support to complete the research and writing of this book. Thank you to my faculty colleagues and the administration for all of their help.

My husband, Simon Zhang, has been living with *(MORE)* as long as I have known him, so I thank him for his patience with me and encouragement as I have worked on it. Day in and day out, he is the reason I have been able to finish this book.

My dad has the skepticism and inquisitiveness of a journalist, and he has always been one of the people I keep in my mind when I envision an ideal reader. And I watched my mom write her own dissertation and begin her academic career when I was in junior high school. She has always inspired me to pursue my scholarship. This book is dedicated to my parents.

PROVOKING THE PRESS

Introduction

The journalism review *(MORE)* was founded in 1971 in the midst of a time of turmoil and self-examination for American journalism. It was a period that has many echoes in contemporary American journalism: a presidential administration openly hostile to the press; a divisive public discourse; and a press that found its established best practices unable to adequately cover new social realities in the country. It was a decade in which many of the most elite practitioners of journalism openly questioned the tenets of objectivity that they had been told—by editors, instructors, older colleagues—were the gold standard of journalistic practice. It was the apotheosis of the age of mass media, with big-city newspapers establishing a sort of mainstream hegemony in dominating their local markets, and only a few national news networks telling Americans that "that's the way it is." Walter Cronkite was never really "the most trusted man in America,"[1] but there is still truth behind that assertion in the way that his brand of detached, seemingly balanced, seemingly unbiased journalism held sway. Of course, this portrait of a monolithic, entirely mainstream media is far from complete. The flashy "New Journalists," as Tom Wolfe—one of their own—called them, were experimenting with radical forms of subjectivity in their journalism. Independent journalists such as I. F. Stone eschewed the traditional clubby forms of access journalism to mine government reports that would otherwise have been overlooked, prying out embarrassing secrets that had been buried deep in their most boring pages. And a long tradition of alternative sources of news—the black press, the socialist press, a rising underground press, works of satire and essays—also circled the mainstream of American journalism, providing outlets for ideas that would be seen as too radical for the papers or the network news or for *Time* or *Newsweek* or *Look* or *Life* or any other of the mass-circulation, general-interest magazines.

But despite this ecosystem of alternatives, it was exactly those papers and television programs and magazines that dominated American media in 1971. And despite attempts by conservative politicians to delegitimize reporting by branding it as "liberal," the mainstream press at the end of the 1960s was actually quite conservative—particularly in the sense that they were unwilling to take major risks. When Abraham M. Rosenthal, managing editor of the *New York Times*, made the decision to publish the Pentagon Papers, he underwent something of a personal existential crisis, worried that he had just persuaded the paper's publisher to print the documents that would lead to the downfall of both the *Times* and, perhaps, the United States itself.[2] The newsrooms of these conservative, mainstream publications, however, were staffed by a new kind of journalist: educated at elite universities, young enough to be a part of, or at least to identify with, the counterculture that had been roiling the country for several years. These were the journalists who founded *(MORE)*.

(MORE) was never a part of the counterculture. But it was certainly anti-institutional, or at least counterinstitutional, set against the bland, staid, small-*c* conservative press that was reaching the mainstream, but which the founders and staff of *(MORE)* never intended to tear down. This book tells the story of *(MORE)* and in doing so, it examines the way that an organ of press criticism shapes the institutions that in turn shape public discourse. The book also tells a history of American journalism in the 1970s through the eyes of one of its keenest observers.

(MORE): A Journalism Review was published in New York from 1971 to 1978. The Pulitzer Prize–winning *New York Times* reporter J. Anthony Lukas came up with the idea for the journal in 1970, when he was covering the Chicago Seven conspiracy trial. There, he met the editors of the *Chicago Journalism Review* and simultaneously began to realize that the "objective" journalism that the *Times* made him produce was insufficient to cover a world that had been roiled by racial conflict, gender disparities, and the generation gap. He enlisted his friend, former *Newsweek* media editor Richard Pollak, to edit the review. An independently wealthy young reporter for the liberal *New York Post* came on board as publisher.

Together with writers and conference panelists including David Halberstam, Mike Wallace, Brit Hume, Tom Wolfe, Gay Talese, Christopher Hitchens, Calvin Trillin, Nora Ephron, Alexander Cockburn, Charlotte Curtis, and dozens of others, these three founders and the two owners who followed them published press criticism that took on issues of media ownership, government censorship, journalism's complicity with institutions of power, and even the bland handsomeness of local news anchors. They covered journalism in the decade in which The Press became The Media;

hosted a series of raucous "counter-conventions"; and chronicled Watergate, the Pentagon Papers, the WBAI obscenity trial, and the rise of NPR, PBS, Geraldo Rivera, and Rupert Murdoch. *(MORE)* showed the power of press criticism to shape the behavior of news organizations, and at the same time witnessed the coalescence of a group made up of a new kind of elite journalist. These journalists felt that the kinds of institutional media available to them were insufficient to describe the world as it had evolved throughout the 1960s. A new culture deserved a new kind of journalism, and not just the New Journalism, but one that was rooted in principles of investigation and public service. Like the New Journalism, though, this new kind of reporting would be free of the constraints that institutional objectivity demands. At the same time, *(MORE)* allowed these elite journalists to network with each other in unprecedented ways, effectively shaping reporting practices for the decades that would follow.

As press criticism, *(MORE)*'s effects were slow, but real. The gadfly goaded the mainstream press into a new kind of self-awareness (call it a consciousness-raising, in the spirit of the '70s), but some of its legacy is more intangible. In a way, *(MORE)* allowed a certain class of journalists to find each other for the first time. What conservatives would today attack as the liberal elite media coalesced for the first time around the magazine and the series of conventions it ran. In a pre-social media era, it allowed the intellectuals of journalism to meet, to discuss ideas, and to transcend the dogged but plodding reporting that earned the *New York Times* the nickname the Gray Lady. *(MORE)* was also there to chronicle one of the most eventful and transformative decades in American journalism. We entered the '70s with The Press. A decade later, news organizations had become far more nationalized and corporate. The Press had become The Media, and the most radical of *(MORE)*'s ideas had been polished into something more acceptable to corporate media and were co-opted by it. *(MORE)* underwent similar changes during this period. What had started as a contentious, probing, and funny anti-institutional publication on newsprint was eventually sold to a former *New York* magazine editor who turned it into a glossy "media magazine." That editor, Michael Kramer, was never able to find the general audience he thought existed, and the magazine struggled through one more period of ownership before ceasing publication. Because of the easy profitability of news in the 1980s that followed, the ideal of objectivity never got overthrown as the dominant model, which means that today, the crisis of objectivity has come to the fore again.

Provoking the Press tells the story of *(MORE)* and of the changes in American journalism in the 1970s through the use of the journal itself; archival documents from *(MORE)* and the publications it covered; and oral history interviews with surviving staff members and participants in the A. J. Liebling Counter-Conventions.

The book follows four main arguments:

- *(MORE)* chronicled a revolt among self-critical reporters against the restraints of institutional requirements of "objectivity" in the American press, a revolt that eventually died down, with some of its ideas being co-opted into the mainstream press, but without ever achieving its goal of dislodging objectivity as the primary mode of American journalism.
- *(MORE)* demonstrates the importance of press criticism in shaping the norms of American journalism.
- *(MORE)* represents the coalescence of the elite liberal media, a class of journalists that had been forming for some time, but that found its voice in opposition to the institutional conservatism of their employers and in the face of critics such as Vice President Spiro Agnew.
- Finally, in its transition from a scrappy newsprint journalism review to a glossy "media magazine," *(MORE)* parallels changes in American journalism between the 1960s and the 1980s, helping to explain how "The Press" became "The Media."

Chapter 1 puts *(MORE)* in the context of the history of press criticism. While there have always been people who were inclined to *attack* the press, very few engaged in actual critical analysis of it. *(MORE)* emerged at a time when calls for public accountability in the mainstream press were reaching un-ignorable levels, and the cultural ferment of the late 1960s and early 1970s provided an opening for the kind of regularly published journalism criticism that *(MORE)* would provide. The magazine's eventual failure says something about the long-term viability of an organ dedicated to analyzing the workings of American journalism, but parallels with the late 2010s suggest that changes in distribution and funding models might support a *(MORE)*-like magazine again.

Chapter 2 tells the story of how Tony Lukas, a Pulitzer Prize–winning *New York Times* reporter, began to feel the limitations of working in the newsroom of even an elite daily newspaper, and how he was inspired by the founders of the *Chicago Journalism Review* and his own experiences dealing with *Times* editors while reporting on the Chicago Seven conspiracy trial to start a journalism review for New York, but with national ambitions, in June 1971. The early days of the magazine provide insight into the crisis of objectivity that inspired many of the staff members and contributors to *(MORE)* to begin to think reflexively about their own journalistic practices and those of their colleagues. This chapter asserts that despite the role of journalists as critics of public discourse, they are actually, on the whole, anti-intellectual when it comes to examining themselves and their work.

Chapter 3 takes on the first era of *(MORE)*'s regular publication. With the addition of its first full-time staff members besides editor Dick Pollak, the fledgling journalism review began to negotiate its role as a gadfly that could challenge the institutional press to do its best work. An examination of the first year or so of *(MORE)* reveals the themes that animated its journalists in the early to mid 1970s: distrust of government, corporations, and advertising; advocacy for interest groups, including women and minorities; new publications and experiments with the forms of journalism; obscenity and censorship; press ethics and accountability; and more generally, the experience of being a journalist at the end of what historians refer to as "the Long Sixties."

In chapter 4, the book relates the story of the first A. J. Liebling Counter-Convention, scheduled, in its first year, counter to the American Newspaper Publishers Association meeting in New York City in 1972. Organized by Tony Lukas and then-journalist Nora Ephron, the gathering grew into a happening, drawing thousands of frustrated journalists, both those at the highest levels of achievement and those doing the grunt work of their newsrooms. It was the first time that a convention of this sort was held and it helped to solidify some of the networks of journalists who had come to be maligned as "the liberal media."

Chapter 5 examines the changing self-regard of journalists as the implications of the Watergate scandal were becoming clear. Using the second Liebling convention as a guide, this chapter follows *(MORE)* into its adulthood and the period of its greatest influence, as the publication wrestled with how to interact with the mainstream press, now that the press had started to adopt some of the anti-institutional stances that *(MORE)* itself had long advocated.

Chapter 6 breaks from the strict chronological narrative of the preceding chapters to look at two case studies of how *(MORE)* interacted with and influenced its main subject of criticism, the *New York Times*. The first of these tests the assertion by *(MORE)*'s founding editor, Dick Pollak, that the magazine's most tangible accomplishment was to persuade the *Times* to begin running a daily corrections department. Pollak's contention turns out to be plausible but more complicated and nuanced than the idea that *(MORE)* suggested it and the *Times* took them up on that suggestion. The second case study follows a Harvard Business School researcher and consultant named Chris Argyris, who wrote a study of management dysfunction at the *Times*.[3] Argyris attempted to protect the identity of the editors and other employees he interviewed, and even the identity of the newspaper itself. However, *(MORE)* decoded Argyris's pseudonyms and published a story with their real names, thus turning Argyris into a sort of accidental press critic himself. In examining this relationship, this case study illuminates the role of the critic in maintaining or altering the operations of the institutional press that he criticizes.

Chapter 7 describes *(MORE)* after the team that founded it sold it to a new owner in 1976. Michael Kramer, a former staff member at the hip, sleek regional magazine and proponent of New Journalism *New York*, bought *(MORE)*, renamed it *More: The Media Magazine*, dropping the "journalism review" and the parentheses, and broadened the magazine's focus to media industries beyond the press, including film, television, and advertising. In his attempt to make *More* into an inclusive general-interest magazine about the media, Kramer mirrored a trend in American society more broadly—the co-opting of the news media into a larger, more amorphous idea of what media is. Accordingly, *More* became a slick, glossy, perfect-bound magazine, where it used to be a tabloid printed on cheap newsprint.

Finally, chapter 8 explores the last days of *More*, as well as its legacy. Kramer sold the magazine one more time, to James B. Adler, the owner of the Congressional News Service. Adler hired a young editor named Robert Friedman to run the magazine, and with Kramer's exit, some of the founders of *(MORE)* returned to consult, or even to take editorial jobs on the masthead. But Adler became ill and found the magazine difficult to run from Washington, DC, and he turned over the magazine and its subscription list to its staid rival, the *Columbia Journalism Review*.

Four decades after its run ended, *(MORE)* has regained relevance in the atmosphere of criticism surrounding the press. Founding editor Dick Pollak has said that *(MORE)* died because it was no longer necessary, that the press had started to do the things that *(MORE)* wanted it to do. And while that may be true to some extent, the press may need reminding of some of those ideas again. Really, though, as a journalism review with no secure advertising base and a group of dedicated subscribers who still could not subsidize an entire magazine, *(MORE)* was more likely just exhausting and forbiddingly expensive to run. Today's lower barriers to entry for press critics have set the scene for a golden age of criticism that the paper-and-ink *(MORE)* could never have dreamed of.

Note: *(MORE)* placed its name in stylized parentheses on the front cover of the magazine during the first period of its ownership. After being sold in 1976, the magazine underwent a redesign, and the name was restyled as *More*. This book follows those conventions. When quoting printed texts, it follows the typographical choices made by each publication, leaving them unchanged from the original.

1. A Culture of Criticism

The Limitations of the American Newsroom and the Societal Role of Press Criticism

In 1974, media scholar James W. Carey published an essay in the academic journal *The Review of Politics*, in which he lamented the state of American press criticism heading in the last quarter of the twentieth century. Carey, who was then a professor at the University of Illinois, found himself perplexed by what he saw as a glaring absence in the public discourse of the time: the lack of what he called a "tradition of sustained, systematic, and intellectually sound criticism of the press."[1] In his opening paragraph, Carey notes that the press, despite being an institution that affects the lives of everyone in a representative democracy, received less critical scrutiny than baseball and only slightly more than soccer. Carey set out "to demonstrate that a tradition of press criticism does not exist in the United States, that a critical tradition is indispensable to the operation of democratic institutions, and that journalism criticism, properly conceived, is the criticism of language."[2]

While there had been sporadic instances of press criticism before the 1970s, Carey was right that no consistent critical discourse about the press—one that regularly attempted to interact with a critical public and bring change to the norms of journalism from the outside—had taken hold. And it is not a coincidence that Carey wrote when he did. The structural, cultural, and institutional factors that could support a culture of press criticism were falling into place from the 1960s up through the time of Carey's writing. What Carey, writing in the midst of cultural and structural changes in both the United States and its organized press, may not have seen while being immersed in that cultural ferment was that 1974 actually represented the last great moment for American press criticism and a chance for the kind of critical culture he advocated in his essay to take hold. All of the conditions for a critical culture were present, except for a sustainable business model to support it and the technology to distribute this kind of press criticism to a broad, general audience. This was something of a golden age for press criticism, one that was born of a crisis of confidence in American journalism, and a moment for press criticism that would not be equaled until another major crisis of confidence in the mid–2010s. The prime embodiment of this moment in American journalism criticism was a monthly journalism review called *(MORE)*, which Carey does not name in his essay but which he alludes to as one of "the new reviews that have sprung up in many cities."[3] *(MORE)* made the best attempt to bring regular critical examination of the mainstream news media to a general audience. Carey also names the *Columbia Journalism Review* and the "coteries of professionals and students that queue up before the *Chicago Journalism Review*."[4] The two *CJR*s—Columbia and Chicago—were important influences on *(MORE)*, one as a foil, one as an inspiration, as will be described in chapter 2.

    (MORE) did something different from the press criticism that came before it. For one thing, it attempted to reach as broad an audience as possible, not limiting itself to being a professional journal read only by working journalists or newsroom managers, but attempting to speak to the interested public who might have an interest in the performance of the press in its various roles as watchdog, gatekeeper, or just as a chronicle of turbulent times. For its entire run, from 1971 to 1978, *(MORE)* had a moderate circulation, never getting above about twenty thousand readers, and never reaching too far beyond the world of working journalists in the United States and Canada, but within that world, it had an outsize influence. One other difference between *(MORE)* and the press criticism that preceded it was that it took a very different worldview from publications such as the *Columbia Journalism Review*, which generally maintained institutional and professional norms supported by the managers and editors of the papers. Rather than *maintaining* norms, *(MORE)* sought to question them, and in many cases, overturn them. The vast bulk of press criticism prior to 1971 worked toward establishing the objective voice in American journalism, which had been developing on a haphazard path since the time of the penny press.[5] While *(MORE)* did not reject objectivity outright as one of many valid norms for the practice of journalism, its editors and writers saw the institutionalized voice of objectivity and detachment as too limiting a way for journalism to describe the world, and they sought a broader understanding of what American journalism could and should be doing to accurately reflect the culture and to serve the public.

Carey had something larger in mind though, imagining that a large, omnibus newspaper such as the *New York Times* would endeavor to print criticism of the press that followed the template of all of the other institutions of American culture that the paper regularly subjected to analysis: "In its pages," he wrote, "particularly the Sunday edition, one finds information, analysis, criticism of every contemporary institution. It treats art, architecture, literature, education, politics, business, religion finance, film, and so forth." This work, Carey argues, attempts to describe and ascribe meaning to human existence. But the *Times* did not, as of his writing in 1974, devote much space at all to criticism of the press. Carey compares the body of critical writing on Plato to that of Homer Bigart (a *Times* reporter whom he employs as an archetype), and finds it remarkable that "most of us" read far more words written by semi-anonymous reporters such as Bigart than we do of Plato, but that volumes of critical analysis of Plato continue to be published two and a half millennia after his death while nothing at all had been published on the work of Bigart. "It is an anomalous fact," Carey wrote, "that all of us consume more words by journalists than any other group and yet our largest and most important literary diet is never given close critical scrutiny in any systematic way."[6]

As it happens, the first issue of *(MORE)*, which had been published in the summer of 1971, three years before Carey's writing, included a piece on Homer Bigart and how his "interpretive reporting" had been turned into a bland objective statement by the editors of the *New York Times*.[7] In it, the staff of *(MORE)* juxtaposed Bigart's submitted draft of an article with the published, institutional, "objective" version. It is exactly the sort of "criticism of language" that Carey called for.[8] The only problem was that *(MORE)* just wasn't able to reach a general audience—though as the following chapters will demonstrate, *(MORE)* did reach an audience of elite journalists who would filter through the world of American journalism, bringing many of *(MORE)*'s ideas with them into the mainstream press.

That *(MORE)* eventually failed tells us about the financially and intellectually draining demands of running a small publication that has no clearly defined audience for advertisers. *(MORE)*'s failure also says something about the limits of public interest in press criticism and about the anti-intellectualism and general bullheadedness of the press, which despite the prodding of *(MORE)* and its successors, remains a singularly intractable collection of institutions.

Many of the cultural divides that roiled the late 1960s and early 1970s are coming to the surface again, and so too is the opportunity to establish Carey's critical tradition. This chapter traces American press criticism from its earliest days to the moment that *(MORE)* entered the conversation, and describes the cultural conditions that allowed it to take root and flourish, intellectually if not financially, for seven raucous and consequential years.

The Proto-History of Press Criticism
and Attempts at Definition

The American press has never lacked for attackers, though as Carey notes, "attack is not criticism."[9] Halfway through his second term, Thomas Jefferson received a letter from an eighteen-year-old man named John Norvell (who would go on to be a newspaper editor and one of the first United States senators from Michigan). Norvell wanted to know what Jefferson thought of newspapers. "It is a melancholy truth, that a suppression of the press could not more compleatly deprive the nation of it's benefits, than is done by it's abandoned prostitution to falsehood," Jefferson wrote in his reply.

> Nothing can now be believed which is seen in a newspaper. Truth itself becomes suspicious by being put into that polluted vehicle. The real extent of this state of misinformation is known only to those who are in situations to confront facts within their knolege with the lies of the day. I really look with commiseration over the great body of my fellow citizens, who, reading newspapers, live & die in the belief, that they have known something of what has been passing in the world in their time; whereas the accounts they have read in newspapers are just as true a history of any other period of the world as of the present, except that the real names of the day are affixed to their fables.[10]

Jefferson's assessment reads like the exasperated lament of a man who had been attacked ruthlessly by a press whose attacks his predecessor, John Adams, had silenced by signing a law making criticism of the president and Congress a crime punishable by fines and prison time. Likely contributing to Jefferson's frustration, the Sedition Act of 1798 explicitly omitted criticism of the *vice* president (Jefferson, at the time), and the acts were set to expire on the day that Adams would step down as president, since it was widely assumed that Jefferson, his political rival, would succeed him.[11]

There are resonances in Jefferson's frustration more than two centuries later, as President Donald Trump attacks the press on social media with

14

regularity. There are, of course, vast differences. Jefferson predicated his criticisms on his own prodigious reading, and many of his complaints were justified. Early nineteenth-century newspapers did not have a commitment to truth or the sort of objectivity that would emerge as the norm for American journalism by the early twentieth century, and many of the attacks on Jefferson were scurrilous lies. But newspapers also exposed the fact that Jefferson was having an affair with Sally Hemings, one of his slaves—and Jefferson denied this inconvenient truth as fake news, centuries before the current attacks on the credibility of the press flared up.

But while Jeffersonian-style *attacks* on the press have been a regular feature of discourse about the press since the earliest days of the American republic, James Carey–style press criticism, "an active and continuous response in terms of factual detail, unemotional language and articulate values" has largely been absent. One of the earliest works of press criticism was Lambert A. Wilmer's 1859 book *Our Press Gang, or a Complete Exposition of the Corruptions and Crimes of the American Newspapers*.[12] Wilmer had been an editor at a variety of American newspapers before undertaking his volume of criticism, which teeters back and forth between *attack* and what Wilmer argues to be constructive criticism of the institution of American newspapers. As the book's subtitle suggests, it was mostly an exposé of blatantly biased, semi-fictional "news" that the American press had been publishing. Writing about a quarter century after the advent of the first mass-market newspapers in the United States—the penny press, as it is usually called—Wilmer actually seems justified in most of his critiques, if we apply the norms of twentieth-century journalism. In that sense, Wilmer may have been ahead of his time as a critic. He also echoes Jefferson's lament that readers of newspapers are hardly well informed about the truly important affairs of the day. "In a country where the newspapers are the principal sources of information," he writes, "it is almost impossible to obtain a strictly-correct account of any thing . . ."[13] A close reading of Wilmer also suggests, however, that there was already a defense for newspapers— that in a market system, newspapers are only giving the public what they demand. Wilmer saw something more pernicious, though:

> I have endeavored to expose the sophistical pretense, that "newspapers are not accountable for their own misconduct, because they are obliged to mould themselves to suit the requirements of the public." I deny that the press of the United States is what the public demands. Instead of adapting themselves

to the tastes and requirements of the people, our newspapers endeavor to innoculate the public with their own morbid humors and purulent morality.[14]

But the important point here is that Wilmer's book, while it might have been one of the earliest surviving examples of published press criticism, was already responding to an ongoing conversation about the press, even if he only puts that conversation into the mouth of a straw man. But even if this conversation was happening, the fact that *Our Press Gang* stands out demonstrates the rarity of *published* works of press criticism and the complete lack of regularly published press criticism. Marion Tuttle Marzolf, in her survey of press criticism between 1880 and the middle of the twentieth century, found much the same thing to be true.[15] In order to trace the critical conversation about journalism, Marzolf had to scour popular magazines, professional publications, and scholarly journals—but no regularly published press criticism. Even the *New Yorker* press critic A. J. Liebling, who began his Wayward Press column toward the end of the period Marzolf studied, published only occasionally (as Jack Shafer also noted). Still, Marzolf found that this nascent discourse about journalistic standards had a civilizing effect on a press that would otherwise have given itself over entirely to the rapacious influences of technology and commerce. "Without the critics—inside and outside the press—the impersonal market forces would have had complete control," Marzolf writes.[16] If indeed Wilmer's *Our Press Gang* was the first published work of press criticism in the United States, the writers who form the basis of Marzolf's study continue the conversation it started about separating the liberal democratic responsibility of a free press from the free market imperatives of a commercial press. That's not to say that the former was always in the interest of the entire society. The main sources of press criticism from 1880 to 1950 were members of the elite classes, and that led to an elitist vision of the press ideal.[17] One other important aspect of Marzolf's survey is her tracing of the first mentions of objectivity as an ideal in American journalism, which she pegs to the 1930s.[18] While that ideal had been developing since the middle of the nineteenth century, it is important to know that it only became an agreed-upon ideal about four decades before the press critics at *(MORE)* would begin to critique its limitations.

Hazel Dicken-Garcia and Yasmine Tarek Dabbous are the only other historians of the press who give much thought to press criticism before World War I.[19] Adding some credence to the claim that pre–twentieth-century press criticism has been sporadic and inconsequential, Tom Goldstein does not even acknowledge that there *was* press criticism before the turn of the century, or even before 1911, when Will Irwin published his series "The American Newspaper: A Study of Journalism in Its Relation to the Public" in *Collier's* magazine. The subtitle of Goldstein's anthology, *Killing the Messenger: 100 Years of Media Criticism*, also hints at his temporal limitation, and this from a writer who claims to "interpret criticism broadly."[20] Goldstein does include the reports of the Robert Maynard Hutchins–led Commission on the Freedom of the Press, speeches criticizing the press by then-vice president Spiro Agnew, and an essay by Joseph Pulitzer arguing for the importance of journalism as a great intellectual profession. But even this broad definition of press criticism, one that encompasses much discourse about the practice of journalism and its role in a liberal democracy, fails to pick up the elements of that discourse that began as journalism began to professionalize in the second half of the nineteenth century.[21] That broad interpretation, taken beyond Goldstein's century of press criticism, would have picked up a discourse about journalism that was largely internal to the profession and to the task of professionalization and the establishment of the profession's norms. Much of this discourse was internal to the profession, appearing in trade journals or textbooks. And when articles about the press did appear in the popular press, they were more interested in explaining what they portrayed as an esoteric, special knowledge that only journalists could truly understand and that was inaccessible to the layperson.[22] While the establishment of specialized knowledge is an important step in creating a profession, it is not the same as press criticism, intended to reform the practice, since criticism engages both the public as interested consumers of journalism and the press as the subject. However, even if we accept a broad-enough definition of press criticism to encompass this professional discourse, it still echoes most pre-(*MORE*) press criticism in the fact that it is working toward the establishment of objectivity as the overriding norm of the professional American press.

For the purposes of studying (*MORE*) as press criticism, something closer to Carey's definition is more useful, one that gets at the nature of the negotiation between an engaged and activist public and the press itself. Wendy Wyatt, in her book on the theory of press criticism, defines it as "the ongoing process of exchange and debate among members of the press and between the press and its audience over the role and performance of the press in a democratic society."[23] Wyatt's definition, which she expands upon in an entry in an encyclopedia of journalism studies, rightly limits the field under consideration to the organized news media and also rightly excludes mere journalistic reporting on media; it emphasizes the interplay between working journalists and the public; and it underscores the importance of criticism as an accountability system, one that is able to affect the practice of journalism without doing so through strict mechanisms of control.[24] In societies that do not have protections for freedom of the press, these controls might manifest themselves in law rather than in the shaping of norms that comes through critical discourse. As such, press criticism should play an even larger role in the United States than in societies without press protections, ensuring that the press serves the public without resorting to stricter, blunter forms of control. The interested public can express its needs through press criticism, and a responsive press should be able to respond to those needs. And while Wyatt's definition focuses on the role that criticism can play in modifying the behavior of the press, it is important to emphasize that criticism also helps to demystify the process of journalism for the public, in what should be a reversal and repudiation of the professional mystification that nineteenth-century journalists engaged in when they wrote that laypeople would never understand the innate sense of what makes a story newsworthy. Journalistic criticism should explain the processes of journalism to the public, never taking for granted that the public understands how the sausage of news gets made.

Press Criticism in the Twentieth Century

Most histories of press criticism do include Will Irwin's studies of the American newspaper, regardless of whether they begin with him. Irwin's series became canonical, eventually even being reprinted in book form. That it was published in *Collier's*, a popular general-interest magazine, was key. But it also railed against the influence of commercialism and the need to attract readers and advertisers, and did so with enough vitriol that a selection from it would be included almost a century later in an anthology of "radical" press criticism.[25] The fifteen-part series (announced as fourteen, but extended with a muckraking-style piece that Irwin's editors requested) tackled journalism history, yellow journalism, the role of the editor/publisher and the reporter in defining the news, the influence of advertising, and the hope that a new generation of well-trained reporters would take over and improve the lot of the industry.[26]

Upton Sinclair, associated with the muckrakers and known to history for *The Jungle*, his novel of the Chicago meatpacking industry, also warranted inclusion in the radical anthology, not least because his self-published 1919 book of press criticism, *The Brass Check*, explicitly compared newspapers to prostitutes working for the wealthy elites whose interests they supported in print. Sinclair was a socialist, so this view is understandable. But Robert W. McChesney and Ben Scott argue that *The Brass Check* actually appeared in something of a golden age of press criticism, when hundreds of examples appeared in mainstream magazines (Irwin's *Collier's* pieces included). They argue that Sinclair's work and that of other radical critics has been ignored by the mainstream precisely because it was radical.[27] *(MORE)* would be acutely aware of the balancing act of trying to push against the mainstream and encourage change without ever completely alienating the institutions from which it came, for risk of having no influence at all.

In the 1920s and 1930s, a handful of other writers also published books about journalism. The columnist and critic Walter Lippmann published three books on the interactions among the press, the public, and a representative democratic government.[28] Lippmann's thinking about the press and ideas of the public sphere grew in part out of his involvement with Woodrow Wilson's World War I propaganda initiative, the Committee on Public Information, from which Lippmann took the idea that the public could be easily manipulated.[29] His ideas found one of their first outlets in a forty-two-page supplement to the *New Republic*, the journal of politics that Lippmann had helped to found. A work of criticism itself, *A Test of the News*, which he co-wrote with Charles Merz, applied the two men's standards for the press to the *New York Times*'s coverage of the Russian Revolution, which they found to be significantly lacking, particularly in the way that "the time honored tradition of protecting news against editorials breaks down. The Russian policy of the editors of the *Times* profoundly and crassly influenced their news columns."[30] Lippmann and Merz conclude their study saying that "newspapers must be prepared for an increasing supervision from the readers of the press."[31] However, they saw this supervision being filtered through press councils and other organizations that would maintain press standards, not through a robust culture of journalism criticism.

The most famous and influential of Lippmann's three books on the press and the public, *Public Opinion*, introduced the idea that people form their ideas based on sketches of the real world, which they receive largely through media. And for Lippmann, news did not necessarily equal truth. Lippmann also argued that the "manufacture of consent" was important for a representative democracy in which not all citizens directly participate in governance.[32] In the 1930s, George Seldes followed in the tradition of Irwin, Sinclair, and Lippmann with two books of his own.[33] In the case of Irwin and Sinclair, he did so by railing against the influence of powerful political and corporate influences on the news. And he "agreed with Lippmann that the press needed better trained newsmen—professionals who adhered to an enforceable code."[34] Like Sinclair, he was seen as a crank by the newspaper industry, and many publishers refused advertising for his books or fired reviewers who gave them positive notice. But still, the books sold surprisingly well, and Seldes influenced a later generation of critics.[35] One of those critics was A. J. Liebling, perhaps the single most famous press critic in U.S. history and a direct inspiration to the editors of (MORE), who would name their series of conventions and an associated award in his honor.

Liebling wrote eighty-three columns about the press for the New Yorker, eighty-two of them under the heading "The Wayward Press." Though he made it very much his own, Liebling didn't originate the column. Former newspaper reporter Morris Markey began it,[36] and humorist Robert Benchley had the most sustained tenure before Liebling, at seventy-four columns. It passed through several other hands too (some pseudonymous) before it finally got to Liebling.[37] Nevertheless, Liebling so took command of the form and published so regularly that he effectively established himself as the archetype of the press critic. Jack Shafer, a press critic himself, later wrote that Liebling had earned a reputation as the "patron saint of press criticism," and while Shafer suspects that this reputation is one of word of mouth rather than of the printed word, his own revisiting of Liebling's works more or less bears out that reputation.[38] Publishers were a favorite target of Liebling (as they were to some of his predecessors) and he famously wrote the axiom, "Freedom of the press is guaranteed only to those who own one."[39] Liebling would become an avatar of press criticism for the writers and editors of (MORE) largely for these reasons, and also because of his humor and sparkling prose, both of which were qualities that the magazine would echo.

The years following Liebling's death in in 1963 and immediately preceding the launch of (MORE) in 1971 saw a new focus on journalism ethics and accountability. In a 1968 book that was part of an "Open Letter" series,

John Tebbel opened his "letter" to newspaper readers in this way: "You are, I assume, a critic of newspapers."[40] His assumption, of course, was based on the idea that every reader is a critic. He goes on to write that the press has many sorts of critics, including disdainful intellectuals and reactionary ideologues. But he admits that he too had been a critic of the press.

But in 1968, Tebbel had likely not seen much press criticism in the same sense as, say, film criticism. For him, and for most observers of the press in 1968, "press criticism" would likely have been synonymous with "criticism of the press," rather than an organized activity or even a profession. There had been some—the *Columbia Journalism Review* had published for five years by then, and A. J. Liebling had only recently concluded his influential Wayward Press column.

In the late 1960s, Tebbel was in the vanguard of this newer sort of press criticism, the kind that sought not just to criticize as in to attack, but to criticize in the sense of analyzing and suggesting paths toward improvement. One of the chief figures in that period was Ben Bagdikian. Though most of his career would occur concurrent with and after the run of *(MORE)*, including his time as the ombudsman for the *Washington Post*,[41] Bagdikian had already published an impassioned critique of American newspapers in *Esquire*, an essay that first got him attention as a press critic.[42] In that piece, he called for newspapers to have in-house readers' representatives, or ombudsmen, and eventually got to serve in the role from 1971 to 1972 at the *Washington Post*. The idea of an ombudsman fit in with the reformist atmosphere of the late 1960s and 1970s in the American press, as did Bagdikian's call for a press council, an idea that would also be realized at the national level, if only briefly, in the 1970s.[43] Bagdikian would go on to publish several books of press criticism, including *The Information Machines*, *The Effete Conspiracy*, and his most famous, *The Media Monopoly*,[44] which has had multiple editions and reprints since then.

Some of this criticism was coming from conservative sources as well. Famously, Vice President Spiro Agnew gave speeches in 1969 and 1970 attacking the press as one of several liberal institutions that he argued were poisoning public discourse (see chapter 4 for more on this). Agnew's speeches fell more into the category of criticism as attack than criticism as analysis, but Edith Efron's 1971 book *The News Twisters* attempted a more nuanced analysis, specifically looking at network news coverage of the run-up to the 1968 presidential election in a quasi-statistical manner.[45] In 1969, Reed Irvine founded the media watchdog group Accuracy in Media (AIM), which states that its mission is to "promote accuracy, fairness and balance in news reporting."[46] Irvine saw AIM as a counterbalance to liberal bias in the press.

By the end of the decade, dozens of books would be published for a general audience examining the workings of the press. In addition to *The Kingdom and the Power* and *The Power and the Glory*, there was Bob Woodward and Carl Bernstein's memoir of their Watergate reporting, *All the President's Men*; Timothy Crouse's *The Boys on the Bus*, about presidential campaign reporting; and memoirs by investigative columnist Jack Anderson; as well as several seminal academic works of criticism, including Gaye Tuchman's *Making News*, Herbert Gans's *Deciding What's News*, and Michael Schudson's *Discovering the News*. The Woodward and Bernstein book became an Oscar-winning film. Enrollment in journalism schools surged during the 1970s. And while this likely had nothing to do directly with Woodward and Bernstein, as has often been claimed,[47] certainly it speaks to a rising interest in the practice of watchdog journalism and the role of journalism in society. People were talking about the press in the 1970s, not just the stories that the press covered.

Those intellectuals who have found themselves constrained by the norms of the professionalized institutional press—and those who find fault with it from the outside—have often turned to press criticism, both to express their own frustration and to attempt to effect change within the press. The best, and perhaps only, way to maintain a press that is both free of government and corporate control and yet responsible to the demand that it function to propagate a democratic society and its attendant culture is to encourage the growth and flourishing of a robust, public, and intellectually probing body of criticism around it.

The rise in awareness of journalistic practice and the critical culture began to spawn some thinking not just about journalism, but also *about* press criticism for the first time. This is the culture that spawned James Carey's call for a culture of press criticism, and also the culture that brought about discussions of press councils (reviving Walter Lippmann's idea), and the underground press that thrived in reaction to mainstream journalism, and also the regional journalism reviews. The regional journalism reviews were not all part of the underground press, despite Carey's characterization of them, but he was right that they did not reach a particularly large audience. *(MORE)* tried, at times, to attract a general audience, at least to the level of the *New York Review of Books*, but perhaps it was too difficult to attract an audience of general-interest citizens to reasoned criticism of the press. Many years later, Robert McChesney and Ben Scott suggested that the power of press criticism (and "radical" press criticism in particular) lies "in its ability to show that the modern commercial press system operates in a manner that is antithetical to the democratic values embodied in the First Amendment."[48] For McChesney and Scott, and for Carey, the value of press criticism lies in the ability of more speech to correct the failings of insufficient or incorrect speech.

The same year that Carey's essay was published, Lee Brown, then a professor at the University of Maryland, published one of the first books that attempted to analyze American press criticism.[49] Brown attempted to classify the various types of criticism of journalism that he saw as extant:

> With the growing movement for a national press council, these have become the principal forms of contemporary press criticism: the resurgent journalist-critic; the journal, particularly the local journal, for criticism of the press; the establishment of local press councils, by individual publishers and under the auspices of the Mellett Fund; the establishment of in-house ombudsmen, on only a few newspapers, to respond to reader complaints; and the reports of presidential and other commissions.[50]

This was the atmosphere that provided the conditions for *(MORE)* to take root: a "critical culture," as press historian and sociologist Michael Schudson would describe it before the end of the decade, one with changing demographics in the press, and one that would allow for as close to a golden age of anti-institutional press criticism as there has been in the history of the American press.

Revolution in the Newsroom

In addition to the rise in press criticism in the late 1960s and early '70s, the American newsroom and practices and norms of newsgathering were changing, and some of those changes prodded many young reporters to chafe at the limitations that their editors were putting on them. A. J. Liebling's aphorism that "Freedom of the press is guaranteed only to those who own one" has become so commonly repeated as to become almost a truism, and certainly a cliché. But the aphorism holds true in at least one seemingly paradoxical way: reporters don't write for newspapers; reporters write for publishers. And for Liebling, publishers were the ultimate threat to the quality of the press, because their money drove the content of their newspapers (and Liebling almost exclusively concerned himself with newspapers). The paradox here is that reporters don't really enjoy freedom of the press, since their work is always filtered through the desires of newsroom management.[51] Reporters working for news organizations at least as early as the 1890s would often feel that their own voices were marginalized,[52] and by the late 1960s and early 1970s, as newsroom demographics changed, moving from being places dominated by hard-nosed working-class reporters to being enclaves of educated journalists, something of a resistance movement sprang up—not just reporters' unions, which had been long established and focused mostly on salary and working conditions, but a real move toward autonomy for a group of reporters who saw themselves not just as hired hacks, but as *writers*. Journalism was changing rapidly in 1970 and '71, as younger reporters who had studied at universities that were roiled by the culture wars of the 1960s graduated and entered the newsroom. This new raft of employees, buoyed by the anti-establishment cultural atmosphere of the 1960s, were beginning to chafe at the limitations put on them by profit-seeking publishers and editors who they saw as staid and conservative, limiting their ability to describe how they, as reporters, saw the world. Michael Schudson argues that this new breed of reporter was instrumental to the rise of the "critical culture" that was becoming more pervasive in the newsrooms of the late 1960s and early '70s:

> Young people, more likely to fit into the youth culture of casual manners and language, open sexuality, and rock music, covered the campuses and social movements and were influenced by them. They often felt uncomfortable in their reportorial roles, almost as if they were agents of "straight" society spying on a subversive culture. They found themselves sympathetic to the ideas and values of the people they wrote about and increasingly skeptical, uneasy, or outraged at the transformation of their stories between copy desk and printed page.[53]

This ferment expressed itself in many ways in the late 1960s and early '70s. Traditionally underrepresented groups—including the largest body of the disenfranchised, women—pushed for new, equal roles in the newsroom.[54] John J. Pauly pinpoints the New Journalism practiced by Tom Wolfe, Gay Talese, and Joan Didion (among others) as the focal point for young journalists "finding themselves" in that period, but he links the form, via the files of the late University of Illinois dean Ted Peterson, to the underground press, debates over objectivity, and even specifically to the founding of *(MORE)*. For Pauly and Peterson, these interconnected events reflect a new "intellectual seriousness" in journalism.[55]

There were other, more direct influences on the creation of *(MORE)* in 1971, however, including several thriving (and more less-than-thriving) regional journalism reviews that had been popping up around the country in the years preceding the launch of *(MORE)*, including reviews in St. Louis, Philadelphia, Colorado, and Southern California among several others (these are the reviews that Carey characterizes as being a part of the underground press).[56] Although *(MORE)* had national ambitions, it was originally intended to be a New York journalism review—a late entry into the regional journalism review movement. There had been at least two other attempts at a journalism review in the city, one published by the New York Media Project and called *Pac-O-Lies* (which had a distinctly underground feel to it), and one put out by some disaffected Associated Press employees. Little evidence of the reach of these publications remains, and while they may have had some of the countercultural spirit that would underlie *(MORE)*, it was really the *Chicago Journalism Review* that most directly inspired Tony Lukas to found *(MORE)*, and it was a lucky coincidence that Lukas met Ron Dorfman when he was in Chicago, finding himself so stymied by his editors at the *Times*.

In March 1970, Dorfman's magazine devoted half a dozen articles to the Chicago Seven conspiracy trial. The lead article, written by Henry DeZutter, viewed the trial as a sort of play, because, as the story says, "Only a dramatist can put it all together, to distill the essence out of the official record of the conspiracy trial and transmit it to those who weren't there. Those who weren't missed a lot. And while a complete transcript would help, it won't do it all."[57]

There was extensive news coverage, but that's the trouble: it was news coverage. This was not a "newsman's" trial. First, there was simply too much to handle, too much drama, too much nuance to capture with the meager tools of pen-and-paper reporting. Second, the forms and formulae of the newsman—the snappy lead, the capsule summary, the few quick quotes, and, yes, the objectivity ("Facts without their nuance," as author Norman Mailer, called as a witness in the trial, derided the idea)—simply did not work for this story. So here may have been another inkling for Lukas that there was "more" to many of the stories that the press purported to cover.

One other item in that issue of the *Chicago Journalism Review* is important for the tale of Tony Lukas in Chicago: a sidebar set in the text of a story about reporters responding to federal subpoenas. Under the headline "Need Help?" is a brief report on a new committee, one of which Lukas was a member:

> Reporters meeting informally at Georgetown University March 8 set up the Reporters' Committee on Freedom of the Press, a 13-man (and 0-woman) group to coordinate the responses of line professionals to the government's attempts to intimidate the media through use of subpoena power. The committee will undertake legal research independent of the media corporations, act as a national clearinghouse for information on developments in the field, and provide assistance to newsmen who request it.[58]

Lukas represented the committee, with his *New York Times* affiliation clearly listed after his name—even though he was not going to be long for the full-time staff of the paper.

In a sense, *The Barnyard Epithet* can be seen as the de facto first issue of *(MORE)*. Lukas would continue to work for the *Times* as a contributing editor (basically a freelance writer who agrees to write on a regular basis), but he would leave the staff under which he found himself chafing. And the story that he told in his book was the first time that he was able to tell the part of the story that his institution wouldn't let him tell.

Two months after the *Chicago Journalism Review* issue that noted Lukas's inclusion on the Reporters' Committee on Freedom of the Press, Lukas popped up as a newsroom rabble-rouser again, this time in *New York* magazine, in an article that provocatively suggested that there was a "cabal" afoot at the *New York Times*. This cabal, wrote Edwin Diamond, "has no officers, no dominant ideology, no agenda, and no definite plans."[59] In an unattributed quotation, one *Times* cabalist insists that "Lukas is not our Lenin," almost making it clear that Lukas was, despite the source's protests, a leader of the cabal. The article goes into some detail about Lukas's discontent in covering the Chicago conspiracy trial, and notes that he had trouble keeping his frustration to himself:

> When Lukas returned to New York earlier this year he shared some of his discontent with other reporters and writers—and with non-*Times* people. At a seminar at Columbia University, for example, a student listened to Lukas'

complaints about the *Times'* trial coverage and then asked him why he stayed. Lukas' half-kidding references to his salary and "perks" (air travel card, etc.) hardly did much to assuage student doubts about the media's integrity.[60]

In addition to Lukas, the article mentions several future *(MORE)* contributors, including the *Times*'s women's news editor Charlotte Curtis, *Washington Post* writer Nicholas von Hoffman, and *Times* reporter Earl Caldwell. (Also noted was a young *New York Post* reporter named William Woodward, who would become essential to *(MORE)*'s beginnings.) But most intriguingly, Diamond writes that some in the "cabal" were pondering a more public version of the *Times*'s interoffice memo "Winners and Sinners," which highlighted good and bad coverage (and grammatical mistakes) among *Times* staffers. Diamond writes that "There is a model in the *Chicago Journalism Review*, an excellent monthly put out by young Second City reporters . . ."[61]

It was in this atmosphere that Lukas suggested that he and Richard Pollak create their own, New York–based journalism review. After all, wasn't New York where most of the national press was headquartered? But in order to make this project work, Pollak and Lukas wanted to make sure they had enough support for and enough interest in their project. To accomplish this, they would go through a two-step trial process. Neither of them had the money it would take to start a magazine, so investors had to be found. More importantly, though, they needed to gauge how much interest journalists would have in writing for—and reading—a publication such as *(MORE)*. There would be plenty: the social and commercial forces shaping journalism in 1970 and 1971 created a sizable pool of journalists who felt the same sort of discontent with their publishers, with their professional roles, and with the greater project of objective journalism.

From *The Kingdom and the Power* to *The Powers That Be*

(MORE) published in an era bookended by two large and influential works of journalism about journalism: Gay Talese's *The Kingdom and the Power* and David Halberstam's *The Powers That Be*. Talese's book portrayed his former employer, the *New York Times*, as a place that was a much less monolithic institution on the inside than it probably seemed to outsiders.[62] The book, published in 1969, was a new animal in that it was an eye-opener to a reading public that hadn't necessarily given much thought to how the news was produced, or to the idea that there could be any dissenters from

the selections that editors and writers made for the newspaper. Perhaps they hadn't even thought about the fact that editors *made* choices. The news was the news. But *The Kingdom and the Power* became Talese's first best-seller, and an era of increased public discussion and scrutiny of the press had begun.

(MORE) contributor David Halberstam published his book about the news media, *The Powers That Be*, in 1979, the year after the magazine ceased publication. It's a colossus of a book, more than seven hundred pages long, and according to the jacket copy, seven years in the making (almost exactly the period of *(MORE)*'s existence).[63] *The Powers That Be* examines four media giants: CBS, *Time*, the *Los Angeles Times*, and the *Washington Post*—four of the most powerful news organizations in the country in the late 1970s—and tells the story of the powerful people behind those institutions and their interactions with the government and corporate interests. The end of the 1970s was when the 1960s' distrust of institutions began to segue into a time when institutions were more widely celebrated and less widely questioned.

These two books fit neatly in chronology just before the launch of *(MORE)* and just after its demise, and both were written by men who had ties to the review (Halberstam was a close friend and colleague of founder Tony Lukas, and Talese was a headliner at the first A. J. Liebling Counter-Convention). But their timing was not just coincidental. The books serve as a convenient shorthand for the changes that roiled the organized press and the broader public in the 1970s, a complex, dynamic, and unstable decade often characterized as a mere transition from the 1960s to the 1980s, both of which have better established identities. In short, *(MORE)* chronicled one of the most eventful and transformative decades in American journalism. The United States entered the 1970s with its news generated by the stolid, historic *press*. By 1980, we had CNN. By 1982, *USA Today*. The Press of the '60s and earlier had become The Media of the '80s and after.

The Kingdom and the Power appeared at a time when distrust of public institutions was beginning to hit an apogee. Distrust of media and government grew throughout the 1960s as the public began to realize the scope of the deception that had brought the country into the Vietnam War and the complicity of the press in furthering that deception. The demonstrations and the violent police response surrounding the 1968 Democratic Convention in Chicago made many people realize that the mainstream news media were slow to recognize new political developments, and often minimized, delegitimized, or moderated them once it did pick up on those movements, as argued by Todd Gitlin, a sociologist and media scholar who participated in some of those political movements as a young man.[64] By 1969 or so, when Talese's book about the *New York Times* appeared, the public was ready to hear about the dissension within the ranks of media institutions. But by the end of the 1970s, the public again seemed eager for strong institutions that had answers and promoted a strong, unified, and more conservative country. A decade of malaise and anti-institutional attitudes had worn off, especially as society began to rediscover the idea of the market, both economically and, really for the first time, even in the realm of ideas and in the academy.[65]

The transition from the 1960s to the 1980s marked a change in the way that journalists thought about themselves. Talese had left the *Times* in 1965 and made a name for himself as a magazine and book author. He was often associated with the New Journalists, including the movement's evangelist, Tom Wolfe,[66] and others who attempted to elevate the style of journalism in the late '60s and early '70s. But tied into the New Journalism was an implicit (and sometimes explicit) critique of objectivity, which some saw as limiting the potential for a new kind of journalistic truth. During this period, journalists became more self-aware and self-critical generally, and made the strongest argument yet that the editorial functions of news-making were the essential element in the publication of a newspaper or the production of a television news show—and that objectivity as a professional ideal was actually being used as a form of control by the publishers who were their employers, enforced by editors who were in an uneasy position of being a part of the management, but usually drawn from the ranks of the reporters. The news-gatherers, writers, and editors began to assert themselves as more important than the publishers—a view that they had likely always held, but one for which they were now able to articulate a coherent and compelling argument. Reporters thrust themselves into the intellectual life of the United States in the 1970s, making inroads against the perception that the norms of the professional press made journalism, counterintuitively, an anti-intellectual profession.[67]

As *(MORE)* began publication in 1971, the profession of journalism was changing; the culture at large was changing; and the business of newspapers, magazines, and broadcast news was also about to be remade. Journalists questioned the professional norm of objectivity with new vehemence and fought with publishers for control of the work they did. *(MORE)* chronicled these changes and played a role in them as well.

Few scholars have looked at the intellectual history of the 1970s, though some works of cultural and political history have begun to take the decade seriously, rather than as nothing more than a bridge between the revolutionary '60s and the corporate '80s. The 1970s were a time of conspiracies, cults, the all-surface-no-depth imagery of Andy Warhol, the self-revelation and self-promotion of the birth of reality television as represented by the television series *An American Family*,[68] and also a period of multiculturalism, feminism, a lack of self-confidence, and an eventual turn to conservatism, with the "squares" becoming the hip by the time of Ronald Reagan's election.[69]

The 1970s, however, were also a period of changes in mass media. It was the decade that saw the Watergate scandal unfold in the *Washington Post*. It was the decade of the Pentagon Papers. It was the decade of the WBAI obscenity trial. It was the decade in which journalism became a glamorous profession when Woodward and Bernstein became Redford and Hoffman. Muckraking became a celebrity pursuit. The "writer's newspaper," the *New York Herald-Tribune*, had gone out of business in 1966, a victim of financial pressures in general and the New York newspaper strike of 1962 to 1963.[70] Some reporters had seen the *Herald-Tribune* as a place where they could have more freedom, and *New York* magazine, which would become a center of literary journalism in the late 1960s and 1970s, had begun life as its Sunday magazine supplement. *New York*'s rival for stylish and politically aware journalism, *Rolling Stone*, had begun publishing in San Francisco in 1967 (and moved to New York a decade later).[71] The newspaper strike of '63 also helped to spawn the *New York Review of Books*, a relative of *(MORE)* in terms of staff and looks.[72]

The death of the *Herald-Tribune* left New York a three-newspaper town. The thorough but boring (at least outwardly, as Gay Talese showed) *New York Times* was the morning broadsheet. The *Daily News* was the morning tabloid. And Dorothy Schiff's evening *Post*, still quite a liberal paper for most of the 1970s, rounded out the trio. Newspapers of the 1970s were still very much like the newspapers that had been around since early in the century, and publishers looked at the changes represented by the New Journalism with skepticism.[73] But by the end of the '70s, even the staid *New York Times* would abandon its two-section format for a multisection newspaper with several magazine-like sections.[74]

The weekly newsmagazines were still seen as strong and important. Most national magazines of importance were based in New York, as were, of course, the national television network news operations, in a world where Walter Cronkite could still be seen by a national public as knowing what really happened in the country and the important news could be summed up in twenty-some minutes of airtime. It was into this atmosphere that *(MORE)* launched as New York's journalism review—but a regional journalism review, no matter what its aspirations, becomes a national journalism review when its region is New York City. And the writers and editors of *(MORE)* knew that what made it into the mainstream news report was only a part of the story. Hence the name.

2. Rosebud Associates

The Crisis of Objectivity in American Journalism and the Founding of *(MORE)*

In mid-May 1971, two men—Richard Pollak and William Woodward III—called a press conference at the Algonquin Hotel on 44th Street in Manhattan. Being members of the press themselves, they could count on a decent amount of attendance. While the Algonquin was famous for being the home of the Round Table and its wits, including the *New Yorker's* first press columnist, Robert Benchley, Pollak and Woodward were there to launch their own publication, which they had founded with a third partner, a *New York Times* reporter named J. Anthony Lukas, and which the three of them called *(MORE): A Journalism Review*. The name and its parentheses (or are they square brackets?)—seem to have flummoxed copy editors for the eight years of its existence. The name was meant to be a play on the marking at the bottom of a page of typed copy, indicating that there was another page to follow. In the case of *(MORE)*, it was intended to imply that there was more to the story of the press than most people were getting.

(MORE) was intended to critique the press from the vantage point of New York City. The founders of *(MORE)* saw the mainstream American press as stagnant, conservative, unwilling to examine itself in a time when the public was losing confidence in institutions. The United States had been in a state of seemingly endless war and reporters such as David Halberstam and Seymour Hersh and I. F. Stone had begun to question the official narratives that people in positions of power had been feeding to the press. The country was also convulsing with social movements, and while the press covered civil rights and the counterculture, the national press—the elite news-gathering organizations of 1970—remained mostly staid, professional, and objective. *(MORE)* sought to explore the limits of traditional objectivity and break up the ossified culture of the nation's newsrooms. *(MORE)* was certainly not the first journalism review in the United States, but it did do something new and different.

The founders of *(MORE)* had come to believe that the tradition of objectivity, which had served American journalism so well for nearly a century, had become a hindrance to reporting the Truth with a capital *T*. Truth was a concept that had become problematic in the sixties, as confidence in American institutions lagged, as it became clear that the government was lying and not always acting in the public's best interest, and as the gap between the World War II generation and their kids was becoming clearer every day. The editors and writers of *(MORE)* recognized that the way the press covered the world had become inadequate—even when the press was executing the old model the best they could. The problem was that the old model wasn't working anymore, and in day-to-day journalism, most reporters and editors had their heads buried too deeply in that day's story to be able to see the bigger picture of how they were approaching the coverage. Only a press critic, at a remove from that daily task, can see the bigger picture. The press needs a gadfly. It probably needs it constantly, but it needs it most acutely at times of paradigm shift.

(MORE) was that gadfly. From 1971 to 1978, the magazine took on issues of newsroom management, diversity of staffing, the treatment of women, the reluctance of news organizations to challenge the government or corporations, and the corporatization of news itself. It ran stories that other magazines or newspapers had spiked, and told the story of why they were killed. At times, it aspired to be the *New York Review of Books* of journalism, with thoughtful, probing essays about journalistic accountability. Sometimes it wanted to be more like *National Lampoon*, running cartoons, or poking fun at the *New York Times* for running multiple column-filler stories about buses in South America plunging into ravines. It occupied a difficult territory. The staff wanted to reform the mainstream press without tearing it down—but they also faced critics who constantly thought that *(MORE)* wasn't going far enough, that the press needed to be torn down and replaced by something new and radical.

Dick Pollak, the editor of *(MORE)* in its first incarnation, and one of the two men at that Algonquin Hotel press conference, did not see himself as a radical, or as a member of the counterculture, or even as particularly anti-institutional. He had been a reporter for the *Baltimore Evening Sun* and briefly worked for a newspaper in Honolulu. But his chief qualification for the job of editing *(MORE)* was a stint at *Newsweek*, where he had been an associate editor and had overseen the newsweekly's press coverage. His other chief qualification was that he knew J. Anthony Lukas. The two had become friends when they overlapped at the *Sun* in Baltimore. Tony thought of Dick when he had the idea for *(MORE)*—an idea he got in Chicago.

Tony Lukas in Chicago

Lukas didn't go to Chicago to cover the 1968 Democratic National Convention, unlike so many of the influential journalists—or writers playing at journalism—who were his age, more or less, and shared, more or less, his political leanings—but the 1968 convention looms large over the founding of *(MORE)*. Hunter S. Thompson, the sui generis gonzo journalist, was there, but he was apparently too freaked out by the behavior of the police and the young protestors to write about what he saw for many years. *Esquire*, one of the great engines of the New Journalism that was all the rage among hip young journos, commissioned a quartet of unlikely writers to cover the event: the French playwright Jean Genet; William S. Burroughs, the junkie author; and even two journalists—John Sack and Terry Southern. Nora Sayre of the *New Statesman* was there. Even the novelist Norman Mailer was there—and while he got half a book out of the experience, his "reporting" mostly amounted to looking out of his hotel window.

To be sure, there were plenty of more mainstream reporters in Chicago too. It was the national convention of one of the two major political parties, after all, and there was going to be some contention over the choice of the vice-presidential nominee. Of course the press would be there. The major newspapers: the *Times*, the *Post*, the local *Tribune*. The networks would be there too, providing live coverage from the floor. And they were all ready for the chaos that could potentially erupt outside the convention hall. *Life* magazine had run a preview of the Chicago police department's preparations for all the young counterculture protestors who were expected to show up.

But Tony Lukas wasn't there. J. Anthony Lukas, as his more formal byline would refer to him, was at the time a reporter for the *New York Times*. He had come there from the *Baltimore Sun*. Before that, he had been at the *St. Louis Post-Dispatch*, and before that, he had gone to Harvard, where he was an editor of the *Daily Crimson*, where he met his friend David Halberstam. It was Halberstam who dashed off a sloppy letter of recommendation (ignoring capitalization and x-ing out typos) for Lukas to his editor, Clifton Daniel, on a typewriter that seems to have had a loose "a" key:

> lukas (who is a friend of mine, so be warned) is just what every young
> newspaperman ought to be. he is very very bright, and he has a high

s ense of the profession and integrity, and unlike xxxxx many bright young guys he has been a nd is willing to do the harder part of the profession—the dirty legwork part. so he is aavery finished and versatile reporter. he is aa guy who has always had his eye on foreign cities but he has also realized that xxxxx the way to get there is to do aa good job covering tough local stories.

he was magna cum laude at harvard (aa phi bete, i believe) and was associate managing editor of the xxxxx crimson; his stories on mc carthy were very good indeed—in fact one interview with professor wendell furry, aa long story xxxxx recounting furry's days in the communist party, was so good that the st louis post dispatch immediately offered him aa job. he went there, worked for the summer. i think he was 19 at the time.

lukas won aa james bryant conant scholarship at harvard which took him to berlin for aa year—hence fluent german; in a ddition he speaks excellent french (the product of aa putney education). he spent two years with the army in japan, then came back and went to work for the xxxxx baltimore sun. has covered aa lot of urban renewal, kept aa watch for african diplomats on route 40, and contributed regularly to the Reporter magazine.

it would be hard to be more enthusiastic (and believe me i have aa lot of friends in this business that I wouldnt wish on the times). but lukas would be a great asset to this xxxxx paper.

Halberstam

(oh yes, he is single, about 28 or 29 now—he was class of 1955 at harvard; and i think his various newspaper clips will tell their own story)[1]

With Halberstam's recommendation, the *Times* hired Lukas, and he made the next part of his career there. Lukas had already won his first Pulitzer Prize and a George Polk Award with the *Times* by the time he began reporting—months after the 1968 Democratic National Convention in Chicago had ended—on the conspiracy trial of several of the leaders of the protests. His Pulitzer had come in 1968 for a *Times* story called "The Two Worlds of Linda Fitzpatrick," in which he chronicled the life and violent death of a teenage girl from wealthy Greenwich, Connecticut, who had gotten involved in the hippie movement and, more disastrously, drugs.[2] Lukas's work on the Fitzpatrick story gave his editors the faith that he would be able to cover the counterculture, even though he would have described himself as a few years too old to have really been a part of it.

The *Times* had also sent Lukas to India, Ceylon, Japan, Pakistan, South Africa, and Zaire. Upon his return to the United States, the paper sponsored him for a Nieman Fellowship for reporters at Harvard University (with some reluctance to have him leave the newsroom, thinking that he might never return, but even more worried that a rising star reporter would be "exceedingly unhappy" if he were not allowed to stretch himself).[3] So he was a seasoned and award-winning reporter who was already familiar with the counterculture and figures such as Abbie Hoffman, Rennie Davis, and David Dellinger when he came to cover the conspiracy trial, even if, in his short 1970 book about the trial, he wrote that his assumptions about the trial, as it began, "were formed partly by inexperience, partly by a liberal's respect for the courts and the law."[4]

In that book, *The Barnyard Epithet and Other Obscenities: Notes on the Chicago Conspiracy Trial*, Lukas tells the story of his frustrating negotiations with an editor at the *Times*, one whom he leaves unnamed. Lukas was covering the trial for the *New York Times Magazine*, for which he had been writing, as well as for the daily newspaper, and one chunk of *The Barnyard Epithet* was originally published in the *Times Magazine*. According to Lukas, it was the news section of the daily paper that gave him trouble. On February 4, 1970, the deputy chief of the Chicago Police Department was testifying about observing David Dellinger leaving Grant Park "at the head of a militant group." According to Lukas, "At that, Mr. Dellinger looked up from his seat at the defense table and said, 'Oh bullshit!'" The judge revoked Dellinger's bail for the rest of the trial to reprimand him for this outburst. Lukas knew that this was an important story for the *Times*, but he was also aware that he was going to be asked to leave out the offending word that led to the story in the first place:

> Knowing the *Times'* sensitivity about such language, I called the National Desk and asked how they wanted to handle Mr. Dellinger's phrase. The editor on duty said he didn't think we could use it and suggested I just say "an obscenity." I objected, arguing that it wasn't, strictly speaking, an obscenity; that if we called it that most people would assume it was something much worse; and that since it was central to the day's events we ought to tell our readers just what Mr. Dellinger had said. The editor thought for a moment and said, "Why don't we just call it 'a barnyard epithet'?" Everything considered, that

seemed like the best solution, and that was the way it appeared in the *Times* the next morning.[5]

Actually, the next morning, it appeared as "a barnyard vulgarity," but even if Lukas misremembered the words he and the editor settled upon, the general sense remained.[6] But while Lukas's reporting continued to appear in the *Times*, and even in the excerpt from *The Barnyard Epithet* that appeared in the *Times Magazine*, the "bullshit" incident was symptomatic of the limitations on Lukas's reporting. "I concluded," Lukas writes by way of explaining why he was adding his book to the pile already being written about the trial, "that the Barnyard Epithet was only one of many aspects which called for fuller reporting."[7] There was more to the story than the *Times* was able or willing to print: in fact, the *New York Times'* commitment to an ideal of "objectivity" kept Lukas from being able to report his real discovery about the trial: that it was a political show trial, not a real criminal trial. Lukas sought an outlet for his frustration with "he said, she said" journalism by writing his book—and also in the magazine article that, in its very title, "The Second Confrontation in Chicago," alluded to the idea that just because the story in the newspaper had come to an end, the story that the article was covering continued onward.

The *Chicago Journalism Review* and the Need for Press Criticism

Lukas had also met Ron Dorfman, editor of the *Chicago Journalism Review*, during his time covering the conspiracy trial. The *Chicago Journalism Review* was by far the most active, regularly published, and anti-institutional journalism review in the country in 1969 and 1970. It had been founded to cover issues of newsroom management and news coverage in Chicago, and it was a part of a spate of regional journalism reviews. Some of these regional reviews—notably the *Montana Journalism Review*—even predated the *Columbia Journalism Review*, which was the one magazine of press criticism that most journalists at the time would have known. That *CJR* had been around for almost a decade by the time Lukas, Pollak, and Woodward founded *(MORE)*. Both *CJR*s (Chicago and Columbia), though quite different in tone and attitude circa 1970, could trace their lineage through a tradition of press criticism dating to at least the early twentieth century. In some ways, the culmination of this movement was the development of the reporter-run journalism review in the 1960s, and the *Chicago Journalism*

Review that Tony Lukas encountered when he was covering the Chicago Seven conspiracy trial in 1969 and 1970. That encounter inspired him, in the face of the newsroom conflict he was experiencing at the *New York Times*, to begin the process of gauging interest in a new, anti-institutional journalism review based in New York. His first order of business: getting his friend Dick Pollak on board.

The Changing Journalist and the Problem of Objectivity

In an interview forty years after he founded *(MORE)*, Dick Pollak said that at one of the A. J. Liebling Counter-Conventions that *(MORE)* hosted, the reporter and columnist Murray Kempton pulled him aside and told him to go easy on most reporters, because "They're doing the best they can." Pollak said he thought that what Kempton meant was that "you don't have to have any special kind of education to be a journalist." Pollak explained:

> I graduated from Amherst and went to work at the *Worcester Telegram.*
> Nobody asked me anything. They took a look at a few clips from the
> Amherst student paper and said yes. And they sent me to the Uxbridge
> bureau to cover high school football and the police blotter, and that's how
> it worked. And so the combination of the staff not having any real intel-
> lectual depth and the management not having a real intellectual depth, or
> at least feeling any demand for it, is why a lot of people leave the profes-
> sion. It's why [David] Halberstam and [Anthony] Lukas and [Gay] Talese
> leave. They can't do the long form. They reach a ceiling beyond which
> you cannot go. And I don't mean money or promotions; I mean intellec-
> tual elbow room. You just cannot do it at a magazine or a newspaper. And
> I think that happens to anybody who has any real intellectual curiosity.[8]

So Lukas and Pollak were aware of the new atmosphere in newsrooms and of the small journalism reviews that were trying to keep their local newspapers honest, and, in the case of the *Columbia Journalism Review*, reach a national audience—though the pair saw *CJR* as being too close to, if not a part of, that staid establishment press, even if they saw themselves as being outside of the counterculture too. Lukas, who was born in 1933, was about ten years too old to be involved in the counterculture himself, according to Pollak (who described himself the same way), but he was aware of it, covering the late 1960s like a concerned older brother.[9] So Pollak and Lukas were outsiders both to the counterculture *and* to the rapidly professionalizing world of daily journalism in which they had both worked. As he stood next to William Woodward in the Algonquin Hotel, about to launch the journalism review *(MORE)*, Dick Pollak brought with him this sense of a system of news media in crisis.

Prior to the rise of the large-city newspaper beginning in the 1830s, there was no real concept of the job of a reporter. Newspapers were usually small operations published as side projects by printers or financed by political parties. Those who were wealthy enough to publish newspapers did enjoy autonomy, but ever since those publishers began hiring writers to work for them, those employees functioned without any real way of expressing their own opinions, for the most part. This was especially true as newspapers began to standardize their "voice" and adopt the posture of objectivity, largely in an effort to avoid losing advertisers or subscribers. Objectivity has roots in the positivist tradition, and may originally have been meant to function somewhat as a scientific method for journalists. But by the 1970s, that meaning had been lost, and it had come to mean something more like "balance" or even a bland disinterestedness that many reporters felt stifled them and denied them their independent voices.

The advent of underground and alternative newspapers, as well as independent newsletters such as *I. F. Stone's Weekly*, allowed journalists to be truly independent for the first time since the rise of mass-circulation newspapers in the nineteenth century. Also, the reporters' power movement (also known as the democracy in the newsroom movement) gave journalists hope that they could have a voice in running larger newsrooms when they weren't able to start their own publications—though the movement, inspired by reporters' strikes in Europe, was mostly ineffective and petered out by the end of the seventies.[10] *(MORE)* gave these independent (and independent-minded) journalists a way to see themselves as a united force across publications, and solidified quasi-professional standards that transcended the industry of journalism.

But in addition to aiding the social status of journalists, professionalization was a boon to publishers, who could see the development of professional standards and a single "voice" for journalists as a way of getting their staffs to fall in line. Also, the key professional ideal that journalists coalesced around—the ideal of objectivity—could be seen as a way of masking a complicity with power.

By the 1890s, the basic structure of a news story had been standardized, though historians differ on the reasons for the development of the "hard news" form, often referred to as the "inverted pyramid."[11] In inverted pyramid news writing, a lead sentence conveys the main news item quickly and clearly, and details about the event proceed from that lead in order of importance. The form possibly grew out of the stilted, concise language of telegraph communications beginning in the 1860s, or because its adoption allowed various news organizations to use the same material from the Associated Press newswires. Publishers and editors controlled journalists' writing in order to ease the work of their superiors or to appeal to the widest possible audience. William S. Solomon argued that "In size, visibility, and influence, the newspapers that became dominant were those that catered to advertisers and treated news as a commodity."[12]

Sometime in the first half of the twentieth century, however, the inverted pyramid and objectivity gained a rationale that elevated them to the status of professional practice rather than production convenience or editorial imposition. Reporters began a march toward professionalism, which would secure them middle-class stability, and as a consequence of this professionalization, journalists internalized the idea of objectivity, which had been an external requirement. It became the best practice. In other words, as employee reporters began to assert themselves as professionals, the objectivity ideal was co-opted as their own, and many reporters would fail to see why it was an ideal that was in the best interest of their publications and not necessarily in their own.

But objectivity also allowed editors and writers the comforting illusion of independence, and in many ways journalists convinced themselves that the noble ideal of objectivity served their own purposes, when in reality, it allowed publishers to exert a kind of unquestioned control over editorial content. Objectivity ensured that newspapers would never be too inflammatory for readers or advertisers. These same concerns would resurface in the 1970s, when (MORE) was published. However, the concern in the later period was more with corporatized editors than it was with the publishers— or at least it extended the concern to the editorial hierarchy.

The critic George Seldes observed, "The reporter throughout our history has been the lowliest of animals. Believing himself to be too good to join in any organization or movement, he has found himself exploited by everyone."[13] Newspaper reporters in the twentieth century were more educated than those who had come before them, but they were entering a more mechanized workplace, and in the division of labor, their work was devalued and considered replaceable. Their stories were subsumed into the larger voice of the newspaper, which was seen by the management classes as being more important than the voice of the individual journalist.[14]

Meanwhile, a new class of editors separated the publishers from the reporters and functioned as a sort of middle management, further distancing individual reporters from any hope of true autonomy.[15] This was certainly true of reporters such as Tony Lukas, who chafed under the leadership of *New York Times* managing editor A. M. Rosenthal, leading in part to Lukas's idea to found *(MORE)*. Rosenthal had been venerated as a reporter—by other reporters—before he became an editor and alienated many of his former newsroom colleagues.

The social function of journalists was a key part of the Progressive movement, the political idea that an active, participatory democracy with a strong basis in scientific rationality could overcome the evils of an industrialized, urban society. The professions could create and secure a middle class and insulate against the corrupting influence of capital through their ethical codes. Through the research component of the professional schools, the professions also connected themselves to the new social sciences, which were becoming established in the universities at about the same time.[16] The scientific rationality of medicine or engineering could thus be applied to pedagogy, social work, psychology, or even to journalism.

Though the valorization of rationality was a boon to those who viewed journalism as a kind of populist social science and contributed to the solidifying of the objectivity norm in journalism, the concomitant standardization has always been an ill fit for journalism, which, in the U.S. system, cannot be a limited-entry profession in the way that medicine or law or even teaching could require a standardized education or licensing. Not all people who practice journalism see themselves as professionals, and so those who worked for newspapers were the main proponents of professionalism. Those who worked to effect social change were often outside the newspaper industry, as the muckrakers were. Also, many of these newspaper journalists were still working-class, not college educated, and viewed themselves more as craftspeople than as professionals.

The peak of journalism's professionalization movement coincided in the 1920s with the articulation of the norm of objectivity.[17] Bill Kovach and Tom Rosenstiel argue that the original meaning of the term was not freedom from bias, but rather one that "called for journalists to develop a consistent method of testing information—a transparent approach to evidence— precisely so that personal and cultural biases would not undermine the accuracy of their work."[18] Walter Lippmann, similarly, wrote of journalists, "There is but one kind of unity possible in a world as diverse as ours. It is a unity of method, rather than aim; the unity of disciplined experiment."[19] Journalists would gather information and analyze it, but accept any conclusion that the evidence pointed toward, rather than the conclusion that the journalists preferred. Then these conclusions would be presented in bland, neutral language, so as not to color these semi-scientific conclusions.

Of course, these are broad historical generalizations, and several newspapers did use a lively writing style to attract readers instead of striving for disinterested blandness, but as Michael Schudson argued, this "story" model was gradually superseded by an "information model":

> While reporters subscribed concurrently to the ideals of factuality and entertainment in writing the news, some of the papers they worked for chose identities that strongly emphasized one ideal or the other. The *World* and the *Journal* chose to be entertaining; the old penny press, especially the *Times* after Adolph Ochs rejuvenated it in 1896, took the path of factuality.[20]

It is these information model newspapers that survived, with newspapers known as "writers' papers" gradually dying out. The *World* ceased publication as an independent paper in 1931, and its successor as the reigning writers' paper in New York, the *Herald Tribune*, could not survive the 1965 newspaper strike and went out of business only a few years before *(MORE)* was founded. This left the *New York Times* as the dominant newspaper in New York, and indeed the dominant newspaper in the United States. This was a clear victory for the objective "information model." As Andrew Porwancher convincingly argues, Adolph Ochs, who had bought and remade the *Times* in the early twentieth century, was the "Prophet of Objectivity," and the key figure in establishing objectivity as a professional ideal. The choice of objectivity was not an altruistic one or one that guided institutional norms. Rather, objectivity was used to legitimize institutional goals of increased advertising and circulation.[21]

The professional model had become well ingrained by the time sociologist Herbert Gans wrote his 1979 book on the culture of newsrooms (published just after the end of the *(MORE)* era), in which he studied two national network television evening news programs and two newsmagazines. Throughout the book, Gans refers to journalists as professionals with almost no explanation. He does, however, touch on the theme of professional autonomy several times. Interestingly, he adds first-person observation to the theorizing of earlier academics. Journalists have some autonomy, he writes, particularly the senior writers who have gained the trust of their editors. He notes that this autonomy may frequently be "illusory," since editors find ways of controlling the newsroom by means other than threats, and by allowing the individual journalists to feel as if they have freedom. "Writers are entitled to select their own facts, draw their own conclusions and come up with their own evaluations, although they may be edited later."[22] Gans, despite his training as a sociologist, wasn't working from the history of professionalism either, and yet he hit on the same point. Objectivity gave publishers and editors a framework for keeping their writers' ideas within what Daniel Hallin calls the "sphere of legitimate controversy."[23]

Over the course of the 20th Century, the professional ideal of objectivity became increasingly ingrained in the culture of journalism, and by the time *(MORE)* was first published, journalism had become, I will argue, an anti-intellectual practice.

Historians of the U.S. press have not devoted much research to examining it as an intellectual activity. And at the same time, intellectual historians often ignore the role of journalists in propagating the ideas of a culture. Journalism is a profession that traditionally has long had writing as one of its core skills; it often concerns itself with public policy and the free flow of information in a democracy; as a subject of academic study, journalism has built up a substantial amount of scholarship; and journalism is taught as a major or minor in hundreds of colleges and universities in the United States (though college-level instruction is not, in and of itself, a guarantee of an intellectual approach to the subject). In fact, the core processes of journalism—reporting, critical evaluation of public events, and investigation—are *inherently* intellectual. Because of these factors and others, one could easily make the commonsense assumption that journalists, as a group, have adopted the probing, questing, questioning, and self-critical habits of mind that characterize intellectuals. Yet despite the near-continual presence of at least some intellectual journalism (as much of the so-called elite media would likely be called), the organized members of the U.S. mass media have on the whole been not merely a non-intellectual group, but rather an *anti*-intellectual group, actively fomenting a press that is populist, anti-elitist, anti-rational, instrumentalist, and blindly professional, and the doctrine of objectivity fed this.

Sociologist and media historian Michael Schudson argues that this "long-term trend toward greater political sophistication and critical scrutiny of government"[24] directly affected journalists because the muckraking tradition of American journalism made journalists feel more disconnected in general from the government, but they also "trusted more in, and cared more about, government."[25] As Schudson points out, an adversarial culture needs a target—something to be adversarial toward—and for journalism, this manifested in a critique of the norm of the kind of journalistic objectivity that purported to be values-free, a brand of popular social science with no political aims. Schudson, writing in the late 1970s, identified three broad aims of this criticism of objectivity:

- "[T]he content of a news story rests on a set of substantive political assumptions, assumptions whose validity is never questioned."[26]
- "[F]orm constitutes content . . . [T]he form of the news story incorporates its own bias."[27]
- The news story is "a social form tightly constrained by the routines of news gathering."[28]

Schudson argues that two journalistic traditions were revived in the 1960s and '70s in opposition to the norm of objectivity: the muckraking tradition and the literary tradition, both of which are strongly reflected in the pages of *(MORE)*.

The literary half of that pairing has long been described under the term "the new journalism," largely because of a long two-part essay Tom Wolfe wrote first for *New York* magazine, and later as the introduction to an anthology also called *The New Journalism*.[29] But at the time, both of these strains—the literary and the hard-nosed muckraking tradition—as well as other forms of advocacy and interpretive journalism were all seen as a part of the same movement away from objectivity, and all of them carried the label "New Journalism" to a certain extent.[30] For intellectual historian Howard Brick, the literary New Journalism was a revolt against positivism, and a move toward the critical, the literary, and the personal. Journalists began to attract the attention of intellectuals, and many of them also took a new kind of intellectual interest in their own work.[31] But Brick sees literary New Journalism and the muckraking tradition as being at odds, since muckraking still relies heavily on the idea of objectivity, if objectivity is interpreted strictly as positivism, the journalistic equivalent of the scientific method. Muckraking still relies heavily on the gathering and analysis of information, rather than just on impressionistic feeling and critical thought. In the eyes of many journalists, "objectivity" encompassed a broader set of ideas, including reporters' autonomy and advocacy journalism. According to John J.

Pauly, one journalism dean and historian who lived through the period saw that the New Journalism represented a change not just in form, but in the sensibility of the reporter. This dean, Ted Peterson of the University of Illinois, also "understood the New Journalism in relation to other forces roiling the profession," including "the underground press, debates over objectivity, changes in the magazine business, the founding of new journalism reviews like *[MORE]*, protests at the annual meetings of corporations and proposals to name working reporters to the boards of directors of wire services."[32] The press was integral to the New Left movement of the sixties, and *(MORE)* appeared at a moment when the truly underground publications such as the *Berkeley Barb* and the *East Village Other* were inspiring a new breed of publications that saw themselves not so much as underground, but instead as alternatives to the mainstream press.[33] The *Village Voice* had been around for almost two decades as an alternative publication, but other papers, mostly weeklies, were springing up to provide an alternative to daily newspapers without being seen as too radical for a larger portion of readers who may have been turned off by the politics, the production values, or the vulgarity of the underground rags.[34] These alternative publications were occupying a constantly negotiated position between opposition and popular respectability. It is a contradiction that Grace Elizabeth Hale describes as "contradictory desires to be a part of the American center and yet separate from it, to fit in and to oppose. . ."[35] This was a position that *(MORE)* struggled with as well, criticizing the mainstream press while going out of its way not to slide from an anti-institutional position to a countercultural one.

Several plausible explanations for the anti-intellectualism of the press present themselves. First, the commercial nature of the U.S. press in general—and the more recent corporate consolidation of the media—have driven journalism's appeal to a populist, middlebrow audience. The effort to maintain a "mass media" requires a mass audience, and like media in general, the press has aimed its reporting at the broadest possible swath of the American public, rather than trying to reach an educated minority or trying to educate the majority. The idea of "infotainment" is very closely related to this: in order to maintain a mass audience, news organizations treat news as just one more element of the media, rather than as an important entity in itself. News, the idea behind infotainment holds, must be entertaining. Importance and relevance are secondary. This leads not only to a focus on entertainment news, sports, and car crashes that have spectacular video available, but also to the sensationalizing of more "serious" news.

But the anti-intellectualism of the press is likely not driven entirely by corporate concerns. The professional norms of journalists themselves sustain anti-intellectual attitudes. Reporters have a long history of vocationalism, preferring to think of themselves as constituting a trade or a craft rather than a profession, with all of the esoteric knowledge and specialized training that professional status would require. Reporting has a strong working-class background, with a tradition of young people working their way from being copy boys, ferrying typescripts between reporters and editors, to being editors themselves. These traditions were beginning to die away by the time *(MORE)* came on the scene, but they lasted at least into the late 1970s. This is not to say that there are not intellectuals within the working classes, because there certainly are, but the tradition (now largely fading) is to be a hard-drinking, tough-as-nails metro reporter who is unfazed by anything he (and with the exception of *His Girl Friday*, the tradition is for it to be a "he") might see down at the precinct or in the back rooms of the ward boss.

Two other explanations for anti-intellectualism in the press also seem likely. The first is public criticism of effete and elitist intellectual snobbery. This is an attack that is leveled against intellectuals of all stripes, in and out of the press, but it can have a particular power when wielded against the press. The paradigmatic examples of this are Sen. Joseph McCarthy's attacks on university professors, writers, and journalists during the red scare of the 1950s and Vice President Spiro Agnew's anti-press campaign as the 1960s turned into the 1970s, but these are only two of many possible examples. These attacks have their particular power over journalists because of the final and perhaps most important reason for the persistence of anti-intellectualism in the American press: the veneration of truth and the organized press's devotion to the idea of objectivity. For at least a century (though some historians debate the origins)[36] American journalists have held to an idea of "truth" as, if not an attainable ideal, at least a goal to strive for at all times. Attacks on the elitism of the press often paint the press as biased toward liberal thinking, and any conclusion on one side or another of any debate is sure to attract attacks from those who believe that the reporters are not holding to the standards of their trade. The veneration of objectivity also leads reporters to value fact over analysis and commentary. The *fact* is the ultimate goal of the American news reporter, and while the collection of facts can be one of the instrumental ends of intelligence, it is not an intellectual activity, or at least is not seen as such by reporters who attempt to dissociate fact from interpretation and thereby ignore the intellectual implications of the process. J. Anthony Lukas, the *(MORE)* co-founder, struggled with the *New York Times'* insistence on objectivity, a key impetus for his creation of *(MORE)*. There had been plenty of careful thinking about the press, but little of it had come from within the organized press. Lukas sought to change that.

The Harvard Club

Before Tony Lukas took Dick Pollak out to dinner on the Upper East Side of Manhattan and suggested that Pollak edit the new journalism review he was contemplating, Pollak—who would become the founding editor of, passionate advocate for, and editorial voice of *(MORE)*—had no thoughts of starting such a publication of any kind, and to determine what kind of magazine they needed, Lukas and Pollak decided to hold a meeting first—an open meeting, bringing in any New York City area reporters who felt the same sorts of frustrations in their work as Lukas was feeling. They both knew quite a few people at New York news organizations, so they spread the word through the grapevine. There was going to be a meeting at the Harvard Club, on West 44th Street, near Grand Central Terminal. Come, they said, share your ideas for a new publication.

Interviewed forty years after this meeting, Pollak doesn't remember who came or exactly what was said by whom (and the same is true for many of the surviving members of *(MORE)*'s first advisory panel, though Calvin Trillin remembered a meeting at some sort of club,[37] and Ron Dorfman confirmed that it was indeed at the Harvard Club).[38] But Pollak does remember that the turnout was far more than he had expected. Apparently, the frustration in the newsrooms was even higher than he and Lukas had guessed. Even though it's not entirely possible to ascertain who attended, it seems reasonable to think that the advisory committee listed on the masthead of *(MORE)*'s first issue may have been there, or at least to form a representative idea of the sort of journalist who was interested in the idea of a new journalism review that would hold news organizations to a higher standard. In addition to Tony Lukas, who was not officially an editor, despite being a cofounder, the advisory committee for the first issue included Paul Cowan, Ernest Dunbar, Pamela Howard, A. Kent MacDougall, Calvin Trillin, and Mike Wallace.

The meeting seems to have occurred sometime in late 1970, given that the magazine's young publisher claimed to have worked for "more than six months" on the publication and he hadn't met the other cofounders before the Harvard Club meeting.[39] There, Pollak and Lukas were approached by someone they didn't know, a young man who asked how the organizers planned to fund the magazine. He was interested in supporting it in some way, and had some family money he could use as he chose. This was William Woodward III, the young *New York Post* writer mentioned in the *New York* magazine article about the cabal at the *New York Times*, who, together with Lukas and Pollak, would become the third founder of *(MORE)*. He was only twenty-six at the time.

Woodward, who went by the nickname Woody, was the son of William Woodward Jr., who was in turn the heir to the Manufacturers Hanover Bank fortune. Woody Woodward was eleven years old when, in 1955, his parents attended a dinner party for Wallis Simpson, Duchess of Windsor. There had been reports that night of a prowler in their neighborhood, Oyster Bay on Long Island. Woody Woodward's parents retired to separate bedrooms, armed and nervous. Sometime during the night, Woodward's father came into his wife's room, and she shot and killed him while their two boys, including the young Woody Woodward, slept in other rooms.[40]

The killing was a sensation. *Life* magazine called it "The Shooting of the Century."[41] A grand jury ruled that the shooting had been an accident, but there were persistent rumors that it was intentional. William Woodward Jr. was known to have been promiscuous with both women and men, so the idea was that his wife had found out about his extracurricular relationships. Truman Capote was also fascinated by the killing and wrote part of a novel about it, with the fictionalized Mrs. Woodward clearly killing her husband intentionally. Several of these chapters were published in *Esquire* magazine in fall 1975, and Woody Woodward's mother reacted: she killed herself. Less than a year later, Woodward's brother jumped from a hotel window on Central Park South and also died. Dominick Dunne later fictionalized the story for his novel *The Two Mrs. Grenvilles*.

But despite his wealthy, and publicly tragic, upbringing, Woody Woodward was not entirely an outsider to the journalistic community that Pollak and Lukas had invited to the Harvard Club, and was in fact quite sympathetic to some of the anti-establishment sentiments that the *(MORE)* regulars harbored. More than a reportorial dilettante, Woodward was determined to find a worthwhile career for himself. According to his *New York Times* obituary,

In 1968, he became a reporter at The New York Post, and if newspapering seemed an unlikely career for a multimillionaire, he embraced it. He paid his own way to cover the Vietnam War, riding around the war on a motorcycle. In New York, he represented the Newspaper Guild in contract negotiations with management, another unlikely role for the heir to a banking fortune.[42]

According to the *New York* "cabal" article, though, Woodward was chosen as the newsroom representative by the *Post*'s publisher, Dorothy Schiff.[43] Woodward's mother had socialized with Schiff and had gotten him his job there,[44] and so Schiff presumably felt comfortable talking to him if he were to become the *Post*'s union rep (Diamond describes Woodward as "both *engagé* and very social").[45] As a newsroom union guy, and the sort of reporter so eager to go to Vietnam that he paid his own way there, Woodward was supportive of the *(MORE)* effort and he agreed to fund a pilot issue of the new magazine, which the founders would use to judge interest in their project. If there was enough, *(MORE)* would begin regular publication. They were inspired in this approach by the *New York Review of Books*, a publication Pollak deeply respected and one that gave the new journalism review advice and assistance in its early days.[46]

In May of 1971, Woodward had lunch with Dorothy Schiff, a meeting that seems to have been at Woodward's request. At lunch, he told Schiff about the publication and about Pollak. He seems to have requested a leave of absence from the *Post* the previous February,[47] but at this meeting Woodward explained his connection to *(MORE)* and that he was going to serve as publisher. In what appears to be something of a sop to his mentor as a publisher, he also told her that "it remained to be seen how the business side and the editorial side got along, mentioning the Harper's situation, which was a clear case of business and editorial sides clashing."[48] Woodward was likely aware, of course, that the first issue of the magazine would carry an article about *Harper's Magazine* forcing its editor, Willie Morris, out. In a memo she dictated about the lunch, Schiff also found it noteworthy that *(MORE)* would have an editorial policy forbidding its writers to write about their own publications. Given the defensiveness with which she would view later *(MORE)* articles and inquiries about the *Post*, it's likely that she already had self-preservation on her mind, and the less interaction that the *Post* could have with a potential journalism review—even through her protégé Woodward—the better it would be for her and her newspaper.

Sometime either at her lunch with Woodward or within the following two weeks, Schiff decided that Woodward could not work at the *Post* anymore—that his leave of absence should become a resignation. In a memo to her files, she wrote, "When I suggested Woody resign because he was now publisher of (More) and there might be a conflict of interest, Woody refused to, saying there was a man on leave from the State Department and was the editor of Foreign Affairs but he didn't have the man's name."[49] Woodward had apparently settled on John Franklin Campbell, editor of *Foreign Affairs*, as his comparison for himself in terms of conflict of interest. But by this point, Schiff and her editor, Paul Sann, had already decided what would be done to demonstrate that the *Post* was not involved in starting up *(MORE)*. They would question Woodward openly at the press conference announcing the first issue, making it clear in their coverage that Woodward was doing this on his own behalf, not Schiff's.

Lukas and Pollak, with their new partner Woodward providing most of the early funding for the magazine from his own pocket, formed a corporation to publish *(MORE)*. They named their company Rosebud Associates, Inc. The name was a sly nod to one of the most famous sleds in the fictional history of journalism, and the *Citizen Kane* reference was yet another way of acknowledging the traditions of journalism. There was, of course, an irony in referring to a fictionalized version of a corrupt newspaper publisher, but it was a foreshadowing of the cheeky tone that *(MORE)* would adopt toward the business of journalism. *(MORE)* would, over the years of its existence, play with several important dialectics, one of which is the interplay between journalism as a practice and its role in society versus the publication of news as a business. Others that they toyed with included being anti-establishment but proud of the traditions of journalism; and being opponents of anti-intellectualism but also given to juvenile parodies from time to time. Criticizing a particular news organization or a pervasive practice within journalism did not mean that the staffers of *(MORE)* disliked journalism itself. Journalism was vital to a self-regulating culture and a self-governing society. The 1960s had shown quite clearly (to a certain subset of people) that criticizing the government did not mean you disliked the country. In fact, in some ways it could be seen as the ultimate in patriotism—defending your country against its government. *(MORE)* occasionally came to see itself as defending journalism against the people who were actually doing journalism, and doing it poorly.

Rosebud Associates was in business, but the magazine itself also needed a name. Pollak says he is unsure who came up with the name for the magazine, but its meaning, at least, was always clear and exemplified a dual approach that would come to define *(MORE)*. Before electronic layout of newspaper copy, reporters would mark the end of each typewritten page with one of two choices: if there was more to the story on the next page, they would type "(more)" to indicate this. If that was the end of the story, they would type —30—. So on the one hand, choosing "*(MORE)*" as the magazine's name indicated the thoughts that Tony Lukas was having in Chicago—that there was more to most news stories than was being told in the mainstream press. On the other hand, the new nameplate spoke to a sense of journalistic tradition that its founders (Pollak and Lukas, at least) felt themselves to be a part of.

To lay out the magazine, Pollak and Lukas brought on Sam Antupit, a well-known designer of publications who was perhaps best known for having designed the *New York Review of Books*, with its matte paper, its bigger-than-a-tabloid-but-smaller-than-a-broadsheet size, and its cartoonish line drawings, most famously by David Levine.[50] The logo Antupit designed was striking and instantly recognizable, though its stylization would cause a large amount of stylistic variation among other publications that wanted to refer to the new journalism review. Antupit cast the letters in a thick, sans-serif, all-caps font, closed in on either side by a pair of what appear to be either parentheses or square brackets. They're likely parentheses, following the tradition from news copy, but they're squarish parentheses, and other publications never seemed quite sure what to do with them when referring to *(MORE)*. Some went with parentheses, some with brackets, some decided to forgo them altogether, even though they were integral to the joke behind the magazine's name. The type of the word "MORE" is aligned with the top of these parentheses, and underneath, lined up with the bottom of them, are the words "A Journalism Review."

Rosebud Associates, Inc., filed to register the trademark on July 29, 1971, more than a month after the pilot issue appeared. Even the trademark office didn't quite get the idea behind the stylized "*(MORE)*," filing the trademark instead as "(MORE A JOURNALISM REVIEW)."[51] That first issue had a publication date of June 1971, but it likely left the presses on May 19, since the trademark approval document gives that date as the first usage of the trademark and the date from which it was in force. The trademark listed the headquarters for *(MORE)* at 960 Park Avenue in New York, which seems to have been Woody Woodward's home address.[52] That first issue bore a cover price of seventy-five cents, and you could subscribe for $7.50 per year. Further discounts were available to generous patrons who believed that *(MORE)* would be around for more than a year: fourteen dollars for two years, nineteen dollars for three.

The Pilot Issue

Paul Sann, editor of the *New York Post*, didn't see much of a need to cover the Algonquin Hotel press conference at first, even though he knew of Woody Woodward's involvement. A few days before the event, he sent a memo to Dorothy Schiff, saying that he "would be tempted to cover only if you said so." Schiff wrote on the memo, "I 'said so' by phone to Paul."[53]

According to the resultant article in the *Post*, *(MORE)* had an initial press run of fifteen thousand copies.[54] *Variety* had the number at only thirteen thousand, though both agreed that the Stern Fund for Investigative Journalism, a philanthropic organization that a few years earlier had helped Seymour Hersh fund his investigation of the My Lai massacre, had also helped to pay for the pilot issue.[55] The *Post* also noted that there had been several small private donations. Among them, Woodward himself had also contributed $2,300 of his own money to the magazine.[56] The *Post* article also contains the answer to the one question Dolly Schiff wanted asked in order to distance her newspaper from the new journalism review:

> Woodward, asked if he had applied for a leave from The Post to serve as pub-
> lisher of (More), replied: "No I didn't. I asked the Post for a leave of absence
> for what I described as personal and business reasons which they asked me to
> elaborate on and which I did. It wasn't until, I'd say, a month or six weeks later
> that I decided that it would be interesting and worthwhile for me to spend
> some time trying to help this publication set up.

While it's not clear if that timeline works out with the Harvard Club meeting and Woodward's initial request for a leave of absence, the answer did seem to satisfy Schiff, as she told the *Post*'s advertising department to work on securing an ad for *(MORE)* that could run in the *Post*. She had seen one that *(MORE)* had taken out in the *New York Times Book Review*, featuring a bald head, shown from the top of the nose up, with slightly menacing eyes. Printed on the head was the sentence, "Every day the press secretly operates on your head: we operate on the press."[57] The ad gave an overview of what *(MORE)* would be trying to accomplish:

(MORE) is a new monthly journalism review which will tell you a lot you don't know about how the press is run.

(MORE) tells you why some stories are killed, why others are "altered," and why what is printed sometimes tells only part of the story.

(MORE) provides you with inside information about newspapers, magazines, radio and television which you can't get anywhere else.

The rest of the ad summarized the content of the first issue—all of which was written on a volunteer basis by its contributors.[58]

The first incarnation of *(MORE)* looked quite a bit like the *New York Review of Books*. Sized at eleven by fifteen inches, roughly the size of a tabloid newspaper, *(MORE)* was printed on cheap newsprint-style paper stock (though the outside pages were often a slightly better-quality paper than the inside), and usually printed in two colors, black and a second highlight color. There were very few, if any, photographs in the first issues, but there were line drawings and cartoons. The *(MORE)* logo appeared in the top left corner of the cover, with an illustration in the top right. In fact, Antupit appears to have recruited his iconic *New York Review of Books* artist David Levine, since Levine drew the first cover illustration. There were several headlines in bold sans-serif type teasing stories that were inside, and, like the *New York Review of Books*, the lead story began on the front cover. It wasn't fancy, but it was clean and focused on the stories. The cover price, for those who hadn't been on the complimentary circulation list for the pilot issue and who wanted to buy a copy on the newsstand, was seventy-five cents.[59]

There hadn't been much in the way of additions to the masthead between the Harvard Club meeting and the pilot issue. Pollak was editor. Woodward got second billing and the title of publisher. Samuel N. Antupit was listed third, as designer. Beyond that, the only names given in the masthead were those of the aforementioned advisory committee. The advisory committee comprised an impressive group of journalists. Paul Cowan was a staff writer at the alternative newspaper the *Village Voice*. Ernest Dunbar had been the first black reporter hired by a national magazine—*Look*. Pamela Howard was the daughter of the former chief of the Scripps Howard media company. Kent MacDougall had recently edited a book of press criticism published by his employer, the *Wall Street Journal*[60] (and would, twenty years later, come out as a socialist who had been working inside the establishment press).[61] Calvin Trillin had been on the staff of the *New Yorker* since 1963, and would continue to be for more than forty years, as well as contributing to the *Nation* and writing books. And Mike Wallace had been working as a correspondent for the CBS News program *60 Minutes* since its debut in 1968. It was a serious and diverse bunch who occupied that first masthead.

In the eight years that *(MORE)* would exist, almost every byline in the magazine would belong to someone who was already a respected and well-known journalist, or was soon to become one. The lineup for the inaugural issue included Stuart H. Loory, then a Washington correspondent for the *Los Angeles Times* who had worked for the *New York Herald-Tribune*, and would go on to work for CNN beginning in 1980 and then teach at the University of Missouri. Lukas contributed a story. George Reedy had been a press secretary in the Johnson administration and was on a fellowship at the Woodrow Wilson International Center for Scholars when he wrote his piece for *(MORE)*. Paul Cowan, also on the advisory committee, contributed. David Halberstam, who had been Lukas's *New York Times* colleague, was already a Pulitzer Prize winner and at work on his book *The Best and the Brightest*, which would come out the next year. He is described in his brief bio as having "recently resigned as a contributing editor of *Harper's*." Charlotte Curtis was editor of the *New York Times* women's pages, which still existed as such in 1971. And finally, Ron Dorfman, editor of the inspirational *Chicago Journalism Review*, wrote a piece for the new magazine.

Almost everything else was written by Pollak, including the brief pieces in the front and back of the magazine, and including the letter from the editor that filled a half column between the masthead and the table of contents. In this long paragraph, Pollak disclaimed any grand purpose for the tenuous new undertaking that he was in charge of:

> Traditionally, a new publication is launched with a Ringing Declaration of Purpose. The trouble with such noble manifestoes, however, is that you then have to live up to them. This often proves exceedingly difficult. Despite your best intentions, little old ladies from Dubuque do pick up your magazine. Or some newspaper editor (or even publisher) momentarily forgets the marble admonition in the lobby and gives the news partially with both fear *and* favor.[62]

Here Pollak was referring to the "without fear or favor" statement of principles that Adolph Ochs, patriarch of the modern *New York Times*, published when he bought the paper and to the type of aged Iowan that the *New Yorker* was decidedly not supposed to be edited for, in the opinion of founding editor Harold Ross. Again, *(MORE)* was having fun with institutions of journalism while simultaneously acknowledging their importance. The editor's note continued,

> Not surprisingly, this causes a certain embarrassment. But worse, it turns out to be quite costly as well. For, having fallen short of your R.D.P., you are forced to keep up appearances by noting your achievements in large, expensive advertisements on the back page of the *Times* and *The Wall Street Journal*. With luck, these advertisements will persuade your readers that at least you are doing something worthwhile. But then there's your staff. They're a pretty savvy bunch and they really know how far you are from the old R.D.P.

Now Pollak is pointing out that reporters are not dupes. Neither are readers. Pollak went on, saying that *(MORE)* was going to

> cover the New York area press—by which we mean newspapers, magazines, radio and television—with a kind of tough-mindedness we think the press should but seldom does apply to its coverage of the world. We hope to do this seriously but not without wit, fairly but not "objectively."[63]

But despite Pollak's stated intention primarily to cover the press in New York, following the lead of the earlier, regional journalism reviews, *(MORE)* clearly had national aspirations. To some extent, that was a reflection of the fact that many national news organizations—*Time* and *Newsweek*, the *Times*, the broadcast network news operations—were based in New York City, and therefore covering the local press meant covering the national press. Still, the articles even in the first issue belie the magazine's national leanings: Lukas's contribution was an article about *Reader's Digest*; Paul Cowan wrote about the press's favorable treatment of the oil industry; Charlotte Curtis told the story of how editor Willie Morris was forced out at *Harper's* magazine. And *(MORE)* also reprinted an article from the *Chicago Journalism Review*, by its editor Ron Dorfman, in which Dorfman detailed the reporters' power struggle at two Chicago newspapers. So *(MORE)* hardly put together a parochial editorial lineup for that first issue.

The quotation marks around the word "objectively" in that introductory note also begin to make clear an attitude toward objectivity that *(MORE)* would espouse more broadly over time. In short, the staff of the magazine thought that it was a scrim that shielded publishers from blame and stifled the troublesome individual reporters who wanted their own voice. The articles in that pilot issue also make clear the theme of the reporter's voice, which played such a large role in pushing the magazine's founders toward the printing press. In the Hellbox column, devoted to shorter pieces and to bestowing "Rosebuds" on reporting they deemed exceptional, the editors ran a side-by-side comparison of two paragraphs of copy that the *New York Times* correspondent Homer Bigart turned in and the toothless one-line distillation that ran in the paper. The column quoted Bigart:

> I never read my stories in the paper anymore. . . . It's a safe way to avoid ulcers. You can't win. You finally get to the point where you either have to take it or quit. People have tried to fight back, but they get nowhere. You can't beat a newspaper bureaucracy any more than you can beat any other kind of bureaucracy.[64]

Paul Cowan's article on the favorable treatment of the oil industry raised the issue of the new class of well-educated reporters and the new sorts of ethical issues they have to deal with:

> It was difficult for a man who would become a dovish writer for the *Times* or *Newsweek* to believe that his classmate, the corporation executive, would become an accessory of an institution forced by the biology of the business world to control large portions of the earth in order to survive.[65]

Charlotte Curtis's article about Willie Morris's forced resignation addressed the limitations of a newsroom given over entirely to the editorial and writing staff; Morris's editing style gave writers room to be themselves, intellectually and stylistically (she quotes David Halberstam as saying that Morris was the only editor who ever understood him), but his editing also made little allowance for the financial continuity of the magazine.

Ron Dorfman's reprinted contribution perhaps most directly addressed the idea of reporters having their own voice. His story told of the reportorial and editorial staffs of two Chicago newspapers—the *Sun-Times* and the *Daily News*, both owned by Marshall Field V—which objected so strongly to their papers' endorsement of Richard Daley for reelection as Chicago's mayor that they fought to buy a full-page ad outlining their objections to Daley and supporting his opponent, Richard E. Friedman. In his closing paragraphs, Dorfman elegantly summarized some of the fissures that had begun to appear in the idea that reporters were opinion-free conduits of pure fact, and he distilled the issue to its core:

> Some reporters have openly demonstrated their sympathy with the anti-war movement. Others have spoken out in favor of the war effort. Some women reporters have announced their commitment to the women's liberation movement. Others have said they are against it. Now some reporters have gone a step further and openly endorsed a political candidate. None of this is especially revolutionary, except in the sense that more such acts are bound to follow . . . and each makes it more difficult for the profession to perpetuate the nonsensical notion that a reporter is a non-human creature who understands everything and believes nothing.[66]

By including this piece, the editors of *(MORE)* were declaring that they would not be that non-human kind of reporter. And in the second issue, four months after the pilot, they also showed that ethical obligation would be stronger than social ties when Dick Pollak wrote a long piece criticizing the *New York Post*, published by Dorothy Schiff, the friend and former employer of *(MORE)*'s publisher.[67]

The most important piece in the first issue, however, was a reaction by George E. Reedy to an essay in *Commentary* by Daniel Patrick Moynihan, an academic and an adviser to the administrations of Kennedy, Johnson, and Nixon. Moynihan had written that there was a growing imbalance between the press and the presidency, with the scales now tipping toward the press. The Reedy piece plays an important role in the history of *(MORE)* for two reasons. One is that Pollak claims that the piece, and a brief editorial inspired by it, pushed the *New York Times* into revising its corrections policy, nudging them into consolidating its corrections in a single box in a fixed part of the newspaper. Pollak claims that this is the most significant direct effect that *(MORE)* ever had on the ethical operation of a news organization.[68] There is substantial evidence to support this claim too, though several other factors intervened as well. The second reason the Reedy essay looms large as a foundational myth for *(MORE)* is that its last paragraph actually makes a better mission statement for the magazine than Pollak's self-effacing disclaimer of high moral purpose. After dismissing Moynihan's call for independent press councils to monitor news organizations, Reedy writes,

As an institution, the press has *not* been sufficiently self-critical and it has been far readier to protect its privileges than to correct its deficiencies. An indictment could be drawn that would make the *Commentary* article pale by comparison.

But a press adequate to the needs of a free society will *not* be produced by press boards which pass upon the "truth" or by rationing the amount of criticism to which individual groups in our society are entitled. This is *not* the road to freedom. It is the road to controlled thought.[69]

Reedy doesn't quite say it, but he does seem to imply that journalism reviews such as *(MORE)* could serve as the proper forum for that journalistic self-criticism.

Reaction to the first issue was mostly positive, at least among those publications that chose to review it. The *Wall Street Journal*,[70] *New York* magazine,[71] and the *New York Times*[72] each wrote up the first issue, though none had much to say about it besides a cursory listing of its articles and occasionally a note about how it was New York's first journalism review. But Nat Hentoff, who, among other tasks, was the media critic for the *Village Voice*, did not even wait for the press conference announcing *(MORE)* to review it. Hentoff didn't like the name, and cracked jokes about it in his column:

There will be enough money by fall, but the bigger the initial subscription response, the less *(MORE)* will have to raise. (You see what happens, Dick, when you have a title like that?)[73]

Hentoff preferred the more prosaic but descriptive title the *New York Journalism Review*. Of course, *(MORE)* had broader ambitions than a title limiting its scope to New York would allow. But still, unselfishly, Hentoff eagerly welcomed *(MORE)* to New York as his competition. "What a pleasure it's going to be," he wrote, "to have a place to send leads instead of guiltily watching them back up because one man in one city can only cover so much space and time." Though he complimented the "many experienced hands" involved in *(MORE)*, it's possible, given the lack of detail in his review and the early publication date, that he was working from the press release alone.

Variety's review was similarly laudatory. The author called it "amazingly good for a first issue, critical but not with that offensive militancy that marks and mars many publications devoted to 'exposing' whatever it is, and those in charge."[74] (MORE) could, in fact, have taken the route of militancy, but even in this first issue avoided that sort of confrontation, adopting a tone that would not alienate establishment press institutions in the same way that more radical publications had. It was a stance that would irritate publishers without angering them (most of the time), and would allow (MORE) to have a greater degree of influence on those they covered. Variety was astute enough to pick up on that tone even in volume one, issue one—though they were less astute on reading the name of the publishers, misprinting "Rosebud Associates" as "Posbred."

Variety picked out Charlotte Curtis's investigation into the ouster of Willie Morris as editor of Harper's as the strongest article, and Newsweek agreed. Dick Pollak had been the editor of the "Press" section of Newsweek, of course, but nevertheless, the praise bordered on effusive. Curtis's piece was a "tour de force." Though the Newsweek columnist noted that New York was late in getting its own journalism review, the columnist picked up on the national ambition of (MORE), unlike Hentoff. Newsweek noted that the "top-flight professional status of its contributors" also set it apart from other journalism reviews, where the contributors might have been just as incensed at the state of journalism but did not have the same preexisting stature coming into their roles as critics. That kind of talent, all of which had agreed to write without payment for the first issue, gave the columnist hope that (MORE) could become "the best publication yet devised for journalists criticizing their own profession."[75]

The Newsweek piece said that Pollak and Woodward would work on soliciting subscriptions and raising more money (so that all future contributors would be paid), but quoted Woodward as saying that they weren't in the publishing business for the money. "Face it," Newsweek quoted Woodward as saying. "There's probably more money in Hula Hoops than in new journalism reviews." Woodward hoped that the magazine would be in the black in five years. And while that never did happen, the first twenty-seven issues, which can be seen as the first of three semi-distinct periods in the history of (MORE), did establish what (MORE) really was up to.

3. The Marble Admonition

Chronicling the Journalism of the Early '70s and Challenging the Institutional Press

In his book about the influential magazine *Ramparts*, Peter Richardson asserted that writing about a magazine is like telling the story of a rock band, with an institutional identity, but as individual personalities leave and enter, that identity changes in subtle or significant ways.[1] A new editor at a magazine could be equated to a major change in a band, like a singer leaving. A lower-level staff member change might be more like getting a new drummer, and freelance writers could be seen as session musicians playing on a particular album. When *(MORE)* launched its pilot issue, only Dick Pollak, the editor, and Woody Woodward, the publisher, represented the magazine at the press conference. Even then, while Woodward was important as a fund-raiser, the editorial identity of the publication was established almost entirely by Pollak. But shortly after it began regular publication in October 1971, *(MORE)* gained a second full-time editorial staff member, Terry Pristin, and her tenure as assistant editor defines the first period of its publication.

The second issue of *(MORE)* came out just when Pollak and Woodward had hoped it would, in the fall of 1971, four months after the pilot issue. Pristin wrote a piece for that issue, as a freelancer. She doesn't recall exactly how she had heard about *(MORE)* in that period between the initial excitement and regular publication. She was young—only twenty-five—and didn't have the same sort of connections that Pollak and Lukas and Halberstam did. After graduating from the Columbia University Graduate School of Journalism, Pristin worked for a television station in Boston and then for an alternative newspaper called *Boston After Dark* (which later became the better-known *Boston Phoenix*). She missed New York, though, and quit to return without a job. But she knew someone who knew someone—maybe Lukas—and she had an idea for a story, she remembers, and Pollak took it for the first issue.[2] That article looked into the success, or lack thereof, of the Harlem-based Community News Service, which was intended to bring black voices into majority white newspapers downtown. The service was failing to bring in enough money to support itself.[3] The table of contents for that issue said that Pristin was a young journalist who had "recently joined the staff of *(MORE)*," but the masthead didn't have a title for her yet. By November, though, she had her name listed next to the title "Assistant Editor." She remembers her pay as $160 or $180 per week, "something in that range. Very little money, but it was fun." She called working for *(MORE)* "a heady experience for a very young person because I was rubbing shoulders with all these famous people. Dick [Pollak] brought in so many well-known journalists and I would go to the kinds of parties that I would never be invited to today. There were always parties. Somehow there were always parties. So I was on a first-name basis with people with distinguished reputations."[4]

While Pristin found that life exciting, she also realized that the mission of *(MORE)* might square better with the career achievements of the more senior contributors to the magazine, since they had the experience both to write more credible stories and to be able to face up to more established journalists and institutions. "It's really better to be a press critic when you actually have done it a little bit," she said. "You should have actually done it so you know what goes into it, what kinds of pressures people are under, and it gives you a little bit more of a humane understanding of what it's like to be a journalist, and I sort of reversed things in my career." Pristin did say, though, that she mostly worked on editing and writing the shorter pieces in the magazine—the Hellbox stories that originally ran on page two and later the Big Apple section that focused on New York City media. Editing duties for the longer pieces mostly belonged to Pollak.[5]

Even with Pristin in the office, the staff of *(MORE)* remained exceedingly small. At most, there were four regular employees who would show up. Pollak and Pristin constituted the entire editorial staff. According to Pristin, Woody Woodward also came to the office regularly, at least at first. And Tom Reeves later joined the magazine as a business and advertising manager. Sam Antupit, the designer, came in toward the end of the production cycle and sometimes accompanied the group on trips to the printer in Connecticut, but he was mostly absent. Tony Lukas, the third founder of *(MORE)* with Pollak and Woodward, mostly stayed away, busy with other parts of his career. According to Pristin, Lukas would come into the office occasionally and help to generate story ideas or to bring in writers—and of course to write stories himself. But he wasn't an editor.

Figure 1. From its launch in 1971 until its sale in 1976, *(MORE)* published as a tabloid, in black and white with a single spot color on each cover. Originally designed by Sam Antupit, who also designed the iconic New York Review of Books, the magazine usually featured cartoons as illustrations, including art by David Levine, Marty Norman, and Jules Feiffer (Courtesy of *Columbia Journalism Review*).

Themes in *(MORE)* in the Terry Pristin Era,
June 1971 to December 1973

In the first incarnation of *(MORE)*, from the pilot issue until December of 1973, when Terry Pristin was replaced on the masthead, the magazine developed several consistent themes and areas of coverage—many of which would remain throughout the magazine's run, or at least through the period in which Rosebud Associates, the founders, owned the publication. At the same time, the first two and a half years of *(MORE)* established the magazine's characteristic tone. The recurring themes included the following:

- Journalists' growing distrust of corporations and for advertising in general.
- Journalists' growing distrust of the government, particularly in matters regarding surveillance and propaganda. *(MORE)* also expressed dismay at the number of journalists and media organizations that willingly complied with government efforts to censor information or mislead the public.
- In the spirit of 1970s identity politics, *(MORE)* was watchful on behalf of several interest groups, advocating for their inclusion both in stories in the mainstream press and in the newsrooms that produced those stories.
- The chronicling of new and promising press ventures, interwoven with an elegiac wistfulness about the dying off of several venerable media properties.
- Advocating protections for journalists, particularly in the area of the protection of anonymous sources.
- Obscenity and censorship of obscenity, which *(MORE)* covered almost as closely as it covered the more serious censorship of information.
- Press ethics and accountability, particularly the discussion over whether the United States needed a news council that could independently review stories in the press.
- Finally, *(MORE)* chronicled the experience of being a journalist in the 1970s in a way that its predecessors, such as the *Columbia Journalism Review*, never did. It was almost as if it were a lifestyle magazine for journalists.

(MORE) was a local journalism review in the way that the *New York Times* was a local newspaper in the 1970s. It was based in New York City, and to

some extent its coverage reflected that fact. New York media organizations were much more likely to come under scrutiny in *(MORE)* than were magazines based in Philadelphia or Chicago, and even more so than dailies in Denver or Dubuque. And the predominantly New York–based staff had a New York–centric view of the world in much the same way that the *Times* often does. It's the New Yorker's view of the world that Saul Steinberg cartooned for the cover of the *New Yorker* in 1976, with Manhattan seen in granular detail and the rest of the country a sketchy rectangle on the horizon. Nevertheless, *(MORE)* did attempt to cover the entire country, as did the *Times*, which already in the 1970s was a national newspaper as much as it was a local broadsheet. Like the *Times*, *(MORE)* would eventually open a Washington, DC, bureau (one staffed by a single man, in *(MORE)*'s case). And also like the *Times*, *(MORE)* had a national influence. Among journals of press criticism, it was the standard-bearer during its brief life. All of these factors influenced the range of coverage that made its way into *(MORE)*, and the beginnings of that range can be seen in its first two and a half years.

(MORE)'s tone in this period also covered a wide range, but coalesced around two poles: a sort of *New York Review of Books* attempt at intellectual seriousness, and a cheeky satirical approach. Both of these worldviews can be seen as an attempt to crack the institutional press's reluctance to engage in self-examination. That reluctance is one of the key markers of anti-intellectualism in the professions, and *(MORE)*'s encouragement of self-scrutiny speaks to the magazine's place as an opponent of anti-intellectualism. Almost always, though, whether it was being serious or mocking, *(MORE)* operated with an awareness of the history of reporting in the United States—particularly the muckraking tradition—while also advocating for change. Theirs was a progressivism rooted in sentimentality for a golden age that was never quite real.

Coverage of Business and Advertising

In its first months of publication, *(MORE)* used a particularly large amount of printer's ink on coverage of two related issues. In establishing its early anti-institutional stance, *(MORE)* ran several articles on the theme of distrust of corporate America. Interspersed with these were several articles about the nature of advertising in news publications and the relationship between money and news in general.

Even *(MORE)*'s pilot issue featured two articles on the topic. Tony Lukas's article about *Reader's Digest* and its favoring of corporations over environmental issues squarely fits into a class of articles in which *(MORE)* faulted publications for failing to hold business accountable. Lukas describes a 1969 *Reader's Digest* article that names "the two main villains" in the degradation of the environment as the growing U.S. population and a failure of oversight by federal agencies, but leaves out any responsibility on the part of corporations. But in 1971, this was old news. The news peg for Lukas's article was an announced supplement that would run in the September 1971 issue of the *Digest* and that promised answers to what American corporations were doing to help the environment. Rather than hard-hitting investigative reporting, however, this was going to be an advertising supplement, which *Reader's Digest* sold to companies as a public relations opportunity. For Lukas, this was a violation of the public service obligation of a large-circulation American general-interest magazine.[6]

As discussed above, Paul Cowan's piece on under-coverage of the oil industry blamed the chummy relationships between oil executives and journalists who attended college with them for the lack of serious reporting. Cowan investigated whether the threat of losing advertising from oil companies might be to blame, but found that it accounted for very little of the advertising income of most publications. Cowan put the blame squarely on reporters, for being "too timid or lazy or unimaginative (or all three) to do the kind of reading and interviewing that would help them understand how complex organizations like oil companies operate. . . . They eagerly accept a bureaucrat's transparent lie if it will allow them to avoid an ominously difficult piece of research."[7]

But while *(MORE)* was never reluctant to put the blame for bad reporting on a lazy reporter, the publication was much more likely to follow the lead of its patron saint, A. J. Liebling, and give the lion's share of the distrust to the publishers. In the first two and a half years of its existence, *(MORE)* ran seven lengthy articles that questioned the relationship between advertisers and publishers. Journalist Chris Welles addressed the issue in a cover article he wrote for the December 1971 issue about how the *New York Times* covered business. Welles analyzed nearly six hundred business articles over a two-month period and diagnosed the *Times*'s soft coverage as a combination of overreliance on corporate public relations—the sort of unquestioning reportorial laziness that troubled Paul Cowan about the oil industry—and the publishers being cowed by advertisers. He illustrated the second point with an anecdote about airline executives storming the office of *Times* publisher Arthur Ochs "Punch" Sulzberger after an editorial pushing for airline deregulation.[8] The point that the *Times* was a lapdog for corporations was driven home by a cartoon depicting a tail-wagging *New York Times* puppy eagerly delivering a rolled newspaper, clenched in its teeth, to a satisfied-looking personification of industry wearing a suit, wing-tips, and pinkie rings, and chomping on a cigar while smoke puffs out of the smokestack that constitutes his head. It was one of the first cartoons for *(MORE)* by an artist named Marty Norman, who would soon become the closest thing the magazine had to a house cartoonist (though he ran this cartoon under a pen name, afraid that he might lose business cartooning for the *Times*, with which he also had a business relationship).[9]

While the piece about the *Times* attacked the relationship between publishers and advertisers obliquely—no advertiser was named specifically—*(MORE)* took on advertising issues directly several times in the period between June 1971 and December 1973. There was an article about how newspapers were refusing to take ads from a computerized car-matching system in order to avoid competition with local car dealership advertising.[10] The same issue had an article about invasive print advertising, where ads would cut at a diagonal across a page of editorial content or take up two quarter-pages at the top left and bottom right, completely dominating the articles that they subsidized.[11] *(MORE)* covered the *New York Times* advertising acceptability policy[12] (an article that also pushed the conversation into First Amendment territory by suggesting that the *Times* was censoring potentially unsavory ads). *(MORE)* investigated the public service ads of the Advertising Council, which *(MORE)* found to be overly protective of "the image and interests of the nation's industrial and governmental power brokers." Some of the Ad Council's "public service" ads were, according to this article, "nothing short of a public hoax."[13] *(MORE)* also looked at propaganda from the strip mining industry[14] and even returned to an examination of the oil business with a more in-depth look at an advertising supplement that Standard Oil had placed in sixteen national and regional magazines.[15]

(MORE)'s pace of coverage of advertising and business slowed a bit from the end of 1972 into 1973, a period in which the magazine ran three pieces on the subject, one on deceptive advertising[16] and one about counteradvertisements to counteract it,[17] and one front-cover piece about IBM's public relations operation.[18] The general focus on advertising, business, and their interaction falls squarely into *(MORE)*'s anti-institutional stance. But really, *(MORE)* doesn't seem to be anticorporate in these articles—in fact, bowing to the need to make money to continue publication, they raised their

own advertising rates in April 1973, with a full-page ad costing six hundred dollars.[19] Instead, the overriding message is one of disappointment, not so much with the corporations—indeed, they're seen as naturally rapacious—but with the institutional press that was supposed to be investigating those corporations. *(MORE)* was goading the watchdogs, not trying to take down the press, but trying, at least, to keep those watchdogs from becoming lapdogs like the one in Marty Norman's cartoon.

Coverage of Politics

In March 1973, *(MORE)* publisher Woody Woodward wrote a Column Two essay about some physical changes to the magazine (a switch from two to three columns and a new subscription price—$10 per year, up from $7.50). More importantly, though, Woodward wrote that the magazine had added a new focus. *(MORE)* had hired a new Washington, DC, editor, and would be holding the second of its A. J. Liebling Counter-Conventions in Washington as well.[20] The new hire was a young reporter named Brit Hume, who had recently worked for the syndicated Washington investigative columnist Jack Anderson and had made his own name with the 1971 publication of his book *Death and the Mines*, which told the story of the United Mine Workers union in the 1960s. He would later publish a memoir of his time with Anderson, further bolstering his bona fides as a reporter.[21] Hume's addition to the masthead and the location of the second of *(MORE)*'s "counter-conventions" were clear signs that *(MORE)* had ambitions beyond New York City.

Given the political atmosphere of the early 1970s and the role of the press in uncovering national political scandals, it is surprising that there wasn't even more reporting on political reporting in the first few issues of *(MORE)*. The cover story of the pilot issue was about Nixon's exploitation of prisoners of war in Vietnam for his own political purposes. And the cover of a publication's pilot issue is a place to make a statement about the magazine's values. But the next two issues barely mentioned politics at all. Perhaps this is owing to *(MORE)*'s New York–centrism. In December of 1972, the coverage of politics picked up quickly, but even then, it ran only in bursts until Hume joined the staff. Likely this is a result of an overwhelmed editorial staff. Pollak and Pristin just couldn't get their heads around more national political coverage than they did, and the majority of their connections in the press were also New Yorkers. Things stabilized once Hume came on board.

The same anti-institutional stance that informed *(MORE)*'s early coverage of business and advertising would be equally evident in the magazine's coverage of the press's relationship with government, though in the era of the Pentagon Papers and Watergate, *(MORE)* would place more of the blame on the government in this relationship than on failures of the press. Still, the press remained the main concern.

From December 1971 to March 1972, each issue of *(MORE)* carried at least one story about the relationship between the press and the government. These included articles lamenting the *New York Times*'s Washington bureau chief James "Scotty" Reston's transformation from a scrappy reporter to a "journalistic statesman,"[22] one about how a North Carolinian named Jesse Helms used his fame from broadcasting on the Tobacco Network to get elected to the U.S. Senate,[23] and one about how law enforcement surveillance of activist groups had a chilling effect on their free speech.[24] But while surveillance and the comings and goings of *Times*men were interesting to *(MORE)*, they were overshadowed by the coverage that began to dominate once the implications of Daniel Ellsberg's leaking of the Pentagon Papers to the *New York Times* became clear and as the revelations of two virtually unknown *Washington Post* reporters started to come to light. After the Pentagon Papers and while the Watergate case was beginning to build momentum, *(MORE)* found its footing as a critic of government reporting and found much to write about on the topics of government cover-ups and leakers in the wake of Vietnam, and more specifically about Richard Nixon himself.

(MORE)'s coverage of the Pentagon Papers case and government leakers began in January 1972, about six months after the *Times* began publishing them. That piece, by Edwin Diamond, criticized the job that wire services and newspapers had done covering the grand jury investigations fishing for government leaks after the Pentagon Papers were made public.[25] In part, wrote Diamond, the news organizations just didn't have enough writers with the intellectual firepower needed to cover such a complex case. Much of the story was taking place in Boston, where one of two grand juries was sitting, meaning that top writers from the national press were not present to dig out facts or cajole grand jurors for quotes. Reporting the case properly would have involved a combination of political and legal knowledge that most stringers wouldn't be able to pick up, especially if they were responsible for other stories at the same time. And grand jury investigations are also particularly closed proceedings, which made the reporting even more

difficult, even for the strongest reporters. Diamond attempted to provide some clarity to the story as it stood in late 1971, when he wrote the essay, attempting to add to the work of Sanford Ungar of the *Washington Post*, the one reporter Diamond praises in the piece. He also examines how the ongoing investigations had begun to have a chilling effect not just on Ellsberg (whose teenage son was subpoenaed) but also on left-wing intellectuals of Cambridge, including linguist Noam Chomsky, historian Howard Zinn, and even *(MORE)* contributor David Halberstam.

Bridging both the theme of Vietnam coverage and the long arm of Richard Nixon, *(MORE)* editor Dick Pollak wrote a piece about a series of paid political columns that the *Washington Post* discouraged from publication in its pages.[26] Several foundations had banded together with the idea of running a series of fifty open letters to Richard Nixon, which would be published as paid advertisements. Some would be written by prominent Americans, and the first batch included letters from historian Lewis Mumford, singer Harry Belafonte, and psychologist Erich Fromm as well as a businessman, a rancher, "and a well-known actor made so nervous by the *Post*'s subsequent behavior in this tale that he asked that his name not be used in this article."[27] What the *Post* did is somewhat murky, but it seems to have required each of the writers to approve his or her individual ad and disclaim any liability for reactions to that ad—even though the *Post* had originally said that batch clearance would be fine. This created enough of a hassle for the group that was organizing the ads to cancel the entire project. Pollak suggested that the *Post* was trying to chill the speech of the more anti-Nixon letter writers, since the *Post* had already caused enough friction with the administration through its Watergate reporting. Pollak admitted that the case was not clear, and that there is no inherent right for a third party to be published in a privately owned newspaper. But, he concluded, "the odds remain unjustly high against the political advertiser with a boatrocking message—even at so relatively enlightened an organization as The Washington Post Co."[28]

(MORE) published two substantial articles about political leaks to the press in 1973, at the height of Watergate. A man called "Anderson Price" wrote the first, but *(MORE)* acknowledged that this was a pen name. Price was an accountant who dealt with politicians as part of his job (perhaps his pseudonym was a conflation of the accounting firms of Arthur Andersen and Price Waterhouse), but who was more interesting to *(MORE)* because of what he called his "hobby": leaking political stories to the press.[29] The

article purports to explain the specific motivations of its author, but also to provide a glimpse into the press and political pathologies that make him and leakers like him viable in the system. Price says that he had always wanted to be a reporter himself, and that leaking to them continues to give him a thrill:

> Why do I do this? Because I like reporters better than any other kind of people. I like to be seen in their company in swank restaurants, to eat their food and drink their liquor as they ply me for leads. I love to exchange bits of political gossip, to join in the reporters' cynical assessment of politicians and their jealous criticism of the columnists, who make so much more money than they for what seems to be easier work. My biggest high comes when, in the middle of a formal dinner party, I let drop a particularly juicy item and a reporter takes his pad out of his dinner jacket and starts making notes. I will give reporters almost anything they want to keep them interested in me.[30]

Following through on the story's headline ("How to Become a Reliable Source"), Price offers just three tips: tell the truth; know who you're talking to; and don't blow your cover. But that headline is also a bit misleading, since the story is really about how "the whole idea of reliable sources has been debased—not by the sources, but by the journalists."[31] Price argues that the vast majority of anonymous sources are unnecessarily anonymous—that most of the stories that use anonymous sourcing could just as easily be reported on the record, or even more tellingly, not reported at all. As much as he enjoys his role as a leaker, he thinks that most of the stories he leaks are actually just gossipmongering or meaningless prognostication, and for the benefit of the reader, they should disappear.

A few months later, Bob Kuttner also argued in a (MORE) cover story that the importance of anonymous reporting is largely overblown.[32] The occasion for the essay was Vice President Spiro Agnew's complaint that he had been the victim of a series of systematic news leaks designed to destroy his career—and the subsequent judicial order that would have allowed Agnew's attorneys to search the private files of members of the press. Agnew had resigned by the time of the article, making that judicial order moot, but Kuttner felt compelled to argue that Agnew's complaints, combined with the reporting of Bob Woodward and Carl Bernstein in covering Watergate, had inflated the importance of leaks in the mind of the public. Real investigative reporting, he argues, requires legwork, even when a leak is involved.

He quotes investigative journalist Seymour Hersh, who says that the real work isn't getting the leak, but instead calling and calling and calling to find someone who is willing (or indiscreet enough) to talk, and then calling again until that first statement can be confirmed or refuted. Kuttner asserts that the growing practice of leaks had given the press more credit than it deserved, since some of its revelations were really only republished leaks of information that had originally been gathered by the Senate Watergate Committee, headed by Sen. Sam Ervin.

Kuttner interviewed the journalists who did much of the reporting that led to Agnew's resignation, and while they wouldn't reveal their sources, he concluded that most of the anonymous information came not from a calculated pattern of leaks but from attorneys on either side of the case—quite normal sources for a reporter. The real lesson of Watergate, Kuttner concludes, is not that government officials are necessarily waging a covert war of words against each other by leaking to the press, but that the press needs to stay more vigilant than ever against those officials' lies and attempts to cover up their own wrongdoing. In the last two words of his piece, Kuttner aptly sums up *(MORE)*'s general attitude toward the revival of muckraking journalism: "keep digging."[33]

(MORE) covered the Nixon administration more than it covered any other single topic in 1973—which should not be surprising, given the timing of the Watergate story and the general anti-Nixon atmosphere. One classified ad as early as January 1972 advertised "Dump Nixon" stickers for sale. And it was the Nixon administration together with Vietnam that spurred the return to the muckraking that *(MORE)* pushed for in Kuttner's article and in others, such as one that pointed out the press's underuse of the Freedom of Information Act.[34] Nixon's Christmastime public relations effort made the pages of *(MORE)* in early 1972,[35] as did an essay trying to determine why Henry Kissinger garnered so much love from the press corps despite his constant evasions.[36] Nixon's press secretary, Ron Ziegler, merited a profile,[37] and in a lighter vein, *(MORE)* asked why the *New York Times* continued to refer to Spiro Agnew as "Mr. Agnew" on second reference, despite a policy that revoked honorifics from other people who had been convicted of crimes.[38] As prospects darkened for Nixon, CBS News correspondent Dan Rather's interview with him also got coverage,[39] as did the general turn in television coverage's tone concerning the president.[40] And a collection of short essays published right after Nixon's reelection asked whether it was the press or the public that was more at fault for that reelection. If a

properly informed public still makes the wrong decisions, *(MORE)* wondered, could the press still be blamed for that shortcoming?[41] The authors who answered that question included Tony Lukas, David Halberstam, Nora Sayre, Joe McGinniss, Timothy Crouse, and Roger Wilkins, all of whom were well known and well respected. Their general conclusion was that the press did what it could—but that Nixon had found too many ways to manipulate the media and control a story that he needed controlled. They also argued that George McGovern could never be up to matching Nixon at his own game.

While the Pentagon Papers, and then Nixon and Watergate, dominated the first two and a half years of political coverage in *(MORE)*—and the cited articles are only about half of those that ran—there was also regional coverage, including stories about Philadelphia, Cleveland, and the quirky fraternity of the New York City Hall press room. *(MORE)* even requested that its readers send in tips for good regional stories to cover.[42] But there is no doubt that in the first two and a half years of its existence, *(MORE)* found the two stories it most needed to cover. The timing was felicitous.

Coverage of the Media Industry

Much as media news sites watch for announcements of new publications today, *(MORE)* excitedly chronicled new developments in what seemed at the time to be a rapidly changing industry. Less than a decade earlier, New York City had a vastly different newspaper industry than it had in 1971, when *(MORE)* began publication. In large part, this was a result of the newspaper strike of 1962, which probably helped kill off four newspapers on its own. In telling the story of that strike, Scott Sherman described pre-strike New York City as a sort of news-lover's paradise:

> New York in 1962 was . . . a place where anyone with a serious newspaper habit lived in a state of perpetual bliss: seven dailies appeared in rolling editions around the clock. There were two upscale morning broadsheets: *The New York Times* and the *New York Herald Tribune*. There were two mass-market morning tabloids with formidable circulations and devoted working-class readers: the *Daily News* . . . and *The New York Daily Mirror*. . . . There was an afternoon tabloid, the *New York Post*. . . . And there were two afternoon broadsheets: the Hearst-owned *New York Journal-American* . . . and the *New York World-Telegram & Sun*. . . . Every few hours bundles containing the latest editions descended on newsstands: the "bulldog" editions of the

morning dailies arrived around nine p.m., ideal for people streaming out of bars, restaurants, and nightclubs, while the first editions of the afternoon papers fell off the printing presses a little after eight a.m.[43]

By 1971, only the *Times*, the *Post*, and the *Daily News* survived. So for serious news or literate ideas, the *Times* had become the only game in town. *(MORE)* would come to focus much of its coverage on the *Times*, for reasons both personal and logical.[44] In its subtle and long-lasting dance with critiquing and supporting the *Times*, *(MORE)* both sought new publications that might challenge the "newspaper of record" and spur it on to better things, and lamented some of the also-rans. This was not an explicit connection, of course. *(MORE)*'s general stance seems to have been support for a diverse and thriving media, and it is only through the accretion of the review's coverage of media beginnings and endings that these conclusions can be reached.

(MORE)'s recurring coverage of the death of beloved media institutions—the wistful, romantic side of the media birth/death dialectic—began with the November 1971 issue. In the early days of *(MORE)*, headlines were often cryptic—more literary than an indication of the content of the articles they sat atop. That November issue included a piece called "Notes from a Bargain Typewriter,"[45] in which Joseph Roddy, a former senior editor at *Look* magazine, lamented the end of general-interest magazines, and *Look* in particular. The headline referred to the typewriter that *Look* sold him for fifty dollars when it liquidated its assets. Already in 1971, *Collier's* had died ("gaudily," according to Roddy) and the *Saturday Evening Post* had come to a "vituperative" end. In his essay, Roddy also writes that even the venerable *Life* magazine was on life support, and that it would probably not be long for this world (and he was right: it ceased weekly publication in 1972, though it has been revived in various forms since then).

In fact, apart from the references to typewriters, very little about Roddy's piece feels anachronistic, even in 2019. No matter how progressive they seem to be to their readers, journalists often romanticize the past—though maybe that is mostly out of concern for the institutions that employ them. Evidence of that worry about a paycheck can be seen in Roddy's lead:

> If only there were a few more mass-circulation feature magazines left to run tests on, I might have an axiom to set down here. In its place I offer only directions for calculating expiration dates to come: 1) watch the magazine's

staff writers closely while they are given new issues fresh from the bindery; 2) when they start counting advertising pages even before they admire their own stories, note the date; 3) add six months—that's when the publisher's salvage crew will begin selling off the typewriters.[46]

Though Roddy takes issue with some of the choices of the magazine's publisher, he writes that *Look*'s demise was all but inevitable, and that editorial changes would only negligibly have prolonged the process. The magazine, he wrote, was strung along in its last months by cigarette ads (an ironic foreshadowing of the final few issues of *(MORE)*).

Just about a year after Roddy's piece, *Life* finally died for the first time, and *(MORE)* memorialized it with an essay by former *Life* staff writer Jane Howard. While *(MORE)* would often take a cynical approach to the press, its writers also knew how lucky they were to work in a field where they could meet wonderful people and have "accessibility to experience," as Howard quotes Marianne Moore saying. This is very much akin to the sort of awe with which *(MORE)*'s assistant editor Terry Pristin viewed the people around her, as noted above. *Life*'s staff had known for some time that their publication was doomed, but at its height, it provided Howard with the chance to meet Rachel Carson, Vladimir Nabokov, James Baldwin, and S. J. Perelman. "In the palmy years before the cutbacks and rumors," she wrote, "there was the heady sense that one might be assigned anytime to go anywhere."[47] She writes that working at *Life* felt like being "among the chosen."[48] Part of that feeling came from the pervasiveness of the magazine even before she began to work there. *Life*, like other general-interest magazines in the early to mid-twentieth century, felt like an immovable part of American culture. For Howard, this paean to the great magazine wasn't just about a personal loss of employment, either. For the last year, she had been working there on a contract basis. This was about the death of an institution.

(MORE)'s coverage of launches was more frequent than its elegies to old media, but also shorter and snappier in most cases. Much of that coverage showed up either in Hellbox, the front-of-the-book department that encompassed most of the pieces that were too short for full article treatment; or, if the publication was local, the story might show up in the Big Apple, a recurring spread, usually across the centerfold of the magazine, that covered New York media. In the same issue as Jane Howard's *Life* essay, the Big Apple included short items about rumors that Bob Guccione, publisher

of the men's adult magazine *Penthouse*, might launch a competitor to the not-quite-as-racy women's magazine *Cosmopolitan*; and about a magazine called *Couples* that would be launched by Clay Felker, editor of *New York*. Neither of those went anywhere. (Later in 1973, *(MORE)* reported that the national pilot issue of *Couples* had flopped, but that two competing magazines on a related theme would be launching on the same day: *Single* and *Singles*).[49] That edition of the Big Apple also had a slightly longer piece about changes at the Long Island daily *Newsday*, which had recently introduced a Sunday edition and a magazine called *LI*, which was derided as "so fluffy, so inconsequential, so trite," by one anonymous staffer quoted in the article.[50]

A longer article in the January 1973 issue looked at plans for a few new evening newspapers that might compete with the *New York Post*. *(MORE)* had confirmation, according to the article, that "New York oil millionaire" John Shaheen would begin publishing a new daily the following Labor Day. Nothing came of that rumor either, though *(MORE)* seemed more interested in running two mockups for an evening edition of the *New York Times*, plans for which had already been abandoned by the time of the article's publication. The *Times* had gone "further than anyone" in planning an afternoon daily, the article said, but the study groups that had been put together decided that it would be too much of a drain on the resources of the *Times*.[51]

While the January 1973 issue seems to have been the one in which *(MORE)* concentrated most of its editorial energies on births and deaths in media properties, the first two and a half years of the magazine did feature several other stories on the subject. *(MORE)* ran a long essayistic and impressionistic review of the *51st State*, an experimental documentary news show on WNET Channel 13, New York City's public television station. Legendary writer and editor Murray Kempton wrote the piece, and he concluded that at least in the sample he had watched, the show fell far short of the promise of its advertising. While the show promised to be vastly different from the restless "Action News" of the 1970s (the kind evoked by the *Anchorman* movies), it in fact suffered from the same inability to give its important subjects the lengthier treatment that they needed.[52] The only real difference, Kempton suggested, was that "the caste mark of the self-serious is the moment they shift to the facetious whenever they feel called upon to prove that, just because they have substance, you shouldn't think they are ponderous."[53] Nearly a year later, though, when the *51st State* was in its second season, *(MORE)*'s editors bestowed a Rosebud (their version of the *Columbia Journalism Review*'s Laurels) on the show, for demonstrating that television journalism could do its own serious reporting and not just recite the day's headlines. This short piece, which ran in Hellbox, also noted that most of the show's staffers assumed that it was doomed at the end of that season, since the show was so expensive to produce.

The *51st State* was one of the news outlets that *(MORE)* outlived. So was *L.A.*, a city magazine for Los Angeles on the model of *New York*. The February 1973 issue of *(MORE)* contained a long autopsy for the short-lived magazine (causes of death: a confusing editorial tone followed by financial mismanagement as the magazine gained its editorial footing).[54] *(MORE)* also chronicled the disastrously short-lived television career of Sally Quinn, *Washington Post* writer and eventual wife of *Post* editor Ben Bradlee. Terry Pristin used the announcement of her debut on CBS to write about the lack of women on television.[55] Joseph Roddy also returned to the pages of *(MORE)* to talk about *Intellectual Digest* as a haven for former writers from *Look*. Roddy's coverage was laudatory, though few magazines billing themselves as intellectual last very long.[56]

In the first two and a half years of *(MORE)*, the magazine did manage to cover a few new publications that would have a lasting impact, though not always in the depth that the failed giants or the spectacular misfires would get. The Big Apple briefly noted the launch of *People* magazine as a spin-off of the People section of *Time*.[57] And in her debut as a writer for *(MORE)*, Claudia Cohen wrote about a rumored new Living section in the *New York Times*, which would mimic the wildly successful Style section[58] (for which Sally Quinn wrote, coincidentally). Two anecdotes do not constitute enough data to substantiate a trend, of course, but it's hard not to infer that the death of the general-interest magazine and the rise of gossip and home publications intimated the end of *Life* as a general-interest publication, and the rise of the general interest in lifestyle publications.

Coverage of the Practice of Journalism

As befits a journalism review for which the primary audience was journalists, *(MORE)*'s most consistent topics were those that addressed the requirements of good, ethical journalism. If, as A. J. Liebling wrote, a school for journalism was worthless without a school for publishers, *(MORE)* aimed to be the printed version of both of those schools. If the magazine's coverage of the media business, as discussed in the previous section, would constitute the school for publishers, then the ethical, critical, and First Amendment issues that *(MORE)* covered, and that are described in this section, would constitute the journalism school.

One issue that dealt specifically with the interactions between editorial and business staff at news publications was the reporters' power movement, which was an inspiration to the founders of *(MORE)* in its earliest days, as we have seen. As noted above, the pilot issue of *(MORE)* included a piece by *Chicago Journalism Review* editor Ron Dorfman about movements for reporters' autonomy at the *Chicago Daily News* and the *Sun-Times*. It was more than a year before *(MORE)* tackled the subject in any depth again, but in three consecutive months, it took up the issue of a staff uprising at the alternative newsweekly the *Boston Phoenix*. The initial piece was written by Bill Kovach, who was working in the Washington bureau of the *New York Times* and would eventually go on to lead it, then edit the *Atlanta Journal-Constitution* and run the Nieman Foundation for Journalism at Harvard University. According to Kovach's article, the owner of the *Phoenix* decided to turn it into something more closely resembling his ideal newspaper—the *Wall Street Journal*—and he fired the editor in order to bring in a new editor recruited from an advertising firm. Nearly forty members of the editorial staff rose up and demanded a say in the operation of the newsroom. They won at least a partial victory, gaining some concessions including a carefully detailed accounting of the process by which an editor could be fired. Kovach saw the prospect of true "democracy in the newsroom" as being a far-off notion, but he also saw the new arrangement as an opportunity for strengthening the paper. On the one hand, the ideas of the owner might tamp down the *Phoenix's* tendency toward stories calculated to shock the establishment. On the other, contributions from the staff could shape cultural coverage in exciting ways. He quotes one staff member as saying that the counterculture was already washed up, but that the *Phoenix* was not about to serve Richard Nixon's "dream of expanding American capitalism."[59] They needed to stay on top of the culture and explain the changes in society in the 1970s.

Kovach's *Phoenix* article began a four-month run of articles about democracy in the newsroom. The following two issues included updates on the *Phoenix* story. In August, after the optimism inspired by the newsroom union's minor victories, *(MORE)* found itself reporting on what it saw as a troubling development. After the strike, the owner of the *Phoenix* was rumored to be in discussion with a more mainstream rival, *Boston After Dark*, in order to arrange a sale or a merger.[60] By September, *(MORE)* had cause to report on the *Phoenix* again. The sale had gone through, and *Boston After Dark* officially changed its name to the *Phoenix*. But the staff who had unionized did not go with the paper after its purchase and instead started a new rival alt-weekly, which they called the *Real Paper*.[61] This new paper lasted until 1981, but the *Phoenix*, which eventually expanded into a small chain of alt-weekly newspapers and other media outlets, lasted until 2013, when it finally ceased publication. In the end, the unionized newsroom sent the paper that the staff wanted to protect into larger, and more corporate, hands.

The next issue of *(MORE)* contained a piece by journalist A. Kent Mac-Dougall, in which he tells the story of the prank he pulled upon resigning from his reporting job at the *Wall Street Journal*, and uses that as an opportunity to critique the management style of the paper. When he quit, Mac-Dougall wrote up a mock wire story declaring his freedom from "peonage" at Dow Jones, the company that owned the *Journal*, and transmitted it to the paper's bureaus. When this led to his being fired immediately, rather than being allowed to resign, MacDougall saw the reaction as typical of a management structure that made no effort to encourage loyalty or to foster journalistic careers. He is careful to separate his complaints about the conditions of employment from the conditions that foster good journalism. In fact, he praises the *Journal* as one of the best places in the United States to practice journalism at the highest level. He even includes a cheeky bar graph showing the paper's yearly accuracy in covering pork belly futures (each bar goes all the way to the top, indicating 100 percent), and sincerely praises the independence and integrity of the paper. But he also charts the paper's profits and documents that the salaries of its employees are lower than those of reporters at less-profitable competitors. While this might not be a story of true democracy in the newsroom—MacDougall made no effort to organize, deciding instead to leave—it is a story of discontent with the management structure. Ultimately, MacDougall finds the conservatism of the paper, its unwillingness to challenge the essential nature of Wall Street or to change itself, to be too overwhelming to continue his employment there.[62] It should be noted that MacDougall saw himself as a radical socialist, though it would be another sixteen years until he was open about that fact.[63]

MacDougall's piece ran on the cover and was one of the longer pieces that *(MORE)* ran in this period. In the same issue, Shelley Fisher wrote about efforts to achieve democracy in the newsroom in Europe, as a comparison to U.S. attempts.[64] An editor's note introducing the piece points out what Kent MacDougall likely already knew: that there was no socialist tradition in the United States, so American journalists looking to organize had to look to Europe for their models.

Firmly rooted in the United States, *(MORE)* seemed to be more concerned with issues of press harassment and whether shield laws designed to protect reporters from testifying against their sources were a good idea for the press. When *(MORE)* began regular publication in October 1971, oral arguments for the landmark (yet muddled) Supreme Court case on reporters' privilege, *Branzburg v. Hayes*, were still a few months in the future.[65] The threat of having to go to jail for a source was very real, and with the Branzburg case's unclear precedent, it would continue to be for some time. In keeping with its ongoing assessment of the state of political reporting, *(MORE)* also kept a close eye on issues of access, harassment, and the rights of newspeople throughout 1972 and 1973.

In April of 1972, two months before the *Branzburg* decision, *(MORE)* ran a piece by Edwin Goodman, general manager of WBAI, a public radio station in New York.[66] WBAI had recorded audiotape of a rebellion inside New York City's detention center, nicknamed "The Tombs." When a judge subpoenaed the tapes, Goodman refused to hand them over and he ended up in jail himself for two days. Goodman's jailers treated him fairly civilly though, and the piece is somewhat tepid, given that it ran in the same issue as Ernest Dunbar's piece on black reporters, which has a much more menacing tone in talking about government harassment, particularly in the case of Earl Caldwell, whose case was decided together with Branzburg's. In June, as the case was set to be decided, *(MORE)* ran another piece on the case, again focusing attention on Caldwell,[67] a reminder that accidents of alphabetization can influence how a Supreme Court decision is remembered. The court consolidated the cases of Branzburg, Caldwell, and Pappas, though *(MORE)* clearly saw the Caldwell case as the most pressing of the three, as it had "become the press' symbol of resistance to subpoenas."[68] As the article, by Fred Graham, went to press, journalists were cautiously optimistic that lower court rulings supporting Caldwell's decision not to testify and reveal the names of his Black Panther Party sources would stand, but Graham cautioned that Richard Nixon had carefully seated enough conservative justices to give pause to that optimism. Caldwell's attorneys, he explained, had asked not only for a new constitutional right to be granted to journalists, but for that right to be taken to its logical extreme, and the Supreme Court, whatever its makeup, rarely liked to move so quickly. In fact, the court's decision was sharply divided, with four justices clearly indicating that they saw no First Amendment right for journalists to protect their sources and four justices indicating that there was, in fact, such a right. And one justice, Lewis Powell, wrote an opinion that said there could be such a privilege, but it was not applicable in this case.

In the face of such a muddled outcome, *(MORE)* kept up its support for reporters' rights, both in reporting on developments and in more ambitiously worded opinion and editorial pieces. *(MORE)* ran at least five additional articles before the end of 1973, three times in support of Peter Bridge, who was the first reporter held on contempt charges after the *Branzburg* decision.[69] One of the essays was written by *New York Times* Supreme Court reporter Anthony Lewis, who would make a name for himself as a strong supporter of the First Amendment.

(MORE) also covered obscenity and profanity issues, which, like shield laws for reporters, is a concern that runs along First Amendment lines, but in a vein not quite as physically threatening as the specter of jail time. *(MORE)* wrote about profanity with all the relish of a preteen discovering dirty language and bodily humor, taking real pleasure in tweaking authority figures, such as when the editors "censored" the headline of one piece by using the word "B——shit."[70] Ethel Strainchamps, who wrote the piece, gives an amusing history of "dirty words" in print, and quotes editors who were frustrated that they couldn't use some words, even as those words became essential to telling the story of counterculture protests. In a way, of course, *(MORE)* was founded when an editor told Tony Lukas that he couldn't write "bullshit" in an article for the *Times*. Reading *(MORE)*'s coverage of profanity and obscenity in its first two and a half years, a sense emerges that *(MORE)* is reminding the media that we're all grownups, and asking, Can't we talk like grownups do and abandon this silly veneer of propriety? But the ironically juvenile way that *(MORE)* approached this commonsense proposition was certainly funny. There was coverage of the obscenity trial surrounding the popular pornographic film *Deep Throat*.[71] There was coverage of newspapers censoring the comic strip *Doonesbury*[72] and the acceptability of an ad for a documentary entitled *Tits*[73]—and of an ad for a French film that contained cartoon nudity that had to be sent back to the artist for some well-placed towels and swimsuits.[74] And there were at least two or three other stories on the subject in the period from June 1971

to the end of 1973. *(MORE)*, it seems, would stop sniggering if only the editors and publishers and judges would allow this discussion out in the open.

As a magazine of press criticism, *(MORE)* had opinions not just about the operations of the press, but also about the best practices for press criticism. Including the piece about Daniel Patrick Moynihan's "scholarly tantrum" in the first issue brought up the idea of press ethics, self-policing, and councils right from the start. That continued with articles written by some of *(MORE)*'s core staff and contributors. Joseph Volz reviewed the first ombudsman of the *Washington Post*, Richard Harwood.[75] Founder Tony Lukas followed up with a piece on the limits of in-house press critics.[76] In February of 1973, Dick Pollak wrote "A Case against Press Councils" to extend that argument.[77] He wouldn't have written the piece himself, he says, but when he assigned a writer to read the sixty-four-page report of the Twentieth Century Fund that led to the creation of a national press council, this writer apparently could not take the report seriously enough to write the piece and begged Pollak to let him off the hook. Pollak didn't take the proposal seriously either, and he also cites a survey of the American Society of Newspaper Editors that opposed the idea three to one, and the strong statement by *New York Times* publisher Punch Sulzberger that they would not go along with the council. However, Pollak argued, his real objection to the idea of a national press council was that any real change in American journalism had to come from within the profession itself. That view jibes perfectly with the ethos of *(MORE)*, which was written about journalism, by journalists, and mostly *for* journalists. Pollak and the other leaders of *(MORE)* had faith that "[t]he newsrooms of the United States are full of journalists with good ideas about how to create a more responsible and responsive press. If they had the power they deserve, the face of journalism in this country might change markedly—far more than it ever will under periodic hot compresses ministered by a national press council."[78] *(MORE)* had faith in journalism, and, more importantly, in journalists.

In an interview, Dick Pollak said he had hoped that *(MORE)* would have an audience beyond professional journalists, becoming something like a *New York Review of Books* for journalism and media, a forum where intelligent people could intelligently expound on the relationship between the press and the culture. And while much of the content of *(MORE)* aimed at bringing in a general audience, the magazine really was, as stated above, *of* journalism, *by* journalists, and primarily also *for* journalists. To that end, though, *(MORE)* served as a kind of lifestyle magazine for reporters in the

1970s, giving working journalists who might not have been at the elite national news organizations a glimpse into the day-to-day life of those who were, and also into the lives of other journalists like themselves across the country. So while it was a magazine of ideas, one that earnestly pondered why there was not more muckraking investigative journalism[79] (or explained the history of the first batch of muckrakers),[80] (MORE) was also a magazine of community, in the way that the best and most successful magazines are. A selection of articles shows the sorts of reporters' issues that (MORE) engaged with.

Early in 1972, (MORE) ran a piece on the special challenges of working in television newsrooms.[81] It called out reporters for being too eager to take freebies from the people they covered,[82] and on the next page exposed the inner workings of the Pulitzer Prizes, which a former Pulitzer judge shows to be rather less formal, organized, or magical than many reporters might have hoped they would be.[83] Tony Lukas profiled gonzo journalist Hunter S. Thompson, parodying Thompson's style,[84] and Calvin Trillin wrote about what it's like to be an out-of-town reporter who swoops into unfamiliar cities and "uses" local newspapers instead of really reading them.[85] NYU journalism professor David Rubin wrote about what it was like to be a reporter senior enough to be invited on a press junket to France with actor Danny Kaye in tow,[86] and at the other end of the spectrum, a young cub reporter named Peter W. Kaplan (who would grow up to be the storied editor of the *New York Observer*) described his experience of being "baptized" by a source who called him "the first sign of a break in the cold and rather killing front of New York journalism."[87] It must have been a heady experience—and an inspirational one for the other young journalists who read (MORE) and, like Kaplan, dreamed of a life as a big-city journalist.

Like a cub reporter beginning to find his feet, (MORE) changed itself physically a bit in the years from 1971 to 1973, switching from two to three columns in March 1973 and bringing on a young graphic designer named Malcolm Frouman as the first full-time art director in July of that year (though Sam Antupit remained on the masthead as having created the magazine's design). The new makeup of the magazine increased its readability quite a bit, both by giving it a slightly more polished look and by introducing subheads and pull quotes that gave readers a better idea of what each particular article was going to be about. Prior to this minor redesign, cryptic headlines occasionally gave little hint as to the content of each article. In the first issue, Tony Lukas's article about *Reader's Digest* and its bowing to corporations on environmental issues was called only "Life in These United States," an oblique reference to *Reader's Digest*'s humor department. Ernest Dunbar's piece about the experiences of black reporters in the newsroom was called only "Notes from the Belly of the Whale."

One thing that was always consistent, though, was the constant injection of levity into the proceedings. In addition to the jokes that made their way into headlines and into the less-ponderous articles, there was a vein of liveliness in almost every issue. The choice of cartoons to illustrate the vast majority of articles helped. Many of these were done by Marty Norman, whose accounting books from the period show that he earned as much as three hundred dollars for a complicated front-page cartoon[88] (but he never earned as much from *(MORE)* as he did from larger national publications). These cartoons, whether by Norman or by other contributors, often had the bulbous style of R. Crumb or Monty Python drawings, sometimes with an Edwardian revival flair that also seemed to crop up on restaurant menus in the 1970s or in the black humor of the macabre cartoonist Edward Gorey.

(MORE) also ran several satirical and parody articles. The first regular issue parodied *New York*,[89] and Clay Felker's city magazine became a regular target. Lynn Sherr took a stab at the style of *Mad* magazine in another issue.[90] The magazine devoted a two-page spread to a brief article about the "poetry" of *New York Daily News* headlines, which was surrounded by more than two dozen choice examples of the art, including "He Has a Flood of Gripes, But No One Gives a Dam," and "Heroin & LSD Used to Ease Last Trip."[91]

Perhaps most famously, though, art director Sam Antupit came to the rescue of the magazine when a story for the Big Apple section fell through. Antupit came into the office with a manila folder full of clippings he had been keeping from the *New York Times*. He had more than thirty of them, all of them one- or two-sentence filler stories that the paper would use to plug holes in the layout when a story didn't reach the bottom of the page. And all of them had headlines that contained the phrase "bus plunge." Someone at the *Times* had made a game of collecting wire service stories about buses in Asia and Latin America that had fallen from cliffs or mountain passes. *(MORE)* ran about twenty of them, filling two columns.[92] They showed a dark sense of humor in both *(MORE)* and the *Times*, as press critic Jack Shafer noted more than thirty years later.[93] They also showed that as much as there was to say about journalism, even a journalism review needed a little filler from time to time.

Coverage of Women and Minorities

(MORE)'s coverage of the Nixon administration so dominated 1973 that political stories almost crowded out cultural stories in that time. But the first year or so of *(MORE)* featured regular and earnest coverage of cultural trends at the end of the chronological 1960s, as a seemingly unified New Left began to splinter into identity politics. Feminism, race, and to a lesser extent a newly visible interest group, gays, all took turns in the spotlight at *(MORE)*. Gay liberation, which borrowed its name from women's liberation, only warranted sporadic coverage, but when it came to race and gender equality, *(MORE)* regularly covered how publications covered these topics, as well as how those publications were making progress toward integrating those groups into their own newsrooms.

The first regular monthly issue, in October 1971, contained articles that touched on women's issues as well as problems of racism in the press. The cover story inaugurated what would become a semi-regular feature in the magazine: running stories that more mainstream publications had "killed" or "spiked," to use the violent language of the newsroom, and usually explaining how those articles came to be excluded from the publications that originally commissioned them. This first instance was a book review by the writer and feminist activist Susan Brownmiller. She had been active in the women's liberation movement for a few years by 1971, but her biggest fame was a few years off, when she would publish her book *Against Our Will: Men, Women and Rape*, which argued that rape had always been defined by men, not by women.

Life magazine had assigned Brownmiller to review *The Prisoner of Sex*, Norman Mailer's critique of feminism, and reportedly told her to "keep it light," which seems like a joke when assigning a feminist journalist to review a book by Norman Mailer. In her review, though, Brownmiller did keep it light, if only by pointing out that no one is better poised to defend manhood than a man who has both the word "man" and a homophone for "male" in his name (though comparing Mailer's chutzpah to Charles Manson's god complex probably didn't help Brownmiller get her story into the magazine).[94] Even though the editorial preamble to the piece focused more on the duplicity and conflicts of interest that the publishers of *Life* engaged in when killing Brownmiller's review, putting it on the front page of the first regular issue of the magazine did make a statement that *(MORE)* identified with the women's liberation movement. The editorial introduction also did much to establish one of the two overriding editorial voices of the magazine: a sneering, sarcastic tone that today would be described as "snarky."

> Yet surely so high-minded a writer as Norman Mailer would not try and tamper with the editorial integrity of *Life*; and certainly the editors would not bow to him if he did. The whole thing was probably Ms. Brownmiller's fault. Here is her Transgression:[95]

Mailer wrote to *(MORE)*, and his letter was published in the next issue. He included the letter he sent to *Life* complaining that assigning a review of his book to a feminist writer would be analogous to asking Spiro Agnew to review the work of the feisty investigative journalist I. F. Stone. Mailer makes a point in his letter to *(MORE)* of refusing to call Brownmiller "Ms.," dismissing it as an irksome neologism.[96]

Two 1972 articles looked at sexism in the media. Pamela Howard wrote a piece on a topic that almost certainly would have grated on Norman Mailer: the casual and careless use of sexist language by reporters. Her piece opens with a bit of satire, another example of the tone that enlivened *(MORE)* when it was sprinkled in between the more serious, heavy pieces. Howard wrote a mock news article about New York City mayor John Lindsay's presidential campaign, written in the way it would have been if it had been about a woman instead.

> John Vliet Lindsay, the svelte, blond, 50-year-old father of four, announced today that he is giving up gardening at Gracie Mansion and setting his sights on more fertile surroundings—the White House and its Rose Garden. As he sipped coffee in the mansion's cozy, aubergine kitchen and his son, Johnny, age 11, whipped up an Angel Food cake, it was hard to imagine that the city's pert, cheery, number one househusband had spent all day traipsing through Bedford Stuyvesant with his best friends, Meade Esposito, the vivacious Brooklyn leader, and Sid Davidoff, his muscular man-in-waiting. His Roland Meledandri suit and his blush of pancake makeup were hardly disturbed by the near-riot he caused when he walked through.[97]

But the serious message of the piece should not be dismissed because of the light tone. Howard's concern was not the blatant, intentional sexism that had been a pressing issue for first-wave feminists, but a more pernicious kind of unconscious, unthinking sexism. Unlike many articles in

(*MORE*), this one directly addressed an audience of working journalists, and ended with six tips for keeping sexist language out of their writing. These included: try substituting the word "black" for the word "women" and see if the phrasing sounds insensitive; don't call anyone eighteen or older a "girl"; and stop referring to women by their first names on second reference. And in one of the earliest calls for reader participation, a request, set off by (*MORE*)'s signature squared-off parentheses, asked for examples of sexist language in the media, which would be run in a future issue. Though (*MORE*) never seemed to follow through on this, the request gave a picture of the editors' attitude when it described Terry Pristin (not by name, but by implication) as "a tenacious feminist" and Dick Pollak as "a beleaguered former male chauvinist."[98]

While the reader-sourced best-of-the-worst sexist writing feature never happened, (*MORE*) did run a piece that looked at sexist advertising. Many of the examples that the author, Barbara J. Siegel, gives are such classics of chauvinist advertising forty years later that they almost feel like museum pieces. There is National Airlines' "Fly Me" ad, and one for Olivetti typewriters that states that the typewriter is smarter than the secretary who uses it. Siegel analyzes a good dozen others in what today might seem like an undergraduate mass communication student's well-done but slightly obvious analytical paper. Even in 1972, these were not new issues but they were gaining prominence, in part because of the launch of *Ms.*, "The New Magazine for Women," which Siegel describes as "schizophrenic"—a step in the right direction, but one that was also "a bitter disappointment to a number of feminists."[99] The advertising in *Ms.* mixed ads that showed women becoming executives with ones that portrayed them as being dressed by men who are taking care of them. So while the issue was not new, it was certainly one that was still pressing.

After 1972, as Watergate came to dominate the pages of (*MORE*), the magazine's coverage of women's issues tapered off somewhat. However, (*MORE*) did contain some coverage of women in the newsroom in 1973. In February, a short piece gave updates on actions by women at *Newsweek*, *Time*, *Newsday*, and the *New York Times*. At *Newsweek*, the women editorial employees seemed to be on the verge of signing an agreement with management and the number of women writers was on the rise. At *Time*, the numbers had dropped. Activity was just getting under way at *Newsday*, and no one at the *Times* wanted to talk to (*MORE*) because negotiations seemed to be moving forward.[100] In August, Terry Pristin, the "tenacious feminist," wrote an update that focused on the successes of the *Newsweek* group, and reported on several other women's newsroom movements that were still ongoing. *(MORE)* said that this was a new moment for executives at media companies, who suddenly found "themselves confronting first-hand a story they have been covering for the past several years, as women all over town organize to fight discrimination with their companies."[101] The *Newsweek* staff who had originally sought to increase their numbers in the editorial departments had filed a second complaint with the Equal Employment Opportunity Commission, and the magazine's executives had responded by signing an agreement to increase the number of women writers (and balance that with an increase in the number of men working in the research department) and even ensure that at least one of the magazine's editorial departments would be headed by a woman by 1974. Pristin also reported on ongoing developments at ABC, NBC, and CBS. She gave a brief update on developments at the *New York Times*, though that paper's organizers in the fight for women's equality in the newsroom remained fairly tight-lipped.[102] A Column Two piece by Pristin in the same issue used the start of a morning news show to be hosted by Sally Quinn as a jumping-off point for noting how few women were on air (at CBS, she noted, there were seven on-air women reporters worldwide).[103]

Coverage of minorities—and in 1971, 1972, and 1973, this meant almost exclusively coverage of black Americans—followed a similar pattern in *(MORE)*, with the main difference coming in the tone of the writing. The first regular issue in October 1971 carried two articles on the subject, and the stories ran fairly regularly throughout 1972 before being crowded out by political coverage, just as coverage of women's issues had been. But coverage of race issues was far more earnest than the often-jocular tone that marked the articles about women.

The more prominent of the two articles, framed by editor Dick Pollak, mostly consisted of a long memo to *New York Post* publisher Dorothy Schiff written by a reporter named Ted Poston (which the magazine consistently misspelled as "Posten"), who had been the only black reporter on their staff for many years. The occasion for publication was a set of findings by the New York State commissioner of human rights, saying that the *Post* had unfairly let go of a black probationary reporter named William Artis. The occasion for Poston's memo was a similar instance, a year earlier, of a black probationary reporter not being hired. Pollak pointed out the irony of the *Post*'s being accused of being unsupportive of a minority group in a time when it was a reliably liberal newspaper. Schiff, an early supporter of (MORE)'s publisher, Bill Woodward, reacted strongly to the piece, and her stonewalling of the magazine is told in more detail in chapter 6.

In May of 1972, Ernest Dunbar reported from the National Black Political Convention, where he concluded that while things were better for black reporters than they had been when he was hired as *Look* magazine's first black editorial employee in 1954, in reality "the barriers have merely been moved back a few paces."[104] In Dunbar's view, "black reporters are still thin on the ground, still dealing with institutional racism of a massive sort in an industry that daily offers ethical standards for others to follow . . . all of us strivers in a profession that kept us out as long as it could and grudgingly accepted a few of us when it had to."[105] Dunbar brings up the case of Earl Caldwell, the black reporter for the *New York Times* who refused to comply with a federal subpoena after he infiltrated and investigated the Black Panther Party. Initially the *Times* supported Caldwell, but eventually left him to fight the case on his own. Dunbar also engages in some criticism of another piece that had run in (MORE)—Joe Roddy's memoir of his time at *Look*. Dunbar recalled telling Roddy that *Look* had never had a black photographer, a point that never made it into Roddy's piece. When Dunbar asked him why it hadn't, Roddy said that further reporting had turned up the fact that *Look* wasn't unusual in that regard. The irony of this was not lost on Dunbar. Dunbar in his piece, and also Bob Kuttner in a later piece on black reporters at the *Washington Post*, echoed the observation that Dick Pollak had made about the *New York Post*: sometimes it was the liberal publications—*Look* and both *Posts* included—that had the hardest time accepting black reporters in their newsrooms, no matter what sort of editorial policy they espoused.

A piece that ran just as 1972 gave way to the Watergate year of 1973 fits into two of (MORE)'s categories. On the one hand, it's an article about black intellectuals. On the other, it's an article about a series of profiles of black intellectuals written by Joseph Okpaku, which was originally written for *Esquire*. The profiles and an introduction ran in that magazine, heavily edited. (MORE), however, ran the edited and original versions of the introduction side by side, in the same spirit of publishing Susan Brownmiller's spiked review of *The Prisoner of Sex*. (MORE) was pretty evenhanded in assessing the two versions. Terry Pristin, who wrote the framing article, clearly prefers the writing of the *Esquire* editor who recast (and severely cut) the introduction and the profiles of black intellectuals, though she understands

Okpaku's outrage at being identified with writers he vehemently disagrees with.[106] While *(MORE)*, as a rule, tended to side with the writer over the editor and the editor over the publisher, this sort of fair-mindedness gives credibility to the other times that *(MORE)* seemed to reflexively side with the little guy. In the end, the Okpaku affair seems to be mostly a matter of style and of a writer not familiar with the editing process being chided for being too stiff in dealing with his editors.

(MORE) could also be accused of being a bit stiff in its writing about minorities in the newsroom. Certainly in 1971 to 1973, an attitude of moral seriousness would be entirely justifiable, though the difference between the lighthearted coverage of women and the serious coverage of blacks does give one pause. Nevertheless, one brief item does raise a bit of a smile, and it ran, coincidentally, in the same issue as the piece about Okpaku and *Esquire*. To illustrate a review of the movie *Hammer*, the *Los Angeles Times* originally chose a publicity photo of the film's co-stars, the black former football player Fred Williamson and the white actress Elizabeth Harding. Williamson, shirtless and muscular, reclines against a pillow while Harding, also shirtless, but partly obscured, rests her head and her hand on his chest. The photo only ran in the first edition, *(MORE)* reports. "Comics run a mere four pages away from movie reviews in the *Times*," the article notes, "causing women's editor Jean Sharley Taylor to fear that impressionable little eyes might catch a glimpse of Fred and Elizabeth."[107] Ironically, in describing the photo that replaced it, *(MORE)* called another actress, Vonetta McGee, "demure," thus denouncing institutional racism while simultaneously using one of the adjectives that Pamela Howard specifically mentioned should be avoided when talking about women. Clearly, *(MORE)* did not have a completely unblemished record on the subject.

4. The Gathering of the Gothamedia

The First A. J. Liebling Counter-Convention and the Coalescence of the Intellectual Elite of American Journalism

On February 25, 1972, Woody Woodward, *(MORE)*'s publisher, typed up a letter to A. M. Rosenthal, managing editor of the *New York Times*.[1] He was writing to ask Rosenthal to sit on a panel called "What Kind of P.M. Paper Should New York Have?" at an upcoming conference sponsored by *(MORE)*. Woodward told Rosenthal that he had already booked at least four panelists—all of them current or former *New York Post* employees. Woodward had worked for the *Post* and had a complicated relationship with its publisher, Dorothy Schiff, who had initially liked the idea of Woodward—a product of New York society—becoming a publisher himself. As the anti-institutional, anti-publisher attitude of *(MORE)* became more and more clear, though, Schiff distanced herself from the project. Anyway, Rosenthal wasn't the publisher of the *Times*. He was its editor. Still management, but at least management on the side of the reporters, theoretically. And as a *Times*man, Rosenthal would have added a little bit of variety.

Rosenthal, a staunch conservative when it came to changing the essential nature of the newspaper he saw himself as guardian of,[2] sent a terse response on March 1: "Dear Mr. Woodward: Thank you for your invitation to appear on the panel. I would rather not."[3]

As a scion of the Manufacturers Hanover Bank fortune and having been raised in Oyster Bay on Long Island, Woodward was no stranger to wealth and power, but now he found himself as the official representative of an anti-establishment journalism review that publishers and editors often wished would just go away. The magazine was still an upstart too. In February of 1972, *(MORE)* had only published five regular issues and one pilot issue, but the topic of Woodward's letter—the first A. J. Liebling Counter-Convention—was going to make *(MORE)* known in newsrooms throughout the United States, as well as abroad. By the end of the decade, the counter-conventions had become enough of a symbol of a certain kind of engaged, thoughtful, crusading journalism that a poster for one of the conventions would be used as set decoration for the television newsroom drama *Lou Grant*.

There were few pretensions to that sort of cultural reach at the first counter-convention. It would be held on April 23 and 24, 1972, a Sunday and a Monday, at the Martin Luther King Jr. Labor Center in New York, a block or two west of Times Square and less than a block away from the headquarters of the *Times*. While that proximity may have been a coincidence, it was certainly one that the organizers of the conference would have enjoyed. The "counter" in the conference's name was intended to refer to the American Newspaper Publishers Association's annual convention, which was being held across town at the Waldorf Astoria, one of the most expensive, most exclusive hotels in New York City, redolent of old money and certainly tonier surroundings than a labor union hall in early 1970s Times Square, in the shadow of the Port Authority Bus Terminal. Times Square was well into its most squalid period, and known for vagrants, peep shows, drugs, and pornography. Though of course the *New York Times*, which gave the area its name, was still right around the corner on 43rd Street, a fact that the organizers from *(MORE)* would have been well aware of.

But while the powerful people behind the *Times* and the nation's other newspapers were meeting at the Waldorf, it was the Liebling Counter-Convention that became a sensation among a group of working reporters who had felt themselves chafing against the strictures of "objective" reporting and the move toward professionalism that had proven to be a stale substitute. They were reporters who were increasingly college-educated, and part of the youth culture of the 1960s. These reporters had seen that there were alternatives to the dry, balanced, unbiased, and uncontroversial reporting that they had been trained to do—and that their editors and publishers insisted that they do. They had seen the stylistic experimentation of Tom Wolfe and Gay Talese and Hunter S. Thompson (whose work was just about as far from traditional objectivity as anything that could be called journalism), and had read *Rolling Stone* and *Scanlan's Monthly* and *New York* and *Esquire*. They had read the alternative weekly newspapers and their more raucous, subversive cousins in the underground press. And they knew that there was still a place in journalism for hard-nosed, independent muckraking, exemplified by I. F. Stone. American journalism was beginning to explode: the *New York Times* had begun printing the Pentagon Papers the same month that *(MORE)* published its pilot issue. The Watergate scandal was bubbling up and would come to a head in the next year. The Vietnam War had weakened the trust that many reporters had for institutional sources. Michael Schudson has called this the rise of the "critical culture" in journalism and the realization that the straight news story was a socially constrained form that contained its own inherent biases.[4]

Reporters across the country were beginning to feel these restraints, but many of them had nowhere to go to talk about these issues, save the reporters' bar at the end of the block. *(MORE)* and a few other, more local, journalism reviews had begun to write about some of the issues that concerned American journalists, beginning with the *Chicago Journalism Review*, which began publication in the wake of the 1968 Democratic Convention and what some reporters saw as the shortcomings of the Chicago press in covering it. But reading about an issue and being able to connect with other people who feel the same way you do about your profession are two different things, and the Liebling Counter-Convention allowed 1,500 or more reporters to meet their idols—which is what got many of them there in the first place—but also let them meet each other and learn that they had shared complaints, which they used the conference to turn into a shared optimism.

The organizers of the convention chose as their avatar A. J. Liebling, the *New Yorker's* former press critic. Liebling worked well as a conference mascot because he was an intellectual who constantly questioned the assumptions of journalistic practice; because he was a fluid and witty stylist; and because he was an inveterate opponent of publishers and supporter of the hardworking newspaperman. In addition to being a co-founder of *(MORE)*, Tony Lukas was also a co-coordinator of the conference and wrote the cover essay for the issue of the magazine that would be current during the conference. It was called "Taking Our Cue from Joe," and said that even though Liebling had died less than ten years earlier, his name was not as well known as Lukas had expected. "For many of our younger colleagues, it appears, Liebling has long since passed into ill-deserved obscurity . . ."[5] For Lukas, Liebling's value as an icon lay in his antagonism toward publishers, his indifference toward editors, and his support of reporters. "For what outraged Liebling far more than error or stupidity was pomposity and pretension, traits he regularly found in the publishers' offices but rarely in the city room."[6]

In the spirit of its namesake, the first A. J. Liebling Counter-Convention marked a shift in the kind of power that dominated professional journalism in the United States. That is not to say, of course, that it was a cause of the shifting power dynamic—that had been accelerating for at least a decade—but there was a symbolic power in the knowledge workers in the newsroom holding a convention directly counter to the convention of journalism's moneyed people. The intellectual elite of American journalism were supplanting the power elite. It would be incorrect to call the first A. J. Liebling Counter-Convention the origin point for the elite media that have become a target for critics of American journalism—particularly those on the political right, who would add the word "liberal" to the epithet. In fact, conservative criticism of the press was already hitting a historic high point, with Vice President Spiro Agnew giving a pair of speeches criticizing the American press in the fall of 1969. Agnew, who thought of the press as part of the "effete corps of intellectual snobs who characterize themselves as intellectuals," privately coined the term "Gothamedia" to refer to the New York–based press, hinting that they were out of touch with most of America.[7]

So while the idea of the "liberal elite media" had already been planted, the idea existed more as a straw man (or as a corps of effete straw men) than it existed in reality. There were a few informal networks of journalists working at the highest levels. Reporters really did meet at bars after deadline. The *New York Times* and the *New York Herald-Tribune* had offices only a few blocks apart in the 1960s. The White House press corps saw each other far more often than they saw their own editors at their individual, competing papers. As Timothy Crouse's *The Boys on the Bus* would chronicle, campaign reporters following a candidate around the country felt the same way about each other in regard to their editors.[8] They were almost a fraternity. And they did exchange notes and enculturate each other into the world of the best practices of journalism, forming what Barbie Zelizer referred to as an "interpretive community" of journalism.[9]

Reporters remembered and recommended each other as they moved from one paper to another, just as David Halberstam recommended his friend Tony Lukas to his editors at the *Times*. And just as Lukas remembered Dick Pollak when he was thinking of starting a journalism review. And just as Lukas and Pollak together were able to summon a group of like-minded newspeople to the Harvard Club to discuss starting a journalism review, a year and a half before the Liebling Counter-Convention brought them together again.

But these were mostly informal networks. Reporters outside of New York or not assigned to the White House might only have their colleagues at their own papers or magazines or television stations to talk to. Some reporters might join regional or national press associations or subscribe to the *Columbia Journalism Review* or *Quill*, but these were professional associations and publications, unlikely to stir up trouble with the moneyed publishers. The Underground Press Syndicate was strong, but its activities were more radical than those of *(MORE)*, which meant that there was a place for a publication—and a gathering—that could split the difference, giving a voice to a group that wanted to critique the status quo, but that still wanted to get along with the squares who gave them jobs.

The sort of journalists that the Liebling Counter-Convention attracted could be described as intellectual journalists, but not in the sense of the sneering baiting of pointy-headed intellectuals that Spiro Agnew would have used. They fit into the definitions of intellectuals posited by historian Richard Hofstadter. The intellect, he wrote,

> is the critical, creative, and contemplative side of mind. Whereas intelligence seeks to grasp, manipulate, re-order, adjust, intellect examines, ponders, wonders, theorizes, criticizes, imagines. Intelligence will seize the immediate meaning in a situation and evaluate it. Intellect evaluates evaluations, and looks for the meanings of situations as a whole.[10]

Counter-intuitively for a profession built around the gathering and dissemination of knowledge, the daily work of journalism can actually discourage the type of intellectual thought that Hofstadter described. Instead, the work becomes routinized, and the perceived strictures of objectivity and the processes of editing limit the range of conclusions a single reporter can come to and encourage a kind of false balance. The process of creating the news actually discourages self-reflection, when those powers of critical scrutiny are focused outward to other institutions of cultural power.[11] Journalists can be surprisingly anti-intellectual. Working from Hofstadter's book, sociologist Daniel Rigney codified three forms of anti-intellectualism: religious anti-rationalism, populist anti-elitism, and unreflective instrumentalism. Journalists are unlikely to be anti-rational, given the centrality of objectivity to their work. But they can be anti-elitist in the sense that they are investigators of power. Unlike many people who fall into this category, journalists do tend to trust experts, but given outside pressure like the criticism of Spiro Agnew, they can often overcompensate in an attempt to balance their reporting, affecting an anti-elitist tone, despite clearly having more

in common with the powerful institutions they cover than with their readership. The third category, though, is the category that would have most
appalled *(MORE)* readers. These readers were the journalists who actively
thought about their role in the newsroom, who questioned whether the way
they did things was really the best possible way. Who asked why their bosses
told them to do things a certain way.

As issues of *(MORE)* began to filter across the country, these reporters began to sense that they were not alone, and the Liebling Counter-
Convention gave them an opportunity to commune with like-minded
people for the first time, and to actively discuss the ideas underlying the
journalism that they did every day.

The . . . New . . . Journalism

Lukas and Pollak, along with assistant editor Terry Pristin (who may have
come up with the idea for the conference in the first place after having
heard of similar "counter-conventions"),[12] and the convention's other co-
coordinator, Nora Ephron (already famous as an essayist and press critic, though not yet as a screenwriter or director), felt that same solidarity
with the reporter. The unsigned editorial at the front of the magazine, likely written by Pollak, explains the reason *(MORE)* had decided to hold a
counter-convention:

> The journalist is one of the nation's most foolishly wasted resources. In city
> rooms and television newsrooms around the country, thousands of men and
> women capable of giving their communities the kind of enlightened, tough-
> minded reporting they deserve are daily demeaned by the feckless institu-
> tions for which they work. And thousands more leave or refuse to enter the
> profession every year because of a system that still rewards stenography and
> discourages enterprise.[13]

The editorial acknowledged that none of these particular gripes was new,
but said that the convention was necessary because "working journalists
are beginning to sense they might be able to do something about it." More
than anything, that sense of optimism pervaded the proceedings of the
convention.

The 1972 A. J. Liebling Counter-Convention wove together several of
the themes that faced American journalism in the early 1970s: the questioning of the objectivity norm; the movement of journalism from being

an anonymous "team sport" to a profession where bylines could become celebrities and writers could have a voice; the growth of press criticism as an activity; calls for intellectual self-awareness in journalism; calls for accountability and ethics in reporting; newsroom democracy and anti-establishment tendencies within the establishment press; a return to muck-raking; and the emergence of journalism as a glamorous profession. These themes came together at the Liebling Counter-Convention because it gave reporters a chance to see themselves as an intellectual community for the first time, allowing them to communicate in ways they could not under the watchful eyes of their editors and publishers.

Around the same time he received the letter from Woody Woodward inviting him to sit on the P.M. papers panel, Abe Rosenthal also received a generic invitation to attend the Liebling Counter-Convention. In the envelope, he would have found two RSVP cards. One card advertised a luncheon speaker: Tom Wicker, a *Times* columnist. The other invited its recipient to an opening celebration of the convention, with former *New York Post* columnist Jimmy Breslin as keynote speaker. The scheduled location could hardly be further, symbolically, from the publishers' convention: instead of dining on Waldorf salad, counter-conventioneers would meet at the Times Square location of Nathan's Famous, the hot dog stand.[14] In the end, the opening party had to be moved; Nathan's employees were beginning what would be a forty-four-day strike against their employer.[15] Instead, the convention convened for the first time at a Chinese restaurant, Sun Luck West,[16] "with its little bridge and trickling pond, tinsel and paper dragons."[17] Charles Long, writing for the *Quill*, the magazine of the Society of Professional Journalists, opened his piece about the conference in the second person, putting "you" inside the restaurant on a rainy spring evening, alongside Nan A. Talese (whom Long demeaned by not naming her and describing her only as "the pretty wife of Gay Talese").[18] The rest of the lead continued the name-dropping, by way of scene setting: Bill Russell, retired basketball player and television analyst; Mike Wallace; Yippie activist Abbie Hoffman; Kurt Vonnegut. Then the keynote speech begins:

A path is made for the bulky form of Jimmy Breslin, the author and former columnist, and he works his way up to a table top, the only place he can be seen by everyone since no one is sitting down. There through the haze of his own cigarette smoke blending with the rest, he sets the stage for much of the vocabulary that will follow tomorrow. "The problem to be discussed here,"

Breslin begins, "is not so much advocacy in the newsroom as it is Shylock in the composing room." [. . .] Breslin disappears from the table with what has been a five-minute keynote address, and thus brings to a close Saturday night in a Chinese restaurant.

Several of the stories written about the counter-convention take this quasi-literary, in-the-moment approach to description, perhaps inspired by one of the two blockbuster panels that opened the meeting the next afternoon (the convention formally opened at noon, perhaps to allow for hangovers to dissipate). That panel, called (with Tom Wolfe-ian playful punctuation) "The . . . New . . . Journalism," brought together a group of writers who were already stars in their field, several of whom would go on to populate literary journalism syllabi in colleges across the country: Gay Talese, Gail Sheehy, Tom Wolfe, Calvin Trillin, Pauline Kael, Renata Adler, and moderator Benjamin DeMott. (Albert Goldman was also listed in the program, but seems not to have participated in the panel.) Wolfe had published the two-part essay in which the New Journalism movement got it its name in February, only a few months before this panel.

The panels at the Liebling Counter-Convention took place in two auditoriums, each seating about 800 people,[19] though several reports suggest that somewhere between 1,500 and 3,000 people attended the sessions.[20] Many were likely drawn by the invitations that the *(MORE)* staff had distributed to the newsrooms of the New York metropolitan area, which asked recipients to invite any co-workers who hadn't gotten their own invitation.[21] Enclosed was a draft of the convention program, which opened with a quotation from Liebling:

> Twelve years ago, the late A. J. Liebling, *The New Yorker*'s press critic, wrote: "The (American Newspaper Publishers Association) convention reaches here at the same season as the Ringling Brothers and Barnum and Bailey Circus. . . . Like the Big Show, the convention bears a certain resemblance to its predecessors . . ." If you're tired of circuses come to: The A. J. Liebling Counter-Convention.[22]

Some of the non-journalists in attendance may also have been drawn by the popular media attention that the conference received even before it opened. *New York* magazine named it one their "Best Bets" for the weekend, and noted that those who couldn't be there could follow the convention on the local Pacifica radio station, WBAI.[23] In fact, WBAI broadcast about fourteen hours of live coverage over the two days.[24] One of New York City's fledgling cable television systems also broadcast much of the conference.[25] But the reach of the conference went much further beyond the New York metropolitan area than the organizers had expected. In part, word spread through the network of regional journalism reviews that had sprung up in the previous three or four years.[26] (*MORE*) had also achieved a national circulation of at least eight thousand copies by this point,[27] and the conference brought in participants from as far away as Iowa, Arizona, and Hawaii.[28] And they were all sorts of people, as Sally Quinn noted:

> There were hundreds of journalism students and scattered emissaries from small-town Midwestern newspapers who had come to see the media celebrities in their New York ego center and if what they aspired to was really all that hot. Some had brought their babies, their tape recorders, their suitcases, their lunch pails, their clips.[29]

The coats and ties on stage, she wrote, were watched by people in "blue jeans and raggedy jackets." The celebrities were certainly a draw, especially for the first panel, but as Quinn insinuates, many were there to find work, to distribute their clips. Some also came for their own political purposes, as will be discussed below, and the whole mix lent something of a circus air to the proceedings, despite the alternative to circuses promised in the invitation.

But many also came to discuss the issues, and at the first panel, the first order of business was to define "New Journalism." Unsurprisingly, Tom Wolfe, the great evangelist of the New Journalism,[30] gave the first statement of the panel, and the first thing he did was dismiss definitions. The second was to add himself to a lineage that includes Boswell, Mark Twain, Chekhov, and A. J. Liebling himself. But in addition to self-aggrandizement, Wolfe also pinpointed what he saw as the new "tremendous appeal" of nonfiction writing: "I don't think that young writers any longer have the obsession, which I had when I left college and which I think most people my age had, which was to write a novel. I think the excitement has shifted into nonfiction now." Pauline Kael, who, along with Adler and Trillin, represented the *New Yorker*, a magazine Wolfe had publicly attacked, accused the New Journalism of being excellent for some stories, but not "an adequate form of journalism for dealing with the issues that most of us are interested in."

Trillin also raised the question of whether New Journalism relied too heavily on big ideas that the facts of the reporting ultimately could not support. He related his "airplane theories" story: when flying out to report a story, he would sometimes get a "brilliant theory" that would sum up the whole story. But after he did the reporting, the whole thrust of the story would change. "[I]t's not just an error or a wrong date or something like that," Trillin said of the problem with the "accountability toward truth" in the New Journalism, "but that the *impression* you got in your impressionistic portrait is wrong because everything you based it on is wrong."

Gay Talese mostly stayed quiet because, as he said, he didn't know where he stood. "I find myself siding with Tom, then with Bud [Trillin] and Renata," he said. "I do not consider myself anything but a journalist, old or new; I do my homework and I stand, or do not, by my record as an accurate reporter."[31]

None of this debate was really new in the spring of 1972. What was new was putting partisans of each side in the debate on a stage together, even if that meant risking a scene. More than one story after the convention said that Renata Adler had come armed with a can of Campbell's soup and a can opener, planning to dump the soup onto Tom Wolfe's trademark immaculate white suit in retaliation for his attacks on the *New Yorker*. But whether or not that was true, she never made good on her threat.[32]

Perhaps even more novel than having New Journalism's advocates and detractors on stage together was allowing rank-and-file reporters to question them. *(MORE)* ran an edited transcript of this panel, but the questions from the floor survive only in notes taken by journalist Nora Sayre. She recorded the West Coast journalist Paul Jacobs saying that he was troubled by the confusion of style and substance in the discussion. He argued that even doing the same work as his subjects—farmworkers, in his example—didn't let him get into their heads. He said that it could only approximate the life of those people, because the reporter has the means to escape back to the newsroom and cannot feel what it is like to be trapped in that job. Referring to Gail Sheehy's *New York* story about prostitution, he said that she could really only say what she *thought* it would be like to be a prostitute, even though, as Sheehy explained, she did everything short of sleep with customers in reporting that story. Sayre punctuated this in her notes with a punchy "Yes!"[33]

Despite the fireworks that could have erupted at the panel, and despite its star power, which was clearly intended to open the conference with strong crowds, some in the audience did not seem to get much of substance out of the proceedings. Thomas Meehan, who wrote the most extensive piece on the supposed Renata Adler plan to dump soup on Tom Wolfe, used the "nonevent" of the soup as a metaphor for the panel as a whole: "chaotic and amusing," but ultimately an empty threat.[34] However, there certainly were issues of ethics and accountability deeply entwined within what the New Journalists were doing. The mere fact of their celebrity showed that journalism was already on its way to becoming a place where individuals could shine, even though it was often thought of primarily as something done as a team, where the individual reporter was less important than the story and the publication that ran it. Press critic David Carr wrote that this transition was happening in 2013,[35] but even in 1972, bylines were already becoming more than just a vanity play for reporters: readers were actually beginning to notice the names. Individual enterprise mattered to them and to reporters.

As well-attended as the New Journalism panel may have been (and as well-reported), the panel that ran opposite it in the same time slot may have been even more important to assessing the state of organized journalism. That was "Democracy in the Newsroom," which brought together Ron Dorfman, editor of the *Chicago Journalism Review*; three correspondents for French news organizations; a newspaper publisher from Iowa; and moderator Edwin Diamond, a *New York* magazine contributing editor. A couple years earlier, Diamond had written of a "cabal" at the *New York Times*, a movement to challenge the power of the editors in the newsroom; Tony Lukas had been one of the instigators.[36] *Le Monde* and *Le Figaro*, represented by two of the French panelists, had won a measure of reporter control, and Dorfman had written about efforts in Chicago to do the same—though the American efforts never went as far as those in France.[37] The Liebling Counter-Convention gave a new sense of "reporter power" to those in attendance, though, and one Monday panel, about the tensions between newsroom management and reporters, would take up the topic again. Dick Pollak, editor of *(MORE)*, also called midnight meetings on both conference days to consider resolutions to adopt. Charles Perlik Jr., president of the Newspaper Guild, was one of thirteen steering committee members who were set to draft a "declaration of independence from news-media management on professional matters."[38] But the first midnight meeting was still more than ten hours off.

Still, these first two panels were not completely devoid of progress in the eyes of all who attended them, even if none of the important questions facing the press had been answered. At least the conferencegoers had begun to realize that they were mostly asking the same questions. The *Chicago Journalism Review* concluded that even the first two sessions had "revealed a surprising consensus" on issues that they had thought were unresolved. One was that "the basic style of newswriting taught in journalism schools and required by American news media is a fundamental obstacle to good journalism." The second was that it should be the reporters themselves, "not the owners, not the editors, not the broadcast producers," who "should have control over what they cover and how they present it."[39]

How They Cover Me

The "New Journalism" and "Democracy in the Newsroom" panels were followed by a panel on covering political campaigns featuring the syndicated columnist Jack Anderson; *Washington Post* columnist David Broder; Joe McGinniss, who had written *The Selling of the President*; Dan Rather, then the CBS News White House correspondent; Victor Navasky, author of *Kennedy Justice*; and U.S. Sen. Fred Harris, whose name was printed on the program in a different typeface, which suggests that he may have been a last-minute addition.[40] Simultaneously, the Committee for Public Justice cosponsored "A Public Hearing on Government and the Press." The late afternoon brought a panel on challenging television licenses, which was mostly a practical affair and which *Newsweek* noted was underattended, like all of the other practical-minded panels.[41] Elsewhere, conference cochairman Tony Lukas moderated a panel on sports reporting with former Major League Baseball player Jim Bouton and writer Leonard Schechter, who collaborated on Bouton's memoir, *Ball Four*. Roger Angell, the *New Yorker* writer; Dick Young, of the *New York Daily News*; and Larry Merchant of the *Post* also pitched in.

After a dinner break, several hundred people came back from bars and restaurants and from milling in the halls—so many jammed into the halls that a closed-circuit television was set up to serve the overflow—and returned to the Martin Luther King Jr. Labor Center for a panel called "How They Cover Me," another blockbuster panel meant to draw a crowd.[42] There was no announced lineup for the panel, which was supposed to be a moderated discussion of how various celebrities saw themselves covered in the press. Nora Ephron said that "[e]very famous person in the world was asked to be on this panel and refused." Hugh Hefner, Henry Kissinger, Tom Seaver, Dalton Trumbo, Alger Hiss, Henry Fonda, Shirley MacLaine, John

Lennon, Bob Dylan, and Daniel Ellsberg all said no.[43] The mobster Crazy Joe Gallo said yes, but he was killed at a clam house in Little Italy between the time he had signed on and the day of the conference.[44] The woman who arranged for him to show up as the surprise guest "made us promise not to tell a soul because they might come here and shoot him," Ephron said.[45] The final group included activist Abbie Hoffman, actor Tony Randall, film director Otto Preminger, writer Gore Vidal, Congresswoman Bella Abzug, and Marvin Miller, head of the Major League Baseball Players Association. Charlotte Curtis, editor of the *New York Times* women's pages, moderated.

The *Progressive* pointed out that any gathering of this size would have "a fair measure of irrelevance, of showboating, of utter foolishness"[46] and the "How They Cover Me" panel was a prime example. Earlier in the day, a group from the underground press and the Zippie party (having recently morphed from the Yippies), had interrupted the New Journalism panel and demanded that there be an underground press representative on every panel going forward.[47] In general, that seems to have been followed. The reporter Claudia Dreifus passed Nora Sayre a note that "by Zippie decree," she had been added to the panel on racism, sexism, and elitism in journalism.[48] Tom Forçade, head of the Underground Press Syndicate, who would go on to found *High Times* magazine, had been added to the panel on covering political campaigns.[49] Forçade was well known for using thrown pies as a method of political protest, and there were rumors that he would be doing so at the conference, though like Renata Adler's soup, that threat never materialized.[50] But Jerry Rubin and Forçade did interrupt the "How They Cover Me" panel to make a statement supporting George McGovern for president.[51] Throughout the two days, Fran Lee, a New York City activist whose latest cause was advocating for a "pooper scooper" law, repeatedly interrupted panels. She took the opportunity of having so many members of the working press around to make her case.[52] The same was true of Hal Koppersmith, a fringe candidate for Congress who wore a sandwich board advertising his platform.[53]

When the television lights turned off and the celebrities went home, the casual conferencegoers filtered out, and the die-hards convened their midnight session to begin the newsroom revolution.

Why Journalists Leave Daily Newspapers

Pat McBroom had come to New York from Philadelphia, where she had been serving six months' hard labor on the obituaries desk of the *Inquirer*.

McBroom had previously been a science writer, but when management found out that she was living with Donald Drake, who was the editor of the *Philadelphia Journalism Review*, they suspected that she must somehow be involved in efforts to democratize the newsroom, organizing editorial staff against management.[54] She says she wasn't, but after attending the Liebling Counter-Convention, she became radicalized and typed out a scathing piece about the "seeds of revolution" that had been planted in New York.

David Fitzpatrick had come from Phoenix, where he worked for the Arizona *Republic*. He became the "casually-dressed young reporter" through whom the *Chicago Journalism Review* would look at the conference. In that magazine's story, Fitzpatrick represented all of the reporters who wanted change:

> What really separated Fitzpatrick and most of the other journalists in the hall from the men on the stage was not the geography of the auditorium, but the constraints of traditional journalism as practiced everywhere in the United States. Most of those in the audience were still fettered; those on the stage had, to some extent, been able to free themselves. The question Fitzpatrick and the others had was, "How?"[55]

Both Fitzpatrick and McBroom would soon find themselves to be unfettered, though not by their own choice. What got them in trouble was their effort to get some power in their newsrooms. They tried to answer the "How?"

One of the first panels on Monday morning was called "Why Journalists Leave Daily Newspapers." Three of the panelists—Tony Lukas, David Halberstam, and Sidney Zion—were former *Times* reporters who had found themselves limited by the objectivity that the newspaper required. They had found it inadequate to cover the Vietnam War or, in Lukas's case, the Chicago conspiracy trial. "The *Times* wanted, as they later admitted to me, [a] virtually stenographic account of what went on the courtroom," Lukas told an oral history interviewer. "I one day refused to write a story, the only time I've ever done it on the *Times*. I told them to use the wire services that day because they were telling me that I could not write the story the way I wanted to write it."[56]

The tensions between the *(MORE)* conference organizers and their former employers were also demonstrated by the simmering anger with which those employers greeted word of the conference. Abe Rosenthal's terse response to his panel invitation only told part of the story. Rosenthal must have noticed some of the names on the provisional program for the conference, and he sent a memo to Punch Sulzberger, editor of the *Times*:

> Tom Wicker and Charlotte Curtis, both editors of this paper, apparently have agreed to participate. I think that this makes the *Times* look just silly. There may be no way that we can prevent Guild employees from participating but I think that we have every right and indeed a duty to insist that editors and other executives do not strike off on their own and make statements or participate in affairs that are not in the best interests of the paper.[57]

Sulzberger sent memos to Curtis and Wicker, discouraging them from participating, but not forbidding it. Curtis, who herself had clashed with Rosenthal,[58] sent a memo to Sulzberger (on Women's News Department stationery) distancing herself from *(MORE)* and the advertising copy that she thought might have implied her approval of the conference's themes, but standing firm in her decision to moderate the "How They Cover Me" panel.[59] Rosenthal seems to have resigned himself to the conference and some *Times* staff participation after that, mustering his own commitment to objectivity, but certainly not making any promises to treat the *Times* people at the conference in any special way:

> While I am away, the ANPA convention will be meeting. Also, "More" will have its counter-meeting. As I have written to Arthur Gelb, we ought to cover the "More" thing on a strict news basis. I would appreciate it if you would watch the copy on this. There will be a number of people like Halberstam, Zion and Lukas, who will be spouting off. If they have anything important to say, we should print it. But we should feel under no obligation to print something just because they are talking. Nor should we feel that simply because they attack the papers, probably including this one, that we have an inherent obligation to print what they have to say. We should be fair but not allow ourselves to be used by them.[60]

This hardly seems like the sort of toxic atmosphere that would drive out a Halberstam or a Lukas (though "spouting off" does imply a certain attitude). But a letter from several years later, when a new editor/publisher had taken over *(MORE)*, betrays a less kind feeling. In it, Rosenthal says that the magazine is a reflection "of the psychic problems and nastiness of some of the people who used to put out More and are now still involved with it."[61]

Downtown, at the offices of the *New York Post*, publisher Dorothy Schiff was also bracing herself for the beginning of the counter-convention. Ever since Woody Woodward had taken a leave of absence from the *Post* to help found *(MORE)*, she had kept an eye on the publication, first with a sense of pride in Woodward's success, but increasingly with a sense of skepticism toward Woodward's creeping radicalism. There had been inklings of the radical in Woodward before *(MORE)*: the Edwin Diamond article about the *Times* "cabal" mentioned that Woodward was working as a labor nego-tiator at the *Post*. But Schiff's opinion of *(MORE)* really soured when Dick Pollak wrote a piece excoriating the *Post* for not giving an African-American reporter the same full tryout that other, white, reporters got. Schiff wrote a scathing letter to the editor, which she never sent, calling the article "ten-dentious."[62] Schiff also wrote on top of a memo that she would consider writing for *(MORE)* to be "gross disloyalty + dischargeable offense."[63] So it should not have been surprising that when she discovered that there would be an entire panel devoted to afternoon newspapers, she would either listen to the radio or watch on television and take angry notes on the panel—which did, in fact, turn out to mostly be a complaint-fest about Schiff. She also procured a complete transcript of the panel and marked it up, with a keen eye for minor inaccuracies and petty slights.[64] She also had a staffer attend the panel and prepare a lengthy report.[65]

These are high-profile cases of editors and publishers who wanted to keep tight reins on their editorial staff, but they seem to be representative of the pressures that even less-prominent reporters were feeling. While it may have been cathartic or inspirational for them to hear the stories of reporters who had escaped, they really got their chance to voice their anger at the two midnight planning sessions. According to Pat McBroom, about seventy people attended one or both of the meetings.[66] As in the daytime sessions, the actual solutions were left for another day. Sidney Zion said, "We'll declare it now and do something about it later."[67]

The biggest dose of inspiration came from a surprise visit on the second night from I. F. Stone, the independent investigative reporter who had just been awarded the first ever A. J. Liebling Prize "For his commitment, car-ried on single-handedly over two decades, to independent and unrelenting investigation of public and private power in America and his defense of individual liberty."[68] In his speech upon accepting the award from Liebling's widow, Jean Stafford Liebling, Stone opened with a joke that made it clear how happy—and surprised—he was to see so many "radical journalists" in one place. As an elder statesman, he had a message for the "kids" in the audience:

> [W]e are up against a whole series of fundamental problems to which we have no answers. And what's so wonderful about the kids, compared to their grandfathers is that they know there are no answers and they're willing to act and to fight and to search and to move without a clear blueprint, knowing that we're in a wilderness.[69]

Stone's call for perseverance in the face of uncertainty—or even the embrace of uncertainty—fit well with the tone that *Times* columnist Tom Wicker struck in his lunchtime keynote address, when he said that "there is no orthodoxy, formula or dogma . . . of new journalism or objectivity or advocacy or activism . . . that can free us from the ills of orthodoxy . . ."[70] And echoing a call that had been issued repeatedly throughout the convention, he said that reporters needed to avoid "spurious objectivity."[71] Replacing old orthodoxies with new ones, he said, would not help journalism, but instead reporters needed to be free to do their own best work.[72] "We must let a hundred flowers bloom," Wicker said.[73] Flowers like Patricia McBroom from Philadelphia, or David Fitzpatrick from Phoenix. In the end, the *Chicago Journalism Review* piece leaves Fitzpatrick still wondering "how." That was for the late-night session. But when Stone showed up that night at the organizing meeting, he spoke to the participants, telling them once again that he didn't have any answers. The best he could do was to rouse the troops, telling them that "The life of the paper comes from the guys who write it, not the guy who happens to own it. . . . They're the ones who make it good or bad or wonderful. They're giving their lives to it, their talents and their devotion and they have a right to a say in it."[74]

Invigorated by this talk and similar speeches and conversations throughout the conference, McBroom went home and wrote her first piece for the *Philadelphia Journalism Review*, which she had avoided so far so as not to make trouble with the *Inquirer.* But her *PJR* piece pulled no punches, and she admits that she probably made a strategic mistake when she paraded copies of the journal through the *Inquirer* newsroom. Within hours, she was fired—and with the exception of a few freelance pieces, she didn't return to journalism for nearly forty years.[75] David Fitzpatrick met a similar fate when he returned home, despite not even writing about the conference. "Fitzpatrick was dismissed for refusing to acknowledge that he owed any obligation and any loyalty to the people who were paying him," his editor told *(MORE)*.[76]

For most people, however, the first A. J. Liebling Counter-Convention did not end so dramatically. There were additional Monday panels, including one on local television news chaired by Nat Hentoff; a panel on racism, sexism, and elitism in journalism that featured Studs Terkel, Susan Brownmiller, Ernest Dunbar, and Jimmy Breslin (years before his own very public racist and sexist outbursts); an alternative media panel; one on the future of women's pages with Lynn Sherr and Gloria Steinem; and a panel about the muckraking tradition, which was part of the celebration of Izzy Stone. There was more drinking, as there is wont to be with journalists. Then people scattered back to their own newsrooms to talk about what they had seen and to look forward to the next conference, which was going to be held in Washington the following year.

Predictably, the more establishment journals that wrote notices of the convention were skeptical and emphasized the silliness and the celebrity worship, while more anti-establishment outlets addressed the spirit of optimism and discovery that many took away. In addition to the articles quoted above, the counter-convention got noticed by the *Harvard Crimson*[77] and even by *(MORE)*'s stodgier older cousin of a press watchdog, the *Columbia Journalism Review*. *CJR* gave the conference a Laurel because "the unrestricted attendance and participatory ambience of the counter-convention made it a landmark."[78]

But the real legacy of the first A. J. Liebling Counter-Convention was the growing sense of community that it—and, more generally, *(MORE)*—gave to attendees and to readers. They were not alone in striving for a more thoughtful, critical, and—importantly—self-critical approach to journalism. Those gathered on stage were, for the most part, elite journalists who saw the problems inherent in the system as it stood in 1972. Those in the audience were the slightly scruffier, slightly younger journalists and students who wanted to follow those elite journalists into a revolution in journalism, one that would remake the profession, break free of the restraints of objectivity, and create a new order where the reporters would be in charge, not just the people with the money at the top of the masthead. As Edward Herman and Noam Chomsky, and Eric Alterman, have argued, the publishers who own newspapers are generally, fundamentally conservatives.[79] The first A. J. Liebling Counter-Convention marked the rise of the liberal voice of the elite media.

5. Get Me Rewrite

(MORE) Adjusts to the Post-Watergate Press

In the spring of 1973, *(MORE)* built on its success with the first counter-convention by moving the proceedings to Washington, DC. A few things had changed from 1972. Instead of being a two-day event, "Liebling II," as the banners behind the panelists called it, had expanded to three days, Friday, May 4, through Sunday, May 6.[1] Instead of being free and open to the public, Liebling II charged convention-goers eight dollars; according to the U.S. Bureau of Labor Statistics inflation calculator, that $8.00 had the buying power of $44.60 in 2017, so while it wasn't an exorbitant amount of money, it wasn't insignificant either.[2] Instead of being counter to the American Newspaper Publishers Association, Liebling II ran counter to the American Society of Newspaper Editors convention. But there wasn't as much of a difference in venue between the two concurrent meetings as there was the first year. While the first Liebling Counter-Convention had been held at the Martin Luther King Jr. Labor Center, a block or two away from the *Midnight Cowboy* seediness of 1970s Times Square, Liebling II moved into the significantly more luxe Mayflower Hotel, the historic hotel decorated with gilded accents and crystal light fixtures just a few blocks away from the White House.

A few months before *(MORE)* would chronicle Sally Quinn's foray into morning television, Quinn attended the second annual Liebling Counter-Convention. She picked up on the new establishment vibe that pervaded the atmosphere there, and attributed it to a sea change in the self-regard of the press between the spring of 1972 and the spring of 1973. The first convention, Quinn wrote, "was still decidedly unestablishment with at least as many freaks as members of respectable journalistic institutions."[3] In Quinn's assessment, Watergate changed everything. It had given journalists a reason to be proud of the mainstream press, she argued. Of course, she might have been biased, writing as she was for the *Washington Post*, which was primarily responsible for breaking the Watergate story—and since she would eventually marry the editor who directed that coverage. Also, she was basing this conclusion on observations she made at the opening-night party, not including any of the actual substance of the conference.

Nevertheless, she did have a point. Coverage of the civil rights movement, Vietnam, and cultural changes in the United States had given journalists a sense that while their work could be noble at times, they were up against an establishment that kept their strongest reporting at bay. Watergate, on the other hand, showed that a mainstream paper that was willing to devote time and resources to a story could actually break through the wall of spin that the establishment put up. And that put the press in the odd position of being both establishment and anti-establishment at the same time. It was a contradiction that *(MORE)* would long struggle with, though the gravitational pull of the establishment is almost always stronger than that of the counter-establishment.

Figure 2. Tony Lukas presents the second A. J. Liebling Award to Pulitzer Prize-winning reporter Homer Bigart at the 1973 A. J. Liebling Counter-Convention, hosted at the Mayflower Hotel in Washington, DC, as David Halberstam looks on. While the first counter-convention, held in a labor organizing hall in New York, felt like a countercultural event, by 1973 the press was dealing with the successes of the *Washington Post's* Bob Woodward and Carl Bernstein's reporting on the Watergate affair, making Liebling II a more celebratory event. (Copyright © Diana Mara Henry/www.dianamarahenry.com)

In a short preview writeup for Liebling II, which included a reprint of the conference program, the *D.C. Gazette*, an alternative paper, complained that the smaller independent papers were being shut out in favor of big-city dailies and wire services:

> As you will note from the program, only a few representatives of the alternative press (including your editor) have been invited to participate and underground and alternative newspapers are being charged $8 a head for the privilege of covering a journalism counter-convention. This all seems a bit odd and leads one to wonder what this convention is counter to. Sleep well tonight, Spiro. As long as it's easier for a big city daily editor to appear at a journalism counter-convention than it is for members of the Underground Press Syndicate, you got nothing to fear.[4]

It should be noted that in addition to the panel that included *D.C. Gazette's* editor, Sam Smith, there was also an entire workshop panel devoted to ideas that the "straight" press could learn from the alternative press.

Nicholas von Hoffman, an occasional *(MORE)* contributor but also a *Washington Post* writer, also noticed the mainstreaming of the counter-convention in its second year. "On other days the younger, farther left and less compromising participants would be counter-conventioning against the American Society of Newspaper Editors concurrently meeting uptown at another hotel. But not in this year of Watergate," he wrote. "The younger ones are so well pleased by the performance of their rich elders that they have invited onto their program editors from The Boston Globe, The Chicago Sun-Times, The Philadelphia Inquirer, The New York Times, and above all, The Washington Post."[5] According to von Hoffman, he and the other "Post Toasties," as he called his fellow *Post* employees in a reference to a breakfast cereal, couldn't help but weep with pride in "the cream" of the accomplishments of Bob Woodward and Carl Bernstein, no matter how little the rest of them had to do with the Watergate story.

In an interview with NPR reporter Robert Conley—one of the first hosts of the iconic *All Things Considered*—Tony Lukas directly addressed the change in tone from Liebling I to Liebling II. NPR was broadcasting one of the conferences panels—on the topic of the journalistic lessons of the Vietnam War—and as they waited for the panel to begin (Conley noted that the counter-convention panels started notoriously late) Conley asked Lukas just how "counter" this counter-convention was.

"Less counter than it was last year, Bob," Lukas replied.

It last year had a very, almost a counter cultural kind of flavor, in part because it was based in New York, and I think last year, some people read it as a kind of "counter-cultural" convention, with people coming in there and saying 'hey man, where are the sitar lessons?' They knew we were counter to something, but they just weren't sure what. This year, I think partly because it's in Washington, and because we're going to focus to a large degree on the Washington press corps, that it's a much less counter affair. In fact, Ben Bagdikian, the former press critic of the Washington Post, is quoted yesterday as having told the American Society of Newspaper Editors, they wondered why a radical like him was speaking to them, and a bunch of establishment editors were speaking to us. We have a number of the country's leading editors speaking to us on our panels.[6]

In the same interview, Lukas also addressed some of the misconceptions that surrounded *(MORE)*'s identity and mission. In his introduction, Conley had identified *(MORE)* as a sort of *Columbia Journalism Review* for the New Journalism. Lukas took issue with that characterization:

(MORE) doesn't really consider itself to be an organ of The New Journalism. What we do consider ourselves to be is an organ of responsible, very hard-hitting press criticism. But New Journalism implies a style. We're not wedded to any one style of reporting. We like and praise often some very traditional journalism. People who write in the very traditional style. Phil Geyelin, who was the editor of the Washington Post editorial page and the so-called keynote speaker of this convention is hardly a New Journalist. But we have great respect for him, and we have great respect for Bob Woodward and Carl Bernstein. . . . This is the best of the old journalism. Far from quibbling with it, we welcome it. And I wouldn't even call it the old journalism. This should be the journalism of the future too. This kind of investigative reporting is what this country needs more of. I think it's unfortunate that people get the impression that *(MORE)* and this Counter-Convention stands for some kind of zonked-out Tom Wolfe style of New Journalism. We stand for good journalism, whether it's zonked-out Wolfe journalism or a very straight Bob Woodward-Carl Bernstein journalism. We want good journalism, not New Journalism.[7]

So on the one hand, Lukas, speaking very quickly and surprisingly eloquently, quickly encapsulated *(MORE)*'s editorial mission in the first several years of its run. But Conley, the NPR reporter, also exemplifies the common perception that *(MORE)* was the journalism review for zonked-out sitar-playing gonzo journalists. It may have appealed to that crowd—and supported some of their work—but the staff and writers were always much more straitlaced.

At the opening night party, Sally Quinn watched as reporters dutifully stood in line for name tags and drink tickets and then stood in line again at the bar to trade them for drinks. The proceedings were almost dignified, compared to the raucous atmosphere of the previous year. Jann Wenner, founder and editor of *Rolling Stone*, even admitted to Quinn that his magazine wasn't an underground publication anymore.[8] The alternative press had begun to move inexorably toward the mainstream. Still, it wasn't so mainstream that there weren't still writers who were scared for their jobs for being at a *(MORE)* convention. A journalist for *U.S. News and World Report* refused to identify himself for fear of being fired.

Another example of that protest from the left came from the National Organization for Women, which held what it called a "counter-counter convention" in the lobby of the Mayflower. Joyce Snyder of NOW said that the organization was disappointed that *(MORE)* apparently regarded women as "a special interest group."[9] Her objections seemed to be more about the way women were represented in the media than with the way *(MORE)* included them on its panels. According to Myra MacPherson, who also covered Liebling II for the *Post*, some women came away from the conference thinking that they would have gotten a fairer hearing across town at the Newspaper Editors convention. She cited two exchanges from the panel on women's issues. In the first, Sally Quinn, in her role as a panelist, said that "If a senator is putting his hand on my fanny and talking about how he's thinking of impeaching Nixon, I'm sure not going to remove his hand." She was hissed by the crowd. And a *Women's Wear Daily* reporter was asked if women who use their femininity in reporting would inevitably lose that power as they got older. Her reply was "Not if she gets a facelift."[10] The Washington Liebling Counter-Convention may have kept some of the "freaks" out by having the gall to charge admission, but in this and future conferences (particularly *(MORE)*'s one foray into the West Coast) it would never entirely rid itself of the protests.

Quinn closed her piece with a quote from Tony Lukas, one which, he hoped, would set the tone for the conference to come: "Last year I said that journalists only get together on two occasions, when they're competing and when they're drunk. . . . Last year they were neither. They were sober and non-competitive. This year we are aiming for higher peaks. This year we hope they will be sober, non-competitive and contemplative."[11]

Unlike the 1972 counter-convention, which was a mishmash of topics that were of concern to journalists, Liebling II had two overriding themes, which Woody Woodward had announced in a Column Two column.[12] Those were political reporting and power in the newsroom. But really, all anyone wanted to talk about was Watergate—and this was before there was definitive evidence linking Nixon to knowledge of the break-in or of the cover-up. It was a lucky coincidence for *(MORE)*.

Nora Ephron had relinquished her planning duties for this conference, though her future husband, Carl Bernstein, was in attendance. Liebling II was put together by Dan McNamee (who would become a *(MORE)* business staff member) and Marjorie Federbush, who would go on to a career in philanthropy. The panels that they put together were remarkably prescient, given that it took at least six months to put together a Liebling convention.[13] Those panels included:

- Journalistic Lessons of the Vietnam War (moderated by Dan Rather of CBS News)
- Press Councils and Press Criticism (which included *(MORE)* editor Dick Pollak)
- Is Anyone Covering the City of Washington? (the panel on which Sam Smith sat)
- Getting Subpoenaed: How to Fight Back (a workshop)
- Reliable Sources: How Reliable? (moderated by Victor Navasky)
- Political Columnists: Can They Be Cosmic Three Days a Week? (Tom Wicker, the previous year's keynote speaker, sat on this panel, as did economist and political adviser John Kenneth Galbraith, who *(MORE)* identified merely as a "gadfly")
- Why Is 90 Per Cent of Washington Uncovered? (activist Ralph Nader and journalists Taylor Branch and Morton Mintz sat on the panel)
- Power in the Newsroom: Who Has It and How to Get It (a workshop featuring Ron Dorfman and four domestic and three foreign journalists)
- How Women Cover Washington: Do They Need a Special Style, View, Eye, Portfolio or Other Refuge (moderated by Lynn Sherr, then of WCBS, and including Sally Quinn, who also covered the convention)

- The Government and Broadcasters: Jamming the Airwaves
- A Deadline Every Minute: Is Wire Service Reporting Obsolete? (Gene Roberts, at the beginning of his run as executive editor of the *Philadelphia Inquirer*, and Seymour Hersh, who broke the story of the My Lai massacre, participated)
- Investigative Reporting: How to Get the Goods on the Baddies (a workshop that featured Carl Bernstein and Bob Woodward)
- The White House: Who's Kicking Whom Around? (moderated by *(MORE)*'s Tony Lukas)
- Who Decides What Is News? (moderated by *(MORE)*'s Brit Hume and including Jann Wenner of *Rolling Stone* and Victor Gold, former press secretary to Vice President Spiro Agnew)[14]

As she had the previous year, journalist Nora Sayre attended the conference and took extensive notes on the panels she attended (though less extensive than her 1972 notes). She started out Friday morning at the "Journalistic Lessons of the Vietnam War" panel. Murray Marder of the *Washington Post* argued that Vietnam and Watergate could not be seen just as "aberrations of justice on [the] part [of the] gov[ernment]." The press, he said, had gotten lulled into accepting the official government view of the war under the Kennedy administration because they liked his "panache." Bob Manning of the *Atlantic* thought that the press had missed the transition from cold war to actual war, and that it took student protests to goad the press into writing that story. He believes that the war "raised a lot of questions about whether the job of the press is simply to inform." Marder chimed in that he didn't think that was enough.[15]

Afterward, Sayre attended the workshop on how to fight subpoenas. The session appears to have been mostly practical tips for reporters. For that reason, though, it is worth noting, since unlike at the first Liebling Counter-Convention, these workshop sessions seemed geared toward real practical advice for working journalists as opposed to more high-minded discussion (or windy bloviating). At one panel called "And Now a Word from Your Editor . . ." which she attended next, she made note of the panelists, but didn't record much of what was said. She did, however, notice that Nora Ephron and Nat Hentoff asked questions. So did Paul Krassner, the counter-cultural journalist and founder of the *Realist*, ("Again," she remarked. Krassner would later take pride in "being the first to ask as meaningful a question as possible at each panel" of every Liebling convention he attended.)[16] Sayre seems to have skipped the panel sessions on Saturday of the conference, but she does have a few notes from a Sunday panel. That was "The White House: Who's Kicking Whom Around?" and thanks to Pacifica Radio, it is the most complete audio recording of a Liebling panel discussion that appears to have survived—though Pacifica clearly favored the liberal panelists in its broadcast.

The panel was less notable for any spirited interaction between its participants than for its laugh lines and speechifying. The panelists mostly seemed thrilled that they had Nixon to kick around. Tony Lukas chaired the panel, which included John Osborne of the *New Republic*; Robert Semple Jr. of the *New York Times*; Henry Trewhitt of *Newsweek*; Andrew Kopkind of WBCN radio, Boston; Sarah McClendon, who ran her own McClendon News Service; and Ralph de Toledano, the conservative author and a friend of Nixon. After an opening montage of one-liners, the Pacifica recording jumps into the middle of McClendon's remarks: "The whole White House operation in my estimation is so staged, so programmed, so controlled, that the Watergate just couldn't have happened without Nixon and his top aides planning it fully." She gets a round of applause from the receptive crowd. "The president," she says, "runs the public relations at the White House, not Ron Ziegler," Nixon's press secretary. "No decision, however small, is made at the White House without the approval of the president." She continues on to her laugh line: "This is why so many mistakes in judgment have been made." And the audience obliges her by laughing. She talks quickly, obviously reading from prepared remarks, but delivering her lines with excellent timing. One anecdote about Nixon's attention to detail has him in a receiving line at the White House with journalists and Chinese visitors, when he sees McClendon across the room, wearing pants to the White House for the first time. He walks over to her, looks her up and down, and says, "My, my. I thought you were a traditionalist!"

Lukas calls on John Osborne next. Osborne wasn't as disappointed in the press setup at the Nixon White House, he says, since he didn't expect more than for the press secretary to deal with the president's interests. And Watergate didn't surprise him either, he says, given the way that he had seen the administration operating. They were secretive and sanctimonious, and while he couldn't have predicted the Watergate break-in or the subsequent cover-up, they seemed of a piece with the rest of the White House's actions.

Lukas moves on to Bob Semple, who opens with his explanation for why the White House press corps didn't break the Watergate story:

The answer to that is fairly simple. The last people who are going to tell you of their own complicity are the people you are covering day after day. And as has no doubt been pointed out here several times, Bernstein and Woodward were not only not White House correspondents, they were not on the national staff of the *Post*. They were aggressive and industrious local reporters who had enough sense not to go to the center to find out what was wrong at the center.

Pacifica gave time only to those three panelists before cutting to questions. In order to cut down on the chaos that might ensue when a rowdy crowd had access to an open microphone, Lukas took written questions from the audience. They were still pointed and partisan. The first: "Why doesn't the press corps identify the administration whores in its midst?"

Sarah McClendon closed out the proceedings with what in retrospect seems like a very shortsighted prediction: "We'll never see such secrecy around the White House again."

On Saturday evening of the conference, David Halberstam gave the second annual A. J. Liebling Award to Homer Bigart, who had recently retired from the *New York Times* after a career spanning more than four decades. Yet another *Washington Post* article about the convention noted that Bigart's winning the award showed again the differences between Liebling II and the first convention. He was "not one of the new journalists," but instead "a silver-haired man honored for his four decades of integrity."[17] *(MORE)* had never set out to be an instrument of the counterculture, but it was also always working to goad the mainstream press. It wasn't counterculture, but it wasn't mainstream. *(MORE)* would always be caught in between. The mainstream press wouldn't accept them, but the alternative press would always protest them.

Following the presentation of the Liebling Award, the conference held its guaranteed big-draw panel in the Mayflower's ballroom. Simply called "Watergate," the panel featured Ben Bradlee and Carl Bernstein of the *Post*. The rest of the panelists were no lightweights either: Frank Mankiewicz, George McGovern's political director; former *New York Times* reporter Robert Smith; writer Garry Wills; Walter Pincus of the *New Republic*; and two former Nixon aides: Richard Whalen and Kevin Phillips. According to Myra MacPherson's account, Whalen and Phillips "locked horns" with Wills and Mankiewicz. Phillips tried to separate himself from the current batch of Nixon aides, saying that they were despised by Republicans in general.

Wills snapped back, saying that it wasn't enough to disavow the staff. "Nixon was doing what he was hired to do."[18]

The Washington Liebling Counter-Convention concluded with a re-convening of the ad hoc committee that had gathered at the first counter-convention. It's unclear what happened, except that they found a publisher for an intermittent newsletter.[19] But as the new focus on the suddenly func-tioning mainstream press suggests, it may very well have been marginal-ized. With editors and publishers as supportive of dogged reporting as Ben Bradlee and Katherine Graham of the *Washington Post* both seemed to have become in the last year, the counter-conventioners appeared to be much less interested in furthering the cause of democracy in the newsroom and far more interested in fawning over the new celebrities of the press. Dick Pollak, in assessing the conference after the fact, said that he was ini-tially discouraged by the lack of interest in real press reform, despite 1,500 journalists being in attendance. He later (by the end of the column, even) re-gained his optimism, but it was probably short-lived.[20] The trend toward the conventions being a celebrity circus would return, with even greater force, the following year, when the Liebling convention went home to New York.

Claudia Cohen Replaces Terry Pristin

No one seems to remember how Claudia Cohen first showed up in the offices of *(MORE)*, but no one could forget her either. She was in her early twenties when Dick Pollak hired her to replace Terry Pristin as *(MORE)*'s assistant editor, only a few months after she graduated from the University of Pennsylvania, where she had been the first woman to edit the college paper, the *Daily Pennsylvanian*. She was whip-smart but had a taste for gossip, particularly about high society. And she was a small part of society too. Her father, Robert Cohen, ran the Hudson County News Company, a newspaper and magazine distribution company, and her family had money as a result. *(MORE)* staff member Kathy Jones described Claudia Cohen as a kind of character she had never met before, a charming one, to be sure, but one whose lifestyle was completely alien to her own. "She'd be on the phone discussing with her brother what they were going to buy their moth-er for her birthday," Jones said, "and it would be something like a trip to Boca Raton, and they'd be discussing what spa to send her to." Jones said that her family was more likely to be baking cookies as birthday gifts. Cohen would come to the office dressed like everyone else, except that she would be dragging a fur coat with her. Cohen and Dick Pollak would also occa-sionally burst out into show tunes, which were apparently a favorite around

Figure 3. The *(MORE)* staff on a retreat on Shelter Island on Long Island, circa 1974. Front: Dick Pollak. Center, left to right: David Lusterman, Claudia Cohen, J. Anthony Lukas. Rear, left to right: Brit Hume, Woody Woodward, Dan McNamee, Malcolm Frouman, Kathy Jones (Photo courtesy of Malcolm Frouman, used with permission).

the *(MORE)* offices in the middle period of the magazine's existence—from about 1974 to 1976, when the headquarters moved to Third Avenue, near Grand Central Terminal.[21] Robert Friedman, who would edit the magazine when it changed formats a few years later, remembers that Cohen would sometimes—and not just on Fridays—slip into the bathroom at the end of the day and come out dressed in a cocktail dress, bound for some party or other.[22]

It's unfair to try to extrapolate from the addition of a single person to an editorial staff to a general change in the tenor of the magazine, but Claudia Cohen is emblematic of a change that did start to come over *(MORE)* in the period from January of 1974 until the summer of 1976, when Rosebud Associates sold the magazine to new owners.

Watergate changed the self-regard of the press significantly. In the Vietnam era, members of mainstream press organizations who found themselves politically to the left of those organizations had bemoaned the failures of their institutions to cover the world and the culture as they were, and the first incarnation of *(MORE)*, and its associated counter-conventions, allowed those journalists a place to commune, to vent, to figure out how best to reconstitute the act of journalism within or outside of the institutional press. But when the *Washington Post* began following the Watergate story, or at least when the import of that story became clear, many journalists began to back away from the idea of overthrowing the existing system and focused instead on improving their own practice of journalism within the systems that they began to see as inevitable. To be clear, *(MORE)* was never a revolutionary magazine. While many radical writers did attend the Liebling conventions, the core staff of *(MORE)* seemed to be content to work within the system. During the last few years of Rosebud Associates ownership, *(MORE)* continued to push up against institutions with the intention of changing them, but not with the intention of toppling them. The magazine wasn't above embarrassing the press in order to advocate for change, either, as several of the stories that ran in this period will show.

1974: *(MORE)* in the Post-Watergate Era

With the addition of Claudia Cohen, the staff of *(MORE)* had grown to eight people on the masthead in January 1974. There was Dick Pollak, still leading the magazine and editing most of the longer stories. Cohen had taken over as assistant editor, managing the Hellbox stories and the Big Apple section. Tony Lukas was still there as a senior editor, but mostly attended editorial meetings and came in with ideas—he wasn't an everyday editor. Brit Hume was running the Washington, DC, coverage. Woody Woodward had also started to show up less to the office, but Rosebud had hired an associate publisher named Dan McNamee and a business manager named David Lusterman. Malcolm Frouman was art director now, fresh from being a Columbia University undergraduate and a member of their chapter of the Students for a Democratic Society.[23]

The first few issues of 1974 were a mixture of the sort of anti-institutional reporting that *(MORE)* had always done with a new kind of article that is a bit more difficult to define. The anti-institutional stuff is easy to identify. There is an article about how the press covers David Rockefeller and Chase Manhattan Bank.[24] Another cover story looks at how reporters have been covering the looming energy crisis, an article illustrated with a Marty Norman drawing of Uncle Sam on his knees, pulling a tourniquet tight with his teeth as he injects oil into his forearm as if it were heroin. A businessman clutching an armful of oil cans and an Arabian sheik look on from behind him.[25] This sort of criticism of the press's coziness with big business is very much of a piece with *(MORE)*'s coverage from 1971 to 1973. As is the April 1974 cover story, about reporters trying to prognosticate the 1976 presidential election, which follows on nicely from coverage *(MORE)* did of political reporting in previous years.[26]

The February 1974 cover story, however, takes *(MORE)* in a new direction. Illustrated with a photograph of a hirsute Al Pacino in the role of Frank Serpico, the article looks at the phenomenon of "movies as journalism," examining the level of truth in films such as *Serpico*. Unsurprisingly, critic Richard Schickel, who wrote the piece, finds the truth lacking, by the standards of journalism.[27] This piece is not the kind of hard-hitting, take-down-the-abusers-of-power story that *(MORE)* specialized in in its early days. This isn't to say that it's an uninteresting or somehow less-valuable piece of journalism, but it does signal the beginnings of a change in the content of the magazine. In 1974, 1975, and 1976, there would be less of the lingering anger of the New Left reflected in the magazine (despite a design director who was an SDS member), and more articles about the role of journalism in society and more lighthearted (but often still cutting) satire.

The May 1974 issue illustrates some of the best and worst tendencies of *(MORE)* when it came to using humor as a tool. Alexander Cockburn, an Irish-American political journalist and critic, wrote the cover story, a satirical look at the use of cliché in foreign reporting. Cockburn starts by picking apart the work of C. L. Sulzberger in particular. Sulzberger was a member of the family that owns the *New York Times*, and was a foreign correspondent for the paper in the 1940s and '50s, and a columnist up through the 1970s. But he was old news in 1974, so why did Cockburn pick on him? "It seems to me that C.L. is the summation, the platonic ideal of what foreign reporting is about," Cockburn wrote.

> It's true that we do not find him courageously observing Cambodian soldiers on the outskirts of Phnom Penh, but this is incidental. C.L. has divined the central mystery of his craft, which is to fire volley after volley of cliché into the densely packed prejudices of his readers. There are no surprises in his work. . . . *He never deviates into paradox.* His work is a constant affirmation of received beliefs. So why spurn the work of the old Zen master?[28]

Cockburn continues in this mode of praising Sulzberger in order to take down cliché-ridden foreign reporting in general, using irony to satirize the fatuous and old-fashioned Sulzberger. He uses much of the rest of the essay as a faux lesson for those who would seek a career as a foreign correspondent, "instructing" them in the proper clichés and received wisdom to spout in various locations. Hong Kong is "a *time bomb*, but also a *listening post*, inhabited by China watchers who will eye you with disdain." And Chou En-lai "is civilized, but a *dedicated revolutionary*. He has an

121

uncanny command of detail. This interview should take place late at night and go on for several hours."[29] In a way, Cockburn seems to be lamenting that all of the really good reporters have focused their attention on Washington, leaving foreign reporting to the lazy and the superficial. It's cutting and funny satire. Cockburn had given disaster coverage a similar working over in December 1973, pretending to give a primer in how best to cover volcano eruptions, typhoons, and earthquakes—and how to maximize their shock effect among readers.[30] Cockburn wrote that piece with the same snide but very funny attitude, and the pieces are effective as criticism and satire as well as being amusing. The same issue that contains Cockburn's piece on foreign reporting, however, also contains a feature that reads more as snide, mean, and holier-than-thou. The piece is called "The 10 Worst," and purports to be an exposé of the most egregiously bad daily papers in the United States. Dick Pollak regretted running the story nearly four decades later, since, as he admitted, the staff of *(MORE)* really didn't know much about regional dailies and didn't really have a team of stringers stationed around the country to give them nominations. Instead they scraped together ideas from friends around the country, and came up with a list: *The San Francisco Chronicle, The Boston Herald-American, The Cleveland Plain Dealer, The Fort Worth Star-Telegram, The St. Louis Globe-Democrat, The Los Angeles Herald-Examiner, The New Orleans Times-Picayune, The San Diego Union, The Memphis Commercial Appeal,* and *The Manchester Union Leader.* Why those ten? The introductory note doesn't explain much, except that they had to have a minimum circulation of 150,000 to qualify. Otherwise, the introduction basically admits that the choices are arbitrary and "impressionistic." The introduction is almost apologetic for following the trend of ten-best and ten-worst lists.[31] The entire exercise feels like pandering to readers and a half-hearted attempt to stir up controversy. Perhaps it's worth noting that the May 1974 issue was tied to that year's A. J. Liebling Counter-Convention, so perhaps the ten-worst list was meant to be a sop to journalists traveling in from the provinces, so that they could look at *(MORE)* and say, "Hey, they make fun of my hometown paper too!" Or maybe it was just meant to give people something to argue about in the hallways of the Roosevelt Hotel.

Around this same time, *(MORE)* began running a fairly incongruous series of ads. Advertising in the magazine had always been thin. The original idea had been to capture some of the same advertising market that ran in the *New York Review of Books* or the *New York Times Book Review.* But publishers mostly did not seem to be interested in buying space in a journal for journalists. Many of the ads were traded space—*(MORE)* would get a free ad in *Ramparts* and *Ramparts* would get a free ad in *(MORE)*. Most of the funding for the magazine had been coming from Woody Woodward's pocket, with occasional foundation support. Subscriptions brought in a little money too, but *(MORE)* had trouble getting its circulation past twenty thousand, and Pollak says that he would sometimes check the subscription lists to see if he could find any ZIP codes outside of the New York tristate area or Washington, DC. Usually it was only a smattering.[32] *(MORE)* was never going to be a general-interest magazine, and so it had to rely on advertisers who wanted to reach its particular niche audience. As publishers have long known, niche audiences with small circulation can be just as profitable as large general interest audiences. *Cat Fancy* can sell ads to cat product manufacturers. An architecture magazine can sell ads to companies that make plumbing fixtures. The problem with *(MORE)*, though, is that journalists are not a niche audience in the same way. *(MORE)*'s business staff could conceivably sell space to typewriter companies or manufacturers of portable recording equipment, but the market would be very small. David Lusterman, *(MORE)*'s business manager in this period, later said that *(MORE)* would never have been viable as a commercial magazine because there is just no product category that makes sense to market to journalists as opposed to the general population—and general advertisers, for the most part, would not be interested in buying space in a magazine with such a small circulation.[33] The ads that started appearing in 1974 were for Mobil, the oil and gasoline company. Mobil had come up with a strategy of targeting opinion leaders with advertisements that were supposed to give the company a better name. It had started taking out ads on the *New York Times*'s new op-ed page, and Mobil apparently saw the high-level journalists who read *(MORE)* as a similar group of opinion leaders. Given the number of anti-Big Oil articles that *(MORE)* had run, this seems like a fair assumption, but it also meant that Mobil would be advertising in something akin to enemy territory. In the July 1974 ad that Mobil ran—a full page—the company showed storyboards for a television commercial it had proposed to the three networks. The commercial asked the public for its opinion on offshore oil drilling. Two of the three networks—ABC and CBS—turned down the commercial. CBS gave the most thorough explanation, saying that it only accepted ads for goods and services, not for "a controversial issue of public importance." Mobil's ad or public relations people clearly knew their audience, and made their appeal to *(MORE)*'s readers on First Amendment grounds. Mobil said it was "dangerous" for the advertising acceptability departments of the networks to be deciding which issues could or could not be discussed over the broadcast airwaves. Whether to accept the ad was an issue that divided the *(MORE)* staff, and probably its readers as well. Should *(MORE)* back a First Amendment argument for access to its pages, or should it effectively censor Mobil? And in the debate that the ad itself sparked, would *(MORE)* support Big Oil or Big Broadcast? Neither was an appealing choice, but *(MORE)* always needed money, so they took the ad—and Mobil ran ads in the magazine for years to come.[34] Later, in the second physical incarnation of the magazine, the back page would be devoted to Marlboro cigarettes, another advertiser about which the staff felt morally compromised.

The September 1974 issue serves as a good example of the state of *(MORE)* in this period, and could even be seen as the archetypal issue of *(MORE)* at its peak under the ownership of its founders. It was also the last issue of *(MORE)* to run a story on its front page. The next month, Malcolm Frouman switched to a more graphic cover, with an image and cover lines. The cover began to resemble a magazine more than a tabloid newspaper, though the same cheap paper stock remained, as did the general layout of the interior pages. And of course, the iconic "*(MORE)*" nameplate also stayed. But those changes would come in October. The September issue ran its last front-page story, one that was very much in line with the magazine's history of criticizing press complicity with the government. With Nixon finally having resigned, *(MORE)* looked at the honeymoon that the press was giving Gerald Ford, and found that this was an tradition worth getting rid of. Surprisingly, given the antagonism between the *New York Times* and *(MORE)*—see chapter 6 for two case studies of this relationship—the Gerald Ford honeymoon article was written by William V. Shannon, a member of the *Times* editorial board.

Inside the issue, however, the relationship with the *Times* felt rockier. Dick Pollak wrote the Column Two piece next to the table of contents, in which he detailed how the *New York Times* fired a reporter named Denny Walsh in what appeared to be direct retaliation for his interaction with *(MORE)* the previous month.[35] Walsh had written an investigative piece about the mayor of San Francisco, Joe Alioto. Walsh's piece, which had taken three months to investigate, questioned Alioto's testimony in a libel case involving *Look* magazine, and alleged connections between Alioto and members of the Mafia. However, the *Times* never ran the story. *(MORE)*'s Washington editor, Brit

Hume, wrote a cover story for the August issue of *(MORE)* in which Walsh claimed that the *Times* had killed the Alioto story. An editor's note that ran alongside Hume's story explained that the original version of the *(MORE)* story included an excerpt from the report that the *Times* had killed. Because *(MORE)* would then be the first publication to make the allegations against Alioto, Hume called Alioto's office for comment. Eventually, *(MORE)* was threatened with lawsuits that—while the magazine would likely win—might very well bankrupt it. So *(MORE)* backed off and ran only Hume's story, not the excerpts from Denny Walsh's. Abe Rosenthal, managing editor of the *Times*, denied that the story had been killed.[36]

The next month, in the archetypal September 1974 issue of *(MORE)*, Pollak reported that Walsh had been fired. Pollak accused the *Times* of hypocrisy, saying that for a publication that speaks out so strongly on behalf of freedom of speech, this censorship of one of its reporters was unacceptable. Pollak justified the accusation of censorship by pointing out that Walsh had offered his manuscript to *Rolling Stone* once he was told that the *Times* wouldn't be running it. It was through *Rolling Stone* that the story found its way to *(MORE)*, since *Rolling Stone* said that the story wasn't written in the style of their usual journalism. Rosenthal claimed that the Walsh manuscript had been held because of concerns about the quality of the reporting. Pollak countered this by saying that it would not have been an issue if Walsh had published with *Rolling Stone* or even with *(MORE)*, since the quality of the reporting would no longer be the problem of the *Times*. Rosenthal was also being hypocritical, Pollak wrote, since it had lambasted the Nixon administration for its use of "plumbers" to stop leaks, and yet Rosenthal was behaving in exactly the same way.

Across the page from Pollak's vitriolic column, the Hellbox section reported on yet another instance of *Doonesbury* censorship, this time for a strip that depicted Republican congressmen falling asleep during the Watergate hearings. Following the Hellbox section, *(MORE)* ran an article by contributing editor David Rubin about the risk of attracting a libel suit when doing muckraking journalism. The piece is part exposure of the overuse of libel and part warning to reporters who sought to do such work.[37]

The ads in the September 1974 issue are also pretty typical for mid-period *(MORE)*. Following Rubin's piece on libel suits, the *Advocate*, which was then a biweekly newspaper covering news of interest to gays, ran a full-page ad focusing on how certain publications wouldn't take their ads. There was also a full-page ad for Mobil, of course, and one for the *American Poetry Review*. So there was one ad for a newspaper run by and for an oppressed cultural minority group, one advocacy ad for a multinational corporation, and one ad—presumably unpaid—for a review of poetry. That broad range of advertisers says much about the state of *(MORE)* in late 1974.

The September 1974 issue also profiled a new phenomenon in broadcast journalism—a long-haired, mustachioed television reporter named Geraldo Rivera. The occasion for the profile was Rivera's recent leap from the local ABC affiliate in New York to his own evening news and variety show. Jane Howard wrote the piece, and like so many people who have tried to assess Rivera since 1974, she was unable to figure out how to classify him: "Is he a swashbuckling muckraker? A name-dropping opportunist? A savior? Or a phony embarked on a one-way deluxe ego trip with no return ticket?"[38] The piece is prescient in seeing that Rivera would be a part of the media for a long time (though Howard speculates, jokingly, about a presidential run in 2000, when Rivera would be fifty-seven). And it demonstrates *(MORE)*'s growing interest in the personalities of the media world. Rivera represented something that had only just begun to exist in the first years of *(MORE)*, a celebrity of the new world of "media," as opposed to "the press." Some of what Rivera did was clearly journalism, but much of it was not. And *(MORE)*, unlike any other publication in the period, was wrestling with what these changes would mean. The next article in the issue dealt with a more recognizable kind of celebrity to a particular generation of journalists—Alexander Cockburn wrote about Frank Sinatra's relationship with the press on a trip to Australia[39]—but Geraldo was a new animal. *(MORE)* may not have known just what to make of him, but it had the foresight to be able to identify him and recognize that his kind would be important in whatever was coming next.

Finally, to close out the archetypal September 1974 issue of *(MORE)*, Joseph Epstein, then a lecturer in English at Northwestern University, examined the possibility that with Nixon gone, the American people would be looking for a new institution to vilify, and that institution might very well be the Media (Epstein capitalized it). Wall Street and Madison Avenue had each had their turn, and the Media looked to be next. The requisites were there, he wrote: the Media are powerful and they have a great potential for manipulation, given their control of information. The only thing that might be missing in the formula for the Media to become the country's next big villain was a motive. For investment banking and for advertising, the motive was clear: money. But for the Media, Epstein argued, the reward was something more intangible: "a sense of being at the center of things, a heady feeling of not merely being where the action is but of having a hand

126

in shaping the action."[40] In short, the media had too much power and too little responsibility, he argued. And that made people suspicious.

(MORE) continued to monitor the media, of course. That was always the guiding purpose of *(MORE)*, particularly under its founding trio and the group of writers and editors they brought into their circle. When *(MORE)* reached the September 1974 issue, it had been publishing for a few months more than three years. They had made themselves an anti-institutional institution. The three A. J. Liebling Counter-Conventions that *(MORE)* had thrown so far had become must-attend events for a certain segment of the elite and aspirational-elite press. *(MORE)* had reached a peak of its influence and also probably of its performance. But underneath that influence, there were real financial problems at the magazine. In November 1974, the magazine published its required report to the Audit Bureau of Circulations, which monitored the circulation of periodicals. The average press run for the previous year had been 17,131 copies, with the latest issue having 18,909 copies. Paid subscriptions accounted for 13,459 issues, with an additional 2,112 issues being sold on the newsstand. The magazine gave away about 2,500 copies. These were not spectacular numbers, barely enough to sustain publication. The ownership disclosure in the Audit Bureau report reflected that. The Audit Bureau required that any shareholder with more than 1 percent be reported. And in addition to the original three Rosebud Associates, *(MORE)* had significant investment now from six other investors (one of which was Woody Woodward's mother). Even at its editorial peak, the magazine was struggling financially. Rosebud Associates would only hold onto the magazine for another year and a half. In that time, the editorial staff continued to do good and important work, with some of the new, more entertainment-oriented journalism mixed in.

Everything You Always Wanted to Know about Counter-Conventions* *But Were Afraid to Ask

Between the 1973 and 1974 counter-conventions, *(MORE)* had become a slightly more polished product. The typesetting was more regular; there were more photographs. Things seemed cleaner and more professional on the page. Some new staff had come on board as well, including a young woman—a Catholic waitress's daughter from Buffalo, as she described herself—named Kathy Jones. Jones wasn't a journalist. She was an alumna of the Peace Corps and had taught in a Montessori school, but she had been turned on to *(MORE)* by her friend Dan McNamee, who had organized the Washington, DC, Liebling Counter-Convention. She was brought on to sell ads—always a difficult issue for *(MORE)*—and to organize the Liebling conventions going forward. Jones did have some party-planning experience, having worked for Daniel and Philip Berrigan—two brothers, both Catholic priests, known for their anti–Vietnam War activism—and also having worked for the composer and conductor Leonard Bernstein and his wife, Felicia. "I think it was on the basis of that," that she was hired, she said. "I've always thrown a good party."[41]

More and more, the counter-conventions were turning into parties too. Whereas the first A. J. Liebling Counter-Convention, held in a trade union meeting hall, had the urgency of a late-night strike-planning session by a group of union hardliners who couldn't get their grievances heard by the management, by year three the conventions had become boozy victory parties and camp reunions, with a valedictory atmosphere. The anticipation of Watergate finally catching up to Nixon had driven the mood in Washington, and amazingly, that still appeared to be the dominant mood when the Liebling convention returned to New York City from May 10 to 12, 1974, at the Roosevelt Hotel near Grand Central Terminal. The price of admission had risen again—and significantly. After having been free in 1972 and eight dollars in 1973, the admission price in 1974 almost doubled to fifteen dollars. Of course, now that included a "free" subscription to the magazine too, but you couldn't renew your own if you already subscribed; you had to start a new one or give one as a gift. Discounted rooms at the Roosevelt were also available, twenty-six dollars for a single or thirty-two dollars for a double.[42]

Friday night opened, as had become expected, with a party. Tony Lukas and Dick Pollak were pulled aside by a *Washington Post* reporter who was covering the conference, and Tony told her that he was "delighted" that Robert Redford would be playing "one of us." Redford had recently announced his intention to play Bob Woodward in a film version of the Watergate investigation story, which would become the film *All the President's Men.* Lukas told the reporter that he wanted Omar Sharif to play him. "The phrase 'star reporter' suddenly assumed all sorts of new meaning," wrote the *Post* journalist.[43] Even though the meat of the conference had been squeezed back into two days, the panels were packed tighter. Instead of having two panels concurrently, there were now three and, at one point, even four. While this was probably meant to spread out the expected crowd a bit more (and Liebling III drew about 2,000, according to one source,[44] though another had the more convincingly specific 1,850 as the paid attendance number),[45] it also meant that attendees began to suffer from what

Dick Pollak jokingly called "panel envy," the Freudian feeling that whatever panel you didn't attend must have been better than the one that you did.[46] (Art Buchwald used the same line in moderating the Watergate panel the previous year, though he had meant that the audience were envious of the panelists for their accomplishments.)[47]

While Watergate may still have dominated the mood of Liebling III, its panels were decidedly more eclectic than those of its Washington, DC, predecessor. The opening panel and the Saturday night gala panel—the one sandwiched between the presentation of the Liebling Award and Saturday's party—were impressive political reporting panels, however. Author and editor Victor Navasky moderated the opening panel, which featured investigative reporter Seymour Hersh and Alger Hiss talking about national security and the press. That evening, *Washington Post* reporter Morton Mintz received the Liebling Award, and *(MORE)* gave a special prize to photographer W. Eugene Smith and also gave out a student prize. Mike Wallace, host of CBS News's *60 Minutes*, then hosted a panel on "The Press and the Presidency" featuring *New York Times* writer Anthony Lewis, wire service reporter Helen Thomas, and gonzo journalist Hunter S. Thompson—an unlikely but probably a lively group.[48] Dan Rather, also of CBS, was scheduled to be on the panel as well, but according to Wallace, he had been called into work to preside over Nixon's "death watch."[49]

There was something of a return to cultural issues at Liebling III. There was a panel on the media and coverage of gay issues. One discussed whether there was "a female sensibility." Nora Ephron chaired a panel about men's magazines that included a *Playboy* writer and Al Goldstein, publisher of the quasi-pornographic *Screw* magazine. Robin Reisig covered the conference for the *Village Voice*, with an eye toward how women were treated. She reported that the women's sensibility panel concluded basically that there were just good writers, "people who make connections" and who "don't filter things out of their consciousness," and bad writers.[50] There was also a discussion of whether the *New York Times* should use the word "Ms." instead of "Miss" and "Mrs." Some of the participants "went into a slow burn" when the editor of the *Times* editorial page, John Oakes, said that he didn't think it was an important question. Reisig also covered the women in the newsroom panel, where participants mostly concluded that they still had "a lo-o-ong way to go."

There was also a panel on cable and satellite technology that everyone seemed to find deathly boring.[51] But what everyone remembers from Liebling III, said its organizer, Kathy Jones, was that the final panel had Woody

Allen on it.[52] Ostensibly, the subject of the panel was failure, and it also featured author Erica Jong. Judy Bachrach, the *Washington Post* reporter who covered the conference, wrote that the celebrities—Alger Hiss, Woody Allen—dominated the conference, and made it seem less like a conference of journalists. And according to Kathy Jones, Allen was a terrible panelist anyway. He spoke quietly, talked through his hands, and mumbled.[53]

The happenings outside the official panels seemed to take precedence for the first time. Press critic Alexander Cockburn, in his *Village Voice* column, wrote that "Large numbers of people paced the corridors of the Roosevelt Hotel, drinking, shouting, and occasionally justifying the long hours of revelry and gossip by attending panel discussions."[54] This sort of camp reunion atmosphere would come to dominate the last two New York counter-conventions as well.

Rather than assigning himself to recap the conference, Dick Pollak put a reporter on it, and picked Calvin Trillin, the *New Yorker* writer who had been on *(MORE)*'s original advisory board. An in-house piece almost didn't seem necessary to Trillin, who suggested, tongue in cheek, that there were so many reporters at the convention "doing a piece" about it that the next year's convention should have a panel on how to cover a Liebling convention. He made up some statistics (and pretended to verify them "employing the methodology of New Journalism, by noting how symmetrical the statistics sounded when I repeated them to myself in the shower"). Though fake, they give an idea of who was attending the conference: "anyone under thirty is part of the audience, anyone from thirty-five to forty-five is a panelist, and anyone fifty-five or over is there to receive the annual A. J. Liebling Award."[55] Trillin found that the Liebling conventions had grown into an institution since their first year (when even then they were accused of being too close to the institutions that they purported to run counter to). But now, Trillin joked, the conference was really only counter to the panelists. For the younger convention-goers, this may have been an opportunity to meet their idols. For more established journalists, it was time for more "panel envy": "a [MORE] convention spectator's first reaction to seeing another writer on the dais," Tony Lukas told Trillin, "is 'why him and not me?'"

Mostly though, Trillin wrote about how the process of a Liebling Counter-Convention had become regularized. Of course there would be drinking ("If it ain't catered, it ain't journalism," Jones said).[56] Of course there would be panel envy. Of course there would be ponderous self-importance. Of course there would be a protest. In 1972, the protestors had been Abbie

Hoffman and his Zippies. In 1973, it had been the National Organization for Women. In 1974, there was a perfunctory protest by the National Caucus of Labor Committees. But in Trillin's telling, even the protestors knew their part to play in the convention. "When the N.C.L.C. speaker went through his allotted two minutes before the Saturday night panel, the audience just waited for the end, like a baseball crowd waiting for the soprano to finish the Star Spangled Banner so the game can get started."[57] And in keeping with its move toward celebrity, *(MORE)* even managed to get a celebrity to take its pictures—the official photos were by Jill Krementz, a noted photographer, particularly of writers.

So even though 1974 was Kathy Jones's first year as convention organizer, she felt pretty confident that she knew what to expect when Pollak asked her to set up a West Coast version of the counter-conventions, something that would focus on the needs and concerns of reporters on the other side of the country, who couldn't necessarily afford to come out to New York City. How different could things be in San Francisco?

Not Left Enough for the Left Coast: The Counter-Convention Comes to San Francisco

San Francisco "was a zoo. That was really a zoo," Kathy Jones said. She may never forgive Dick for the idea, she said. "This was really hard. All I remember are the pickets." When *(MORE)* showed up at the Sheraton Palace Hotel—a setting more like the Mayflower Hotel in Washington, DC, than like the Martin Luther King Jr. Labor Center—in February 1975, the conference staff found a fancy hotel full of young, smart, but unemployed and very miserable writers. More than one thousand people attended, small by the current standards of *(MORE)*'s conventions, but still a large number. "I've never met so many unhappy people," Jones said. "You couldn't do anything right. The price was too high. Everyone wanted to get in for free— and they all wanted to get in for free to something that was clearly racist and sexist and everything else. Just personally, it was one of the hardest experiences I've had workwise. I can't talk about it as the kind of fun that New York was. It wasn't fun."[58]

The best document of the conference is a two-part radio documentary put together by the left-leaning Pacifica Radio of San Francisco, KPFA.[59] Pacifica thought that the conference was mostly "a pretty tame affair" and that the alternative press was mostly quite well represented, though with a few glaring exceptions. Pacifica opened its coverage with part of a panel on local broadcast news, which started from the premise that local news was more entertainment than information. It was one of the best-attended panels, partly because it was, as had become the norm at Liebling Counter-Conventions, "star-studded." Chief among the stars was Van Amburg, host of the Bay Area KGO-TV's newscast, which was a pioneer in "happy talk" news. The panel began with Phil Jacklin, a San Jose State philosophy professor, who pushed for open access to broadcast media. His impassioned rant in favor of the fairness doctrine harkened back to the passions of the first Liebling Counter-Convention. He ended by reading a story lineup from a recent KGO newscast that concluded with a story about Marilyn Monroe look-alikes. "Our source at KGO says that Van Amburg had a hard-on the whole time," Jacklin said, leaving a mixture of shock and laughter in the meeting room. Van Amburg disarmed the crowd immediately, though, showing the charm that earned him six-figure salaries on a mainstream newscast: "I don't see anything wrong with having a hard-on, number one. I think it's a nice thing to have." He then mounted a fairly convincing defense of news about people rather than issues. He was unapologetic about it, but it didn't seem to convince the crowd. And Van Amburg became the target for most of the audience's accusatory questions.

According to KPFA, the only happening of any consequence at the panel was the appearance of black members of the Coalition for Media Change, who circled the podium, as they had at other sessions that day, saying that whatever else the shortcomings of the panel, the lack of minority participation was the most glaring omission.

A panel on alternative media and the power structure in San Francisco now feels particularly local and dated, though a panel on coverage of the Middle East had more lasting interest. The panelists included Robert Scheer, former editor of *Ramparts* magazine, and Russ Stetler of Internews news service, who lamented how long it took the press to give any coverage to the Palestinian side of the Palestine-Israel conflict. Sidney Sober, a representative of the State Department, also spoke at the panel. "With reasonably rare exceptions," he said, "the news we read in the press doesn't surprise us." Robert Scheer called the State Department "a fog machine" for that kind of attitude.

The first episode of Pacifica's coverage ended with a look at how racism was handled. "One serious drawback to the conference was the obvious omission of third world media organizations," the final report began. A black media attorney who had been on the panels accused *(MORE)* of "white liberal racism." Penny Gentilly, who was *(MORE)*'s West Coast coordinator for the conference, then found herself under attack from an activist from the Community Coalition for Media Change. He pointed out some of the racial inequality of the panels. Gentilly was defensive, and sounds young. She explained that there had been two large meetings that tried to come up with ideas for panels and panelists. They felt that it was better, Gentilly explained, "not to ghettoize" the panels, but to include black panelists and women on all of the panels. The activist challenged her, saying that it was "ridiculous" that the panel on the Symbionese Liberation Army didn't include the organizer of its food distribution efforts. He said it must have been a conscious exclusion on the part of the *(MORE)* organizers. "It wasn't conscious, really it wasn't," protested an increasingly overwhelmed-sounding Gentilly. "We left it up to moderators to put together panels, and I wasn't on top of it, and I regret that." The activist continued, "Black people do exist. Latinos do exist. But they've been left out of history, and now they're left out of the conference."

"I'm sorry," Gentilly said, finally. "I thought they were represented."

Pacifica opened its second show with excerpts from a panel about multinational corporations. This was followed by a panel about the financial crisis, which included Anita Frankel, general manager of KPFA, and Stewart Brand, founder of the *Whole Earth Catalog*. More interesting than either of those two panels, however, was a panel on women's issues, which the Pacifica show calls "by far the least coherent of the conference" but "in many ways the most revealing." Susan Hallis, a freelance journalist, told the panel that they should forgo opening statements. "The session began in a vacuum," Pacifica's narrator said. Black media activist Edwin Terry from the Coalition for Media Change broke any illusion of unity right away (despite not being on the panel) with an opening statement of his own: "That two honky females who decided how this conference would be conducted, and who would be invited, shows that they have no sensitivity, only to try to go to bed with a black man." The feminist audience was outraged, but the panel tried to get on track. After a few turns of interesting discussion, things seemed to fly in several directions at once. One group of women wanted to break into small groups to discuss how to take action. Another group wanted the panelists to decide on some unified themes to guide the discussion. This group didn't want to discuss how to get women into more executive roles in mainstream media, and accused the main panel of being the most conservative panel at the conference. The black women in the room walked

133

out. Some women did break into small groups and began caucusing. It was an incredibly fractious session, and one that illustrates the anger and confusion that made Kathy Jones blanch when talking about the West Coast conference even four decades later.

Anita Frankel, Bill Sokol, and Larry Bensky of KPFA held a roundtable for themselves, asking what they had learned from the conference. One thing that came out was the lack of real investigative reporting in San Francisco, particularly in relation to a panel on Mayor Joe Alioto—who also attended the conference.[60] One of the panelists also noted that on his way to any panel he had to pass through five lines of people who were looking for jobs, so the lack of solid reporting wasn't because of lack of talent. They saw too that there were two conflicting lines: the yearning for professionalism, the ability to maintain standards and make a living; and the need to examine politics. But the conflict came, the KPFA panel asserted, in that journalists were unwilling to examine the politics of the news organizations that allowed them to do their work.

As for the politics of *(MORE)*, Larry Bensky said that he had interviewed Tony Lukas and Woody Woodward, two of the three founders of *(MORE)* a few years earlier, and that they had made it clear to him that *(MORE)* was founded by reporters who were employed not by alternative media but by the mainstream media and yet who found themselves significantly to the left of their employers, and *(MORE)* was intended to express that point of view. They didn't necessarily want workers' control of the media, but they wanted fairer coverage of Vietnam. And the professional strain of *(MORE)* also influenced the underrepresentation of non-white people at the conference, according to the KPFA group, since they wanted to show the media as it was, not as it should be, and they didn't give much thought to how to include those voices that were excluded. *(MORE)*, the KPFA group suggested, didn't understand the Bay Area's network of alternative publications that the group saw as being much more vital than the alternative media in New York. Perhaps, they admitted, this was because the underground press was less necessary in New York because the overground press there was much stronger than it was in San Francisco. In any case, *(MORE)* was happy to return to the New York media world, the world that it knew.

Meanwhile, the San Francisco *(MORE)* conference did continue one tradition: partying outside of the conference rooms. There was plenty of drinking at the Sheraton Palace Hotel, and upstairs, according to *Rolling Stone*, there were other substances being inhaled:

Upstairs, the editors of *High Times* magazine had installed two huge canisters of laughing gas in their hospitality suite. Dozens of guests were happily frying their brains and by 2 a.m. the floor was three inches deep with discarded balloons. Serving as host was Underground Press Syndicate founder Tom Forcade, who shares *High Times*' New York office, decked out in a three-piece suit. Also on hand, ex-Yippie Jerry Rubin, shaved and scrubbed and dressed like a fraternity lounge lizard, and Garry Trudeau, the reclusive author of the comic strip "Doonesbury."[61]

Conference-goers from the later years in New York would remember similar scenes of debauchery even more than the panels. But of course, there were panels too.

Liebling IV

The original Rosebud Associates who founded *(MORE)* held one more conference in New York while they owned the magazine. After they sold it to a new editor/publisher, Michael Kramer, Kramer held one final conference before they finally ran out of steam. The last two conferences, Liebling IV and V, followed the pattern set by the 1974 counter-convention, with an increased level of veneration of journalistic celebrity, an increasingly boozier atmosphere in the convention itself, and one that was almost circus-like in the hallways. The socialist journalist Kent MacDougall referred to the later counter-conventions, with their love of celebrity journalists (and other celebrities), as "starfucks."[62]

The conventions gave the world of journalism an iconic poster, one that would live on in the offices of journalism professors for decades, and in the toolkits of set dressers for at least a few years after *(MORE)*, the magazine, finally folded. That poster, a bold rectangle of pure 1970s burnt orange, featured a Marty Norman cartoon of a stereotypical 1920s or 1930s newsman, his striped sleeves rolled up and his tie loosened between his suspenders, but with his fedora firmly pulled down to his brow (with a card reading "PRESS" tucked into the brim, of course). He clutched a two-piece antique phone and shouted into the mouthpiece, "Hello, sweetheart, get me rewrite!" The image first popped up in the ads for the 1974 convention, but the newsman became an icon of the magazine and a symbol of its valuation of hard-bitten news values. Later, owing to popular demand, Norman and *(MORE)* would add a second poster, a woman in a pinstriped suit with the caption "Hello, handsome, get me rewrite!" on a much calmer blue background.

135

Figures 4 & 5. Cartoonist Marty Norman contributed regularly to *(MORE)*, enough so that his style helped define the look of the first several years of the magazine. The "Hello, Sweetheart" poster, which he drew for the fourth A. J. Liebling Counter-Convention, became an iconic symbol for journalists in the 1970s, even showing up as set decoration for the newsroom of *Lou Grant*, the TV drama spun off from *The Mary Tyler Moore* Show.

Women and minorities made up a substantial portion of *(MORE)*'s contributors and audience, and they wanted to see themselves represented in the magazine's pages and at its counter-conventions. Among the requests was a poster showing a woman reporter that would mirror the "Hello, Sweetheart" poster that Norman had created. *(MORE)* and, later, Norman sold reprints of the poster by mail order (Courtesy of Martin Norman).

The magazine sold posters with both images. "Hello, sweetheart" would be the logo for the admission badges to the West Coast Media Conference.[63] Norman would also sell a version of the image to the *Washington Journalism Review* in 1981, with the reporter now holding a contemporary phone, and *WJR* gave it the caption, "Hello, sweetheart, get me the computer!"[64] At least *WJR* thought that the phrase and the image still had resonance three years after *(MORE)* had gone out of business. Norman asked the *Columbia Journalism Review*, which had acquired the rights to the image, if he could reprint and sell the posters in the early 1980s, and he made a small business of it for a while. This is the poster that found its way onto network television when a set dresser decorated the newsroom set of the 1977 to 1982 newspaper drama *Lou Grant*.

But even if the image now seems bigger than the conferences it advertised, those conferences did take place. There was an ever-increasing tilt toward celebrity and debauchery outside the meeting rooms, but a continued attempt to both challenge and celebrate the press when the panels were in session.

The 1975 New York counter-convention came less than three months after the San Francisco foray. Held from May 8 to May 11, it was the last of the regular rites of spring that *(MORE)* would hold. Liebling V, organized by *(MORE)* under new editor Michael Kramer, would be held in the fall of 1976. The party had moved a few blocks to the Hotel Commodore, right next to Grand Central Terminal, and the price rose again, to twenty dollars, though still getting conference-goers a new or gift subscription to the magazine.[65] *(MORE)* did not publish a full program for Liebling IV, though its ads gave teasers of who would be there: *(MORE)* regular Nick von Hoffman; Jack Newfield of the *Village Voice*; Pauline Kael again; Joe Klein of *Rolling Stone*; Halberstam, Lukas, and Hume from *(MORE)*; Gay Talese again; and Gloria Steinem from *Ms.* Steinem was a particularly important "get" for Kathy Jones and the conference planning staff, given the reaction of women's groups in San Francisco and in the 1974 New York conference. In fact, *(MORE)* went a step further and sponsored a full day on the Friday of the conference devoted to something they called the National Conference on Women and the Media. Other panels would include covering the CIA, "Why the Working Man Hates the Media," self-censorship, New Journalism revisited, and the role of the critic. There would also be a screening of the documentary *Antonia: A Portrait of the Woman*, which would be introduced by Gloria Steinem. The ads also teased something called a "media midway," which turned out to be a carnival of journalism in the hallways of the Commodore.

Even Dick Pollak admitted that something had changed significantly from the first Liebling Counter-Convention. He said it was hard not to see a sort of "creeping institutionalism" in the conventions. The attendees, he said, had accepted management as a given of working in the news business, and so (MORE) aimed to give them a "useful" convention more than a "counter" convention. Sure, there were critics, Pollak admitted: "too many stars, too few blacks, too much preoccupation with The New York Times and feminists." But he felt that there was still no danger of becoming the American Newspaper Publishers Association convention under another name. "Self-satisfaction hardly seemed the rule" at the conference, Pollak wrote, and he said that it would continue that way as long as readers continued to tell (MORE) what they wanted from the magazine and the convention.[66] But it is revealing that the one convention panel they chose to transcribe in the magazine was nothing revolutionary, but rather "The Art of the Interview," in which Nat Hentoff of the Voice, Mike Wallace of CBS, Sally Quinn of the Washington Post, and Richard Reeves of New York Magazine shared anecdotes about their interviewing escapades and gave helpful tips to their audience of fawning, envious, and also genuinely interested journalists.

The Chicago journalist and oral historian Studs Terkel won the 1975 Liebling Award, the awarding of which was followed by what was supposed to be the marquee panel that year—the one on self-censorship. But Jules Witcover, writing for the Progressive, said it was perhaps the most disappointing of the convention. The panelists, ironically, seem to have censored themselves and never got deep into the issue of why the press won't run certain stories. The conference had become a bit staid, Witcover said, with jackets and ties becoming the uniform on the dais. Though in the end, he said, the convention still worked, even if it had become a bit boring.[67]

The Village Voice found the '75 convention to be interesting enough to put on the cover—though disappointing enough to say that the convention "never really jelled" that year.[68] The author, Karen Durbin, put the blame on the lack of a single galvanizing issue the way the previous years had had them. She said that in the first three conventions, there was nowhere else you wanted to be if you were a journalist. This one lacked some of that energy, so the journalists in attendance used their excess energy instead in the Media Midway that (MORE) had promised. Durbin found the entire day of talks on women and the media to be a boring rehash, and said that it gave (MORE) an excuse to leave women off panels the rest of the weekend. There was one all-woman panel in the rest of the conference, and it was

devoted to women "invading" traditionally male beats such as sports reporting. That panel did have one moment of interest, though, when a group
of women promoting a book of women's humor attacked the panelists with
whipped cream pies. Durbin also went to the panel on criticism, which she
enjoyed, since it made her want "to go home and write," which most panels
of writers don't do. Afterward, she ran into several people who told her that
she had missed the best panel. "I would worry," she wrote, but people say
this to each other at the (MORE) Convention every year.[69]

Durbin paid a visit to the Media Midway out in the meeting room lobby.
According to her, it consisted of these things:

- a life-sized photographic cutout of Elaine Kaufman, the woman who
  owns Elaine's, a status restaurant for writers and other famous people.
  Next to the cutout is a sign saying "Get your picture taken with Elaine."
- a game called "Spot the Typos," which features some pencils and a
  couple of bedraggled copies of the New York Post.
- a game called "Test your Headlining Skill," with copies of the Daily
  News for reference.
- the aforementioned Media Heavy machine. For fifty cents, you take a
  mallet and hit a lever that will make a ball shoot up a chart. Depending
  on your heaviness you may ring the gong at the top. At the top of the
  chart is "$500,000 Book Advance," with "Pulitzer Prize" just below
  and "White House Correspondent" just below that. In the middle is
  "(MORE) Contributing Editor." At the bottom, just below "Copyper-
  son," is "Rock Critic."

On Saturday evening, Durbin attended a party not sponsored by (MORE),
featuring "joints, hash brownies, and balloons of nitrous oxide." She went
to the Liebling Award panel, where someone who was less high than she
was told her that the panel was boring. She remembered that the last time
she had been that high was at the Rolling Stone party at the 1973 (MORE)
convention. Clearly she had missed Tom Forçade and the High Times hospitality suite in San Francisco.

One night, away from the conference, she and her friends discussed the
elitist liberal racism and sexism inherent in (MORE), but like the panels
at the conference, the discussion didn't seem to go anywhere. At least the
Voice ran a cartoon of real items overheard at the conference to keep things
interesting.

1975 to 1976: The Endgame for Rosebud Associates

(MORE) celebrated the peak of its influence in 1975 by releasing an anthology of some of its best work. The book, *Stop the Presses, I Want to Get Off!*, was published by Random House and edited by Pollak. It featured a ketchup-red dust jacket with mustard-yellow type, an illustration by Marty Norman of a foot bursting through newsprint, and promotional blurbs from four famous and influential journalists: Studs Terkel, Gay Talese, Dan Rather, and Murray Kempton. Talese wrote that "The best journalists in America write for *(MORE)*." Dan Rather wrote that he often disagreed with it, but that *(MORE)* was "one of the most important publications in the country." Pollak wrote an introduction to the book discussing what *(MORE)* had accomplished to date. He wrote that Woody and Tony didn't share his vision for democracy in the newsroom, but that *(MORE)* had been a pretty effective nudge when it came to embarrassing publishers into doing better work.[70] The anthology contains pieces by many of *(MORE)*'s regulars, divided into themes, including The Big Picture, Between the Lines, Profiles, and Institutions. Regular readers of *(MORE)* wouldn't have gotten much that was new out of it, unless they wanted a volume to keep on their shelves. Its real value would have been in exposing some of the best material from *(MORE)* to a more general audience than it normally reached. A review of the book in *Library Journal* called the prospect of a wider distribution of these stories "altogether healthy."[71] Everette Dennis, who was a professor of journalism at the University of Minnesota at the time, reviewed the book for the academic journal *Journalism Quarterly*. He said that it contained "much good writing and some thoughtful analysis" of journalism.[72] He found the book generally worthwhile, but took issue with some of the titles, which he found to be too cutesy and of little value for information retrieval. Curiously, he also called *(MORE)* anti-intellectual. His complaint seems to be that *(MORE)* had little knowledge of the history of journalism or of other press criticism. Perhaps one could come to that conclusion from reading only the book, but the magazine in general was well aware of the history in which it was operating, openly evoking the legacy of the muckrakers and of A. J. Liebling as a press critic. On the whole, *(MORE)* was actually a vociferous opponent of anti-intellectualism in the American press, constantly pushing for the press to move toward the sort of self-scrutiny that is the hallmark of the intellectual.

(MORE) soldiered on as usual through 1975, with little immediately visible change in its coverage or its themes. Dick Pollak admitted that running

the magazine essentially on his own had taken a physical and mental toll, as well as a toll on his personal life, and it is possible that some of this was tempering the energy and enthusiasm that had been the hallmark of the first few years of *(MORE)*. The publication had scaled up in ambition and complexity too, with more longer stories, many more shorter pieces, and a more complicated design makeup. Also, of course, external factors affected the kind of coverage that *(MORE)* attempted, and the magazine seems to have gone into something of a lull of creativity following the successive twin highs created by the energy of New Left anti-institutionalism and by the long Watergate saga. *(MORE)* seemed to fall into a bit of a malaise, just as the country famously would at the end of the 1970s.

There were a few notable stories in 1975 and 1976, of course, with an increase in the number of stories that covered media outside of news-gathering organizations. But *(MORE)* also continued to excel at forcing the press to examine itself. In that vein, *(MORE)* assigned journalist and historian Garry Wills to critique an entire year's issues of *(MORE)* and to publish the resulting criticism in the magazine. Wills took the opportunity not just to critique individual articles (in fact, he knew that as a consumer of the elite media, he was exactly *(MORE)*'s audience), but in fact used the piece to expose and undercut the very premise of the magazine. *(MORE)*, he writes, misses the point. It spends all of its energy nitpicking the very few elite news outlets that conform at all to the vision of the press that *(MORE)* has internalized. He uses the "Ten Worst Newspapers" feature as his jumping-off point. Of course this feature turned out to be bland and almost meaningless, he writes. *(MORE)* was trying to judge the local news-papers of the United States by the standards of the *Washington Post*. And most newspapers in the United States in the 1970s were not trying to be the *Post*. They were trying to serve their readers, who wanted sports and local event coverage and service journalism. Wills makes a distinction between two groups that he calls "The Media" and the press. I would use the terms differently, but what he is suggesting is that there is an elite media, a group of newspapers and news magazines and a few national news programs who conform to those *Washington Post* or *New York Times* definitions of what makes something news. Most of "the press," as he uses the term, don't care to play by those rules, since their circulations are gigantic by playing to the lowest common denominator. He cites circulation statistics for the high-brow and lowbrow publications, and the contrast is startling. *(MORE)* does not understand, Wills writes, that it is overlooking and even dismissing most of the publications that are consumed by most of the United States, and is therefore even more of a niche publication than it probably already saw itself as being. The great "invisible journalism" doesn't interest *(MORE)* because it doesn't interest *(MORE)*'s readers—and so *(MORE)*, in a way, is playing by the same rules as local newspapers or the *Reader's Digest*. What it does do, Wills writes, it does pretty well.[73] Wills is right, of course, that *(MORE)* neglected to cover most of the media, but there is value in pushing for change from the top. They may also just have been a group of elite media members themselves, who thought that they were somehow smarter than the people they covered and were smug about it. Certainly both attitudes come through in the magazine's coverage.

What was really wrong with the magazine, though, wasn't just its coverage. Even if Wills was right and *(MORE)* was pandering to its audience as much as any other publication—even if *(MORE)*'s audience craved gossip about the *New York Times'* internal machinations instead of about Patty Hearst's kidnapping—and even if that pandering was working, the audience wasn't big enough to support a journalism review, and *(MORE)* was beginning to run out of both money and energy. In September of 1975, the *Washington Post* reported that *(MORE)*'s inspiration, the *Chicago Journalism Review*, would be folding. That review's subscription list had dwindled to 2,500, according to the article, down from a peak of 9,000 in 1970. The *Post* article is confusingly edited, and it seems to be referring in places to two different New York–based journalism reviews that are discussing the assumption of the *Chicago Journalism Review*'s debts and subscription list, but only the *Columbia Journalism Review* is named. At one point, the article says that the *Columbia Journalism Review* "had in recent years become more like its nonacademic counterpart," which Ron Dorfman, the editor of the *Chicago Journalism Review*, helped to organize. The sentence seems to refer to *(MORE)*, though that review is never named, perhaps edited out by someone who found the nomenclature confusing and assumed that "the New York based journalism review" must refer to Columbia's. At any rate, the omen of the *Chicago Journalism Review*'s death could not have been a happy one for the staff of *(MORE)*.

Less than a year later, the *New York Times* ran an article reporting that a sale was being negotiated for *(MORE)*. In March 1976, the *Times* interviewed a young *New York* magazine writer named Michael Kramer, who was the leader in a group of investors who were looking to buy the magazine. *(MORE)*, Kramer said, was "the classic case of an undercapitalized publication," and he planned to put a substantial amount of money into it to expand it, and possibly hire another editor. According to the *Times*, Dick Pollak would stay on as editor even after Kramer and his group purchased the magazine from Pollak, Lukas, Woodward, and Robert Livingston, who was the last publisher of *(MORE)* in the Rosebud Associates era.[74]

Dick Pollak didn't want to sell. He would rather have seen the magazine fold than watch it go into someone else's hands, at the risk of the founders' vision being perverted or destroyed. But Woody Woodward didn't want to be the owner of a publication that failed. And Pollak had personal pressures. He said in an interview that when Kramer approached the Rosebud group with his offer to purchase the magazine, Pollak was in the midst of a divorce from his wife, who told him that if he could get away from his all-consuming magazine and give himself a normal work schedule, she would not contest joint custody of their daughter.[75]

Kramer gave more detail about what he planned to do with the magazine in an article that ran in the *Washington Post* a day after the *Times* story. Kramer hoped to convert the magazine from a thirty-two-page tabloid into a sixty-four-page saddle-stitched magazine that looked more like a news-stand glossy. He also hoped to bring up the circulation and appeal to a more general audience, one that was not all working journalists. He foresaw a magazine that was so successful that it could ramp up to biweekly or even weekly production. *(MORE)*, in Kramer's vision, would be a slick magazine with appeal to the general public. According to the final terms of the sale, Rosebud Associates would continue publishing through the June issue. Despite what the *New York Times* reported, Richard Pollak would not be listed as the editor when *(MORE)* relaunched in a July/August double issue. Michael Kramer would be both publisher and editor of the new incarnation of the magazine.

In the first issue of *(MORE)* that came out following the reports of its sale, the magazine devoted the cover to the biggest celebrity moment in the history of journalism: the release of the movie of *All the President's Men*, an adventure story that had a pair of journalists played by the glamorous Robert Redford and Dustin Hoffman. *(MORE)* reviewed the movie in that issue. It reviewed the movie eight times, in fact, hiring as temporary film critics the following luminaries: Russell Baker, Dick Cavett, Jane Howard, Jeff Greenfield, Kurt Vonnegut, Sam Roberts, Roy Cohn, and Frances Fitz-gerald. Mostly the reviewers praised the film, happy that it did not stray too far from the facts (though some complained that not knowing the identity of Woodward and Bernstein's secret source, Deep Throat, left a shadowy hole at the center of the movie). But here were journalists being played by movie stars, journalists turned into heroes. Despite the fact that the issue was marred by one of *(MORE)*'s sillier conceits (a mosaic of nearly identical local television news anchormen who were supposedly competing in some sort of beauty pageant),[76] this issue, the third-to-last in the five-year run of Rosebud Associates, feels like a sort of valedictory moment. As the cover line said, "News Biz Goes Show Biz." *(MORE)* had chronicled the press from a moment in which reporters felt equally stymied by their government and their own employers into an age when reporters had brought down a corrupt president.[77] To top things off (and perhaps to counterbalance the frivolity of the Anchorman Face-Off), *(MORE)* also ran an article about how Mobil Oil was confusing the debate over the energy crisis with its propaganda.[78]

Two months later, the last page of the last issue of *(MORE)* to be produced was devoted to a full-page ad placed by Mobil.

6. The Gadfly

How Press Critics and Their Targets Interact:
Two Case Studies of *(MORE)* and the *New York Times*

From the moment that *(MORE)* debuted in 1971, it was clear to some observers that the new journalism review existed in large part to antagonize the *New York Times*. A *Newsweek* article announcing the new review said that the lack of a journalism review prior to *(MORE)*'s launch was "a notable lapse for a city that is the nation's television center as well as the home of its two leading newsmagazines and two of its most important dailies, The New York Times and The Wall Street Journal." *Newsweek* (which—it should be noted—did call itself one of the nation's leading newsmagazines) then quoted Dick Pollak, the founding editor, who said, "This is the town where the targets are." Though none of the major articles in the first issue of *(MORE)* were specifically about the *Times*, cofounder Tony Lukas had helped establish the magazine in part owing to his frustration with the constraints of the institution that the *Times* had become, reinforcing a particular culture of un–self-questioning professionalism that a certain breed of reporter found stifling. And in addition to Lukas and his former *Times* colleague David Halberstam, the issue also featured an article by Charlotte Curtis, editor of the paper's women's page, as the section was still called in 1971.

The interplay between the venerable watchdog newspaper and the gadfly that would circle it for the next eight years began with a short item in *(MORE)*'s Hellbox column. Homer Bigart, the respected war correspondent who, *(MORE)* noted, was then a year from retirement, had covered the court martial of Lt. William Calley, who had been convicted for his role in the My Lai massacre. The Hellbox column ran Bigart's original copy and the edited version that ran in the *Times* side by side. In the original, Bigart made the point, in two paragraphs, that despite being convicted of the heinous crime, Calley had been treated gently by the army as he was escorted out of court. The edited version was a single line saying that Calley had not been handcuffed, but without any of the nuance or context that Bigart had put into his report. The editing incident at the *Times* has clear connections to some of the battles Lukas had with his own editors at the paper, and also foreshadows the snarky relationship that *(MORE)* and the *Times* would have over the next eight years.

A. M. Rosenthal, managing editor of the *New York Times* in this period, kept several files on *(MORE)*; an examination of those files, along with other sources, including oral history interviews with *(MORE)* editors and contributors, sheds some light on the relationship between an organ of press criticism and the mainstream publications that it covers. That relationship is complicated, at times indirect and subtle, but also influential. This chapter argues that *(MORE)* did, in fact, influence the behavior of its favorite and most consistent target in significant ways. Though the chapter will outline *(MORE)*'s coverage of the *Times* in general, it focuses on two case studies about which substantial records can be found: the influence *(MORE)* had on the standardization of the *New York Times* correction policy, and *(MORE)*'s revealing of the identities of *Times* employees who had participated in a confidential academic book project by a scholar of organizational behavior—a book project that found the paper's hierarchy to be stubbornly resistant to change and self-examination in exactly the ways Tony Lukas and Homer Bigart might have complained about. This focus on the interplay between *(MORE)* and the organization toward which it most frequently directed its critical powers illuminates the ways in which press criticism works. In order to do this, this chapter puts the *New York Times/(MORE)* relationship in the context of theories of press criticism from James W. Carey and Wendy Wyatt and the press theory of Daniel Hallin.

One might expect that the organized press would be less than thrilled about having to deal with a new publication that existed almost entirely to point out its flaws. The *New York Times*, in its relationship with *(MORE)*, was certainly no exception to this. But *(MORE)*'s nuanced relationship with the *Times*, led editorially by managing editor Abe Rosenthal, differs to some extent from the relationships *(MORE)* had with some of the other news organizations it covered regularly. One point of contrast, the *New York Post*, is instructive.

Dorothy Schiff had been an early, if conflicted, supporter of *(MORE)*, seemingly proud that Woody Woodward, a protégé of hers, had left to become the publisher of his own magazine, while also making sure to distance the *Post* from whatever editorial policies this new anti-institutional journalism review might espouse. That caution appears to have been warranted, as

(*MORE*)'s publication of a memo from *Post* reporter Ted Poston ended any sympathy Schiff might have had for it. She drafted a two-page letter to the editor that she never sent. Her main complaints were that Poston's name was misspelled, that Poston's memo and her response were quoted only in part, and that she had never said that the *Post*'s defense of the case might cost more than $100,000 in legal fees, as a sidebar had claimed.[1] A few days later, Schiff received a memo from her assistant, Jean Gillette, saying that a reporter named Claudia Dreifus had called, asking for comment on a story she was writing about employment conditions for women in the media.[2] Even though her inquiry had nothing directly to do with the Poston case, Dreifus became the first (*MORE*) reporter to be flatly turned down for an interview by Schiff. Once she had been angered by the Poston piece, Schiff shut (*MORE*) out completely. Schiff called Dick Pollak that afternoon and asked her assistant to monitor and transcribe the call. In the transcript, the estimate of the *Post*'s legal fees is her main concern. Pollak stood by his reporter, but offered to correct the mistake. Schiff replied that she was "going to write you a letter anyway, because there are many, many other things in the article I need to correct."

Pollak: In other words, you no longer will speak to anyone associated with (*MORE*).

Schiff: On the grounds that I don't dare to since this happened and I don't know how experienced these reporters are, because if they are going to get things that terribly wrong and damaging, I can't take the chance. Normally, being in this business, I talk to reporters because I don't like it when people won't talk to us, but I can't take the chance.[3]

Schiff drafted another version of her letter, which was significantly terser and more curt than her first draft. It was only a series of questions to which she demanded yes or no answers. The article, this draft of Schiff's letter asserted, was "replete with factual errors, half-truths and unchecked statements. Because so much space would be required to call attention to all the mistakes, I shall confine myself to a half a dozen questions."[4] This letter upped the ante from her earlier draft, which had been written before her conversation with Pollak. She and *Post* editor Paul Sann exchanged memos that afternoon about revisions to the draft, but by the next day, she had changed her mind about sending it. "Why make a contribution to (*MORE*), even in the form of a letter signed by me?" she said in a memo sent to Sann and to former editor and then-editorial page editor James Wechsler. And she handwrote on top of the memo, "Not going to dignify by contributing a letter."[5] Claudia Dreifus, who was a freelance reporter, found herself cut off from the *Post* entirely, no matter who her employer was at the time. At the end of the same month, Dreifus called on assignment from *Ms*. When the memo reached Schiff's desk, she scrawled across it in dull pencil, "She's from 'More.' <u>Do not call her back.</u> No reply."[6]

When Abe Rosenthal of the *Times* first encountered the upstart journalism review *(MORE)*, he also bristled at the idea that these journalists—one of whom was the reporter J. Anthony Lukas, whom he had supervised—would try to tell him how to run his newspaper, the great trust that he had been asked to take care of. But he never reacted quite as strongly as Dorothy Schiff did, in the way that she cut off all access to the *Post*. Instead, the ideas that *(MORE)* advocated eventually found their way into the pages of the *Times*. Not directly, but subtly and through a process of negotiated levels of authority. This chapter looks closely at two instances of interaction between *(MORE)* and the *Times* to demonstrate how that relationship worked. *(MORE)*'s influence was indirect but real, and these two episodes give examples of how the process worked. The first looks at *(MORE)*'s attempt to get the *Times* to run corrections in a dedicated space on a prominent page of the paper every day, as a demonstration of accountability and transparency. The second incident involves a *(MORE)* article that put names to a confidential study of the management style of the *Times*. This section shows the overlap between the academic findings of a scholar who studied the newspaper and the journal of press criticism that pursued a similar goal of press reform. It shows that the public accountability to which *(MORE)* could hold the *Times* made the newspaper see that it could not exempt itself from the kind of scrutiny it applied to the rest of the world. *(MORE)* did for the *Times* what the *Times* did to other institutions. It forced the *Times* to scrutinize itself.

A System of Self-Correction

Even to many serious consumers of the news, the newspaper correction must feel like an institution, something as old and as consistent as the funny pages or coverage of baseball. But even though corrections boxes now seem essential to the credibility of a newspaper, the fixed corrections box, under a standing headline, has been a fixture only since the early 1970s, arising in the midst of a broader ethics and accountability movement in the late 1960s and early 1970s.

While the *New York Times* may not have been first to establish a corrections box, it was the first national newspaper to do so and, as the newspaper of record, was influential in modeling the practice for smaller dailies nationwide.[7] Regardless of whether the *Times* was first, its editorial policy changes were widely noted and widely copied in the newspaper industry. Relying in part on the archived papers of then-managing editor Abe Rosenthal and on interviews with contemporary journalists, this section traces the history of the newspaper corrections box in the *New York Times*, which was already an influential national newspaper by this time, and examines the outside critical voices that compelled the paper to burnish its credibility with this acknowledgment of its own errors. In that way, this is a case study in the effects of press criticism and its influence on institutional change in news organizations as much as it is a study of corrections policies at newspapers. This section also corrects and fills in details of the historical record on how the *Times* came to establish its corrections box.

When *(MORE)* put out its pilot issue in June 1971, one of the stories in the issue was a long response to an essay published in *Commentary* a few months earlier, written by Daniel Patrick Moynihan, who was then working as an adviser to the Nixon administration.[8] The main *(MORE)* essay, titled "Moynihan's Scholarly Tantrum," was written by George Reedy, who had served as press secretary to Lyndon Johnson. But *(MORE)* also ran a second, shorter item based on Moynihan's essay—an editor's note, on the inside back page of the magazine, at the end of a column *(MORE)* called Hellbox:

> Although much of Daniel P. Moynihan's *Commentary* essay on the Presidency and the press seems at best wrongheaded and at worst petulant . . . his final plea that the press establish a systematic method of self-correction is altogether valid.

The editorial, which was written by *(MORE)*'s editor, Dick Pollak,[9] then quotes from Moynihan's essay before continuing:

> Traditionally, newspapers, magazines and television stations have been reluctant to run corrections for fear of losing credibility with their readers and viewers. But a system of self-correction, of course, would have just the opposite effect, conceding (to no one's shame) that journalism even at its finest is

an inexact art. Equally important, a regular process of correction (at the end of the network news shows, at the beginning of each day's "A" wire, on page two of the *Times* every day) would make reporters and editors far more accountable than they now are and help put an end to much of the sloppy journalism that pervades the press.

By way of setting what we hope will not be too frequent an example, in future issues we will devote this final Hellbox item to correcting our own mistakes.[10]

This editorial goes beyond Moynihan's essay to suggest a format for prominently displaying corrections—the "standing head," or regular column and headline, and *(MORE)* may be the first publication to have done so.

Just over a year later, another Hellbox item in *(MORE)* called attention to the fact that the scrappy magazine's primary target, the *New York Times*, had finally realized that a corrections box, published in a predictable part of the paper under a recurring headline, would actually add credibility to the paper rather than detract from it. The editorial's tone is hardly crowing, though, and only the first sentence gives any suggestion that *(MORE)* might have been taking any credit for the innovation: "When we started *(MORE)* eleven issues ago, we promised to devote this final Hellbox item to the systematic correction of our own mistakes," it reads, then quotes from its own earlier editorial, in which it challenged other publications to follow its lead. The overall tone is congratulatory (if snarky):

> There has not exactly been a pell-mell rush in the media to establish fixed, highly visible correction boxes. But at least *The New York Times* has now come along. Until several weeks ago, *Times* policy (if that is the word) called for the running of corrections in easily overlooked nooks and crannies of the paper under the type of headline usually reserved for fillers. Now, managing editor A. M. Rosenthal has instructed that corrections appear regularly under a bold, boxed headline at the end of the index on the second front page. And if the correction requires more space than that portion of the index permits, it will be keyed to another page in the paper and run there at length. The rest of the media, please copy.[11]

There is not much self-satisfaction here, but more than forty years later, Dick Pollak remembered this as one of *(MORE)*'s most important accomplishments:

I think we helped start a movement that has taken hold and the press is better for it. I think the movement of self-criticism, which has become established throughout journalism today, was basically started by the early journalism reviews, and I think we are partly responsible for the correction movement that began after Moynihan's piece. Because he didn't really throw down the gauntlet, and we did. We said we're gonna do it, starting at the next issue, and you guys should too. And eventually they did.[12]

Could Pollak be correct? Could *(MORE)* have pressed the *Times* into running corrections under a standing headline? Was Rosenthal even aware of the startup magazine? Pollak has a point in that his editorial does directly challenge other publications in a way that Moynihan's *Commentary* essay does not. Instead, Moynihan weaves together a complicated argument about objectivity, epistemology, and ombudsmen, and even his two examples of mistakes that should have been corrected take three whole pages of the magazine to explain. The closest Moynihan comes to a prescription for correcting corrections is this: "As to the press itself, one thing seems clear. It should become much more open about acknowledging mistakes."[13] Because Moynihan, who was more scholar and policy wonk than newspaperman, is vague in his prescriptions, the *(MORE)* Hellbox item may actually be the first statement of the idea that corrections should always run in the same place.

Moynihan's essay is important for the development of correction policies, however, in that it does provide the intellectual framework for the argument about the ethics of correction. Moynihan puts it this way:

The final, and by far the most important, circumstance of American journalism relevant to this discussion is the absence of a professional tradition of self-correction. The mark of any developed profession is the practice of correcting mistakes, by whomsoever they are made. . . . Ideally, also, no discredit is involved: to the contrary, honest mistakes are integral to the process of advancing the field. Journalism will never attain to such condition. Nevertheless, there is a range of subject matter about which reasonable men can and will agree, and within this range American journalism, even of the higher order, is often seriously wide of the mark.[14]

These are the same sentiments embedded throughout *(MORE)* and Rosenthal's high-minded memos.

Unquestionably, Rosenthal knew of Moynihan's essay at the time of its publication. Rosenthal's papers indicate that he and Moynihan exchanged several letters both before and after the *Commentary* essay. Furthermore, Rosenthal received a copy of a long letter from fellow *Times* editor Max Frankel to Moynihan in response to the *Commentary* essay. Frankel's response is balanced in much the same way as Moynihan's essay, with corrections getting only a small bit of attention toward the end of the fifteen-page, single-spaced typescript. "In one sense, of course, we correct ourselves every morning, a requirement and an opportunity that most other institutions, including the Presidency, lack," Frankel writes. For the most part, he dismisses Moynihan's arguments, but does acknowledge that "there is need, in another sense, for more correction or expansion and amendment of what we report."[15] More importantly, though, the copy of the letter in Rosenthal's files shows that he was aware of Moynihan's essay, and Frankel's attached handwritten note on *Times* stationery also indicates that Rosenthal had been thinking of the essay even before Frankel shared his response. "This went off just an hour before you called about Moynihan's piece tonight," Frankel's note, which is dated March 15, 1971, begins.[16] This is the same month that "The Presidency & the Press" appeared in *Commentary*, and three months before *(MORE)* would make its debut. Also, perhaps not coincidentally, this was about two weeks before Rosenthal would issue his reminder to the news staff about corrections policy, one that focused more on high-minded ideals of journalism ethics, and that closed with this: "What I am trying to do, simply, is to insure [*sic*] attention in each case to the elemental but essential question of journalistic fairness."[17] And as far as Moynihan's influence on Rosenthal, Allan Siegal, Rosenthal's former deputy, writes that "Rosenthal was an admirer and friend of Moynihan, and he tended to adopt suggestions from people he admired, though he did not often convey the source to his associates."[18]

But Moynihan's essay and Rosenthal's subsequent memo were about ideals, not policy; if *(MORE)* did pioneer the idea of the regular corrections column, and if Rosenthal had been thinking about corrections for at least two years, and if he knew of *(MORE)*'s idea, why would he not implement it in the summer of 1971, when Dick Pollak proposed it, instead of waiting a year? The simplest answer would be that in the spring and summer of 1971, Rosenthal was preoccupied with preparations for and dealing with the legal and cultural aftermath of the publication of the Pentagon Papers. A dense section of Rosenthal's journals contains a detailed account of the months of research leading to publication. Additionally, a letter from Rosenthal to, coincidentally, Moynihan, in response to one from Moynihan praising the *Times*'s writing quality, alludes to the pervasiveness of the Pentagon Papers in Rosenthal's professional life: "I must admit that in the last week or so, I haven't paid a hell of a lot of attention to literary style," Rosenthal wrote on June 24, 1971, "except as expressed by various benches."[19]

Another possibility is that Rosenthal was reluctant to take a suggestion from *(MORE)*, a magazine he was aware of, at least by the time of the new corrections policy in 1972, if not necessarily at its 1971 debut. As Siegal writes in an email, "I believe Rosenthal was NOT an admirer of *(MORE)*, which he associated with New Left sympathies that were anathema to him in the 60s and 70s."[20] In addition, one of the founders of *(MORE)* was Tony Lukas, a *Times* reporter who had butted heads with his editors when he was covering the Chicago Seven conspiracy trial in 1969. His experience of being constrained by his editors led directly to conversations with Pollak about starting *(MORE)*.[21] David Halberstam was also a contributor to the first issue of the magazine, and Halberstam had also clashed with the *Times* over his reporting. Quite possibly though, Rosenthal just missed the first issue of *(MORE)*, distracted as he would have been by the Pentagon Papers. By the following summer, however, the magazine had forced its way into his consciousness. In a memo to his deputy Seymour Topping, Rosenthal noted that he would be away from the paper during the American Newspaper Publishers Association meeting (which he did not attend). At the same time as the ANPA meeting, *(MORE)* planned to hold a "counter-convention" across town (as discussed in chapter 4). Halberstam, Lukas, and Sidney Zion, who had also written for the *Times*, were all scheduled to appear on a panel called "Why Journalists Leave Daily Newspapers."[22] In 1971, Zion had publicly revealed the identity of Daniel Ellsberg, the source of the Pentagon Papers. Rosenthal never grew to respect *(MORE)*'s work. In a 1976 letter to Michael Kramer, the new editor-publisher who took over from Pollak and Lukas, he called *(MORE)* "professionally rather adolescent" and said that its coverage was less a reflection of reality than "of the psychic problems and nastiness of some of the people who used to put out" the magazine.[23]

Perhaps, then, Rosenthal's lack of respect for *(MORE)* made it difficult for him to accept the magazine's suggestions, even if he liked those suggestions and even if they fell in line with his own thinking on corrections. But Rosenthal had read Moynihan's essay, which introduced some of the ideas he incorporated into his own explanations of the *Times*'s correction policy, and he knew of *(MORE)*, which first called upon the paper to publish them under a standing headline.

A 1986 study of corrections policies at twelve newspapers observed, "The literature on newspaper corrections systems is remarkably sparse."[24] In part, this was because corrections policies themselves were so new. Before this period, most newspapers used corrections as filler, printing them in tiny type at the ends of columns. They were haphazard, and their use was usually determined by the dictates of space and the whims of department editors and copy editors. As the writer Craig Silverman, a popular expert on corrections, put it,

> At the time, the *Times*, like many other publications in North America, ran its corrections throughout the paper. They would appear in every section, in different places, written in different ways, and often under different headings. If you read the initial error, the chances of your happening upon the correction were slim. It was accuracy roulette.[25]

A 1973 study by the American Newspaper Publishers Association found that nine out of thirty-eight large newspapers (defined as having a circulation of more than 100,000) used a standing head for corrections as one of their systems of accountability, demonstrating that the practice had begun to spread. Of the 135 papers surveyed overall, though, only seventeen had instituted a corrections box or section, so more than half of the papers that regularly ran corrections fell into the largest circulation category.[26]

By the 1980s, however, the practice of consolidating each day's batch of corrections in a single, predictable location had become commonplace enough that researchers began to examine newspapers' policies, though the authors of a 1983 study still called the corrections box "a new approach to journalistic admissions of error."[27] That study looked at the *Times* and the *Washington Post* and found that relatively few mistakes were being corrected, despite new corrections policies, and that most of the corrections were of objective errors, such as misspelled names or incorrect dates, not of more subjective errors of interpretation, fairness, or judgment.

Three years later, in 1986, the erroneous idea had come into being that corrections had *always* been a part of a responsible newspaper's system for maintaining the trust of its readers. Thomas Winship, a former editor of the *Boston Globe*, said "that nothing is more crucial to a news organization than its reputation for accuracy, and that nothing is more crucial to establishing this reputation than the honest, timely and public admission of errors," according to a Gannett Center study of corrections. "This," the study report quoted Winship as saying, "is the way it always has been, and the way it always will be."[28] The study examined the corrections policies of six large and six smaller papers, and found that most of them had policies to print corrections underneath standing headlines, but that the majority of corrections were—as the 1983 study had also found—of simple factual errors, rather than subjective errors.

Though the corrections box became a staple of newspapers during the 1970s and 1980s, the reality seems to be that corrections are more for show—for increasing public trust in the institution—than for real admission of error. Stephen Hess, a fellow of the Brookings Institution, wrote that real self-criticism and admission of error were rare among newspapers. In addition to a brief review of much of the above literature, he quoted Geneva Overholser, who was then (in 1998) serving as ombudsman for the *Washington Post*, as saying that editors did not even want to hear from their reporters that mistakes had been made.[29] That trend continued into the next decade. A 2001 content analysis of corrections and ombudsman columns, by Neil Nemeth and Craig Sanders, came to the same conclusion as several earlier studies: newspapers were correcting their objective errors, but not engaging in deep criticism of their own work.[30]

A 2005 study by Scott R. Maier found that this cavalier attitude toward subjective errors significantly harmed the credibility of newspapers, as these were seen as the most egregious. The perception of inaccuracy was particularly troublesome according to Maier because this led to decreased trust and participation from news sources necessary to the papers.[31] In a later study, Maier found that while journalists contended that they quickly correct mistakes, fewer than one in ten mistakes, as perceived by the news sources, were corrected, leading to "a sense of futility" among the sources.[32]

Newspaper corrections are popular enough with the reading public to have launched Craig Silverman's book *Regret the Error* and supported the blog that he ran under the same name for several years, before it was eventually picked up by the journalism think tank the Poynter Institute. Silverman has also been a regular year-end guest on broadcasts such as NPR's *On the Media*, where he names his corrections of the year.[33] Michael Bugeja and Jane Peterson took the popularity of Silverman's book and blog as the starting point for one of the most recent studies of newspaper corrections, in 2007. They found that editors had come to accept corrections as a responsibility to their readers, and as a way to increase credibility. Bugeja and Peterson also found, as the previous studies had, that most corrections were of objective fact, not of matters of interpretation. And, despite the title of Silverman's blog, most corrections boxes no longer apologized for their errors.[34] Bugeja later wrote a paper codifying the ethics of news organizations corrections, settling on these seven commandments:

1. Identify the error (what it was, when and where it occurred).
2. Correct the record.
3. Do so as soon as possible.
4. Do so prominently.
5. Provide an explanation to the audience or clientele.
6. Disclose how the error could have been avoided and/or how it will
      be prevented in the future.
7. Issue an apology to those damaged by the false disclosure.[35]

But that list was written in 2007, when corrections had become an accepted part of the credibility rituals of news organizations. As these studies have repeatedly shown, despite the boost to credibility that running corrections gives to a paper, editors are still loath to admit errors. And in 1972, when the practice was still virtually unheard-of, it took a confluence of outside influences to nudge the constitutionally conservative *New York Times* toward adopting the policy.

In her book *Critical Conversations*, Wendy Wyatt develops what she calls a discourse theory of press criticism.[36] For Wyatt, press criticism occurs through conversations that occur at and among three levels of discourse, which she presents as three concentric circles. She calls the first level, at the periphery, the "critical public," by which she means the self-appointed members of the public who are engaged with the press and offer suggestions for institutional change based on what they feel would best serve them as a public. One step in from the critical public in Wyatt's model are the critics who filter ideas from the critical public and engage in conversation with the press itself. They are the intermediaries who refine and elaborate on the ideas of the critical public (and may be members of the critical public themselves) and then present the refined ideas for change to those who occupy Wyatt's third level: the press, who sit at the "institutional center" of her model. This is where "members of the press engage in discourse with one another to make decisions about the opinions introduced at the second level and then act on those decisions."[37]

This case study positions the *New York Times* as the institutional center making decisions about policy. Two journalism reviews—the *Columbia Journalism Review* and *(MORE)*—and the politician Daniel Patrick Moynihan are slightly more difficult to place in Wyatt's structure, however. Moynihan, who wrote an influential essay that contained the germ of the idea for the corrections box, probably works best in the model as the "critical public," a consumer of news who had an idea for its betterment. But at the same time, Moynihan also corresponded directly with Abe Rosenthal, a friend at the *New York Times*, making Moynihan somewhat more of an insider than the model would suggest. Also, while both the *Columbia Journalism Review* and *(MORE)* are journalism reviews, they occupy slightly different spots in Wyatt's model. *(MORE)* had a reputation for irreverence and took an openly anti-institutional stance, or at least a position that argued for change within existing institutions, if not for their wholesale overthrow. The *Columbia Journalism Review*, on the other hand, was more staid at the time, and while its ideas may not have been as revolutionary, the writers at *CJR* had an easier time getting the ear of the leaders of the institutional press.

Daniel Hallin's model of the spheres of debate can easily be adapted from its intended use as a model for analyzing press coverage of ideas to explain how ideas infiltrate the management of the institutions of the press as well.[38] Conveniently, Hallin's model also consists of concentric circles, so it overlays easily on Wyatt's. For Hallin, the core of the model is a sphere of consensus—ideas that are so widely agreed-upon that there is no need to discuss them. At the outside is the sphere of deviance, which is the realm where ideas are so beyond the pale that they, too, are not worth discussion. In between is the sphere of legitimate debate, wherein those ideas that are moving from one extreme to the other are worked over in the press. *(MORE)* could be seen as operating within the sphere of deviance in the eyes of Abe Rosenthal, as this case study shows, and even though the *Columbia Journalism Review* advocated an almost identical position, Rosenthal was receptive to the ideas of the latter and not the former. In fact, he implemented *CJR*'s suggestion so quickly that *CJR* was acting almost as a part of the institutional press in Wyatt's model, since there was almost no discussion between the suggestion and the implementation. Of course, history is messier than any one or two models, so the actors do not fit neatly into the categories. But these two models are helpful in understanding the process by which the standardization of corrections moved from an inchoate idea to a challenge, to a suggestion, and then finally to a daily feature of the most respected newspaper in the United States.

The first anchored correction in the *New York Times* ran on June 2, 1972. Except for its place in newspaper history, the correction itself seems less than momentous:

> The obituary of Theodore L. Bates in yesterday's *New York Times* reported that Mr. Bates had once briefly served as a consultant to Investors Overseas Services. Actually, it was T. Rosser Reeves, a former chairman of Ted Bates & Co., who worked for the mutual fund organization.[39]

The correction appeared, as Allan Siegal described, at the end of the News Summary and Index, a feature the *Times* had been running for some time on the second front of the paper. On June 2, 1972, that meant page thirty-nine of the paper overall, but the placement was prominent for two reasons: first, because of the way the paper was produced at the time, there were no sections in the same way there are four decades later. Arts, sports, and business news appeared in discrete areas of the newspaper, but they did not each get their own pullout section. They were folded together into two folios of paper, which made the second front the second most prominent page in the paper. (As the *Times* is a broadsheet, the back pages of the sections aren't quite prime editorial real estate the way they would be in a tabloid.) Although the first correction appears at the bottom of the page, it is noticeable, under a boxed headline reading "correction" in all caps. The other reason the location chosen for corrections was prominent is that editors knew that people sought out the News Summary.

Over the first five months of 1972, before the new policy went into effect, the paper had followed its usual practice of scattering corrections throughout the paper, though there was some logic behind their placement, at least sometimes. A correction running on the television listings page on March 9 corrected a mistake that had appeared on that page (the actress Peggy Ashcroft had been misidentified in a photo caption as Helen Haye).[40] But sometimes, the placement seemed to be dictated as much by where filler was needed, as in the case of a dateline correction for an international news item that was sandwiched between the bottom of the bridge column and an ad for a captain's bed.[41]

In *Regret the Error*, Craig Silverman repeats the story that a single memorandum in 1970 from *Times* managing editor (which was then the top editorial position at the paper) Abe Rosenthal led to the standardization of corrections. This misconception likely stems from assumptions Silverman made after reading his source, the introduction to a 2002 compilation of amusing *New York Times* corrections called *Kill Duck before Serving*. Former *Times* assistant managing editor and standards editor Allan Siegal wrote the introduction. Though Siegal gets his former boss's title and the location of the original corrections right, the way he describes the relationship between the 1970 memo and the regular printing of corrections "two years later" may very well have led Silverman to conclude that there was a direct connection, even though Siegal likely intended only to note a temporal relationship, not a causal one:

> Perfect accuracy is elusive, but accountability need not be. Years ago, reporters sometimes appeased a complainer by burying a correction in their next story. No longer. In 1970, A. M. Rosenthal, then managing editor, told his department heads that "corrections or denials or amplifications don't really catch up with the original because they are not given proper display." Two years later, he created a reserved space where readers could always find the corrections, just below the News Summary (then on the front of the second section, since moved to Page 2). The publisher, Arthur Ochs Sulzberger, wondered in a memo whether "we are not over-penalizing ourselves," but he overcame his misgivings after *The Times* won applause in the industry and other newspapers followed its lead.[42]

This brief account seems to have become the basis for our understanding of the advent of regular corrections in the *Times*, and it is not incorrect—though it *is* incomplete. In fact, between 1970, when Rosenthal seems to have first contemplated running corrections, and 1972, when the policy was implemented, quite a bit of discussion occurred in the intersections among Wyatt's levels of critical discourse, which eventually pushed the *Times* into establishing its permanent corrections policy. A fleshed-out version of the story brings together Rosenthal, two rival journalism reviews, and Daniel Patrick Moynihan, at the time an adviser to President Richard Nixon. And this version puts the story of corrections in the context of broader movements toward press accountability and self-criticism that have broadened and continued even to the present.

The 1970 memo Allan Siegal references appears to be one that Rosenthal sent on December 21, 1970, to eight editors and the "bullpen," the term the *Times* used for an area where top editors collaborated to make decisions about the next morning's paper (and also for those editors):

> One of the problems that has troubled all of us, I think, is giving adequate attention and display to corrections of stories that turn out to be wrong in whole or in major part. It happens on *The Times* as on other papers that the corrections or amplifications don't really catch up with the original because they are not given proper display.
>
> I know we have all had this in mind and that our record is pretty good but pretty good is not good enough. I would appreciate it if, from now on, all corrections, denials or major amplifications of important stories are brought to my personal attention so that a careful decision can be made on how to play them. I am not talking about minor corrections which will continue to be handled in the usual way but about stories involving corrections of substance.[43]

So while Rosenthal had apparently not hit on the idea of consolidating corrections by 1970, he had at least been thinking about the problem of how best to emphasize the importance of corrections at this early stage in his career as managing editor. And it remained on his mind between the 1970 memo and the beginning of the new corrections policy in 1972. On March 31, 1971, Rosenthal sent several top editors another memo that reads as much as a disquisition on the ethics of journalism as it does a directive to his staff:

> There are three areas involving fair play in which all newspapers, including our own, do not, generally speaking, live up to their own standards.
>
> One is making sure that a correction gets decent display. The second is making sure that a denial of a charge gets decently equal treatment with the charge itself. The third is making sure that when a man is acquitted of charges against him, the acquittal gets as much attention as the original charges.[44]

The memo goes on to remind the editors of the policy of bringing major corrections to his attention, but it is notable more for its high-minded tone than for any policy change. The memo appears to be most directly triggered by a less-than-prominent correction the *Times* had given four days earlier, but certainly by the time he authored the memo, Rosenthal had already decided that corrections were an important and underplayed part of the newspaper he was editing. They were so important, in fact, that Rosenthal stapled copies of his December 1970 memo and this March 1971 memo into his personal journal, a hodgepodge of news clippings, memoranda, and more traditional journal entries bound into three-ring binders that were assembled to document his years at the *Times*. Perhaps he did so with an eye to his legacy, of which corrections have become a part, even if, as the historical record shows, he did not invent the *Times*'s new format out of whole cloth or entirely by himself.

If the *New York Times* gave birth to a new corrections format on June 2, 1972, this first case study of the interaction between the *Times* and *(MORE)* has shown that the baby had been gestating at least since 1970, about a year after Rosenthal took the managing editor position. Birth is a labored metaphor, so to speak, but in this case, the metaphor is Rosenthal's. On June 1, 1972, someone named "Steph" (perhaps a secretary or news assistant) gave Rosenthal a copy of a typescript written by Edward W. Barrett, director of the Communications Institute and a former dean of the Columbia University Graduate School of Journalism. Barrett had written a piece about corrections and Steph's attached note asked Rosenthal to look over the draft by that afternoon. Rosenthal's detailed response is dated the same day, June 1:

> I think that your piece about corrections touches on a most interesting and important subject. But, as I said on the phone, I think that your thrust is a little awry. The thrust is that *The Times* has not been doing anything about this and should take leadership.
>
> Actually, this is a subject that we have not only been talking about but moving on in recent months. I share the feeling that *The Times*, like other newspapers, has not given enough attention or prominence to corrections. . . .
>
> We have devised a special typographical format that will be used only for corrections, abandoning the old K-head format. See the attached sample. We have gone one step further, and an important one. We plan to anchor the corrections in one of the most prominent positions in the paper—the second front. I had the sample made so that you can see

that not only is the correction type prominent but that the anchored position entirely changes the quality of the correction, as far as calling it to the reader's attention is concerned. I think that before long people will be turning to this to see what the correction of the day is![45]

Rosenthal attached a sample showing the corrections box at the end of the News Summary and Index, as it would appear the next day. But the text for the sample is a correction about the director of the film *Fools' Parade*, a correction that had appeared in print only that morning. Clearly, even if the staff of the *Times* had been working on this project "in recent months," this mock-up had only been prepared that day. June 1 was also the day that Rosenthal sent a memo to his top editors telling them of "his" idea and asking for their feedback. So either the memo was merely a reminder to his staff of an ongoing project, or, as the memo seems to read, this was the first time Rosenthal had mentioned these key typographical changes, and his insinuation to Barrett that this had been a long time in coming was a face-saving exaggeration.

At the end of his typewritten letter, Rosenthal scrawled a handwritten postscript: "As you may have seen, we started tonight. *The Times* editors are the parents of the new approach but you certainly helped induce labor!"

After receiving the draft article by Edward Barrett at *Columbia Journalism Review,* Rosenthal began the process of changing to the new style in a memo to several news department editors—Seymour Topping, Lewis Jordan, Lawrence Hauck, and Socrates "Chick" Butsikares—in which he laid out what appears to be his own, original idea of consolidating the corrections, and asks for suggestions about implementation:

> Every editor is entitled to a few bugs and I'm buggy about corrections. Actually, this is a matter that concerns a great many readers as my mail shows. I don't think we have done right by corrections and I think it would be to The Times's credit if we took some leadership in this.
>
> I think that we are a little too stingy about printing corrections. I think that they are too small under the K-head format, that they tend to get buried at the bottom of columns, and that they are difficult to find. I think we have an obligation to our readers to do something about this. . . .

> I think we should have a new typographical format for corrections, either a box head, or preferably something distinctive and confined only to corrections, perhaps an overline type thing.
>
> I also think that we should have an anchored place in the paper for corrections—someplace fairly prominent, perhaps page two or the op-obit page, or even the second front so that readers would know where to look to find any correction. . . .
>
> Please do put your minds to this as soon as possible. I would like to put some variation of this into effect within a week.[46]

But as noted above, the process took not a week, but rather less than a day to implement. Another memo, dated the next day, went out from Lewis Jordan, addressed to all of the paper's news desks, as well the editors of the news summary and index and to the composing room, where the paper's layouts were pasted up:

> From now on, all brief corrections of errors that have appeared in the paper will, whatever their nature and whatever desk is the source, be carried at the end of the News Summary and Index (as one was in today's paper). . . .
>
> The desks will, of course, continue to be responsible for checking the corrections or the reference paragraphs in the Index in the first edition.[47]

And with this memo, a one-day experiment in how best to display corrections became the policy of the *New York Times*.

On June 1, the day before the new corrections policy went into effect, the *Times* ran three corrections, and true to practice, they were scattered throughout the paper. One was a correction of the misidentification of Burt Kennedy as the director of *Fools' Parade* (it was actually Andrew V. McLaglen), running on the same page as the film and theater listings. Another listed the wrong winner of the discus throw in a sectional championship of the Catholic High School Athletic Association, on a sports page beneath a story on Lee Trevino's performance at the Kemper Open. Seven pages after that, between business stories and public notices of stock offerings, the final item corrected a typo in a story about a lawsuit concerning franchisees of Chicken Delight, Inc.[48] So when the new policy went into effect the next morning, these somewhat haphazard-seeming corrections would have been consolidated—losing their attachment to the general subject matter they were associated with, but gaining visibility and predictability.

When Barrett's piece appeared, it ran in the July/August 1972 issue of the *Columbia Journalism Review*, the older, stodgier, more establishment-friendly rival to *(MORE)*.[49] The draft copy of the piece had included a call for "forthright, well-displayed correction" of errors, and pointed out that *CJR* had been advocating improvements in corrections since 1968, though the earlier article that Barrett referred to was not specific about asking for a fixed, prominent corrections box.[50] Barrett added two paragraphs toward the end of his final printed article, applauding the beginning of the *Times*'s new corrections policy and noting that Rosenthal had been shown a draft of the article. But Barrett still wanted to see the *Times* do more, including an "unfinished business" column that would allow for letters of clarification to be printed more regularly. It remains unclear whether Barrett had read either Moynihan's *Commentary* essay or the subsequent *(MORE)* editorial, but he at least had read a common ancestor, a piece of press criticism written for the *New York Times Magazine* by the *Times* editorial writer A. H. Raskin, an essay that Moynihan cites specifically too.[51] At any rate, it was, in the end, a journalism review that pushed the *Times* to begin running corrections regularly, but it was not the impish *(MORE)* but the more palatable *CJR* that finally got results from its prodding. *CJR*, to Rosenthal, existed in the sphere of legitimate debate. In fact, Rosenthal's rapid response to the ideas in the *CJR* draft make it seem almost as if *CJR* existed within the central sphere of Wendy Wyatt's critical model: "the level of will formation,"[52] where members of the institutional press discuss critical ideas and implement them. *CJR* almost seems to be a part of the institutional press in this case.

(MORE), the *Columbia Journalism Review*, and even Daniel Patrick Moynihan were not completely independent actors in the run-up. A. H. Raskin published his critique of the press in the *New York Times Magazine* in 1967, and that lofty platform allowed for his essay to become one of the touchstones of the journalistic accountability movement, a culture of ethical critiques of news that was going strong when the *Times* introduced its new corrections format. Even Raskin was not the beginning of that movement. Notably, the Hutchins Commission report in 1947 had called for greater self-policing among members of the press and also for the development of press councils, another movement of the 1960s and

1970s.[53] Raskin advocated for the institution of ombudsmen, internal critics of the newspapers who were insulated from editorial pressure and answerable instead to the public. Moynihan and Barrett both cite Raskin in their arguments for more internal criticism (and against news councils as outside critics). But Norman Isaacs, editor of the *Louisville Courier-Journal* and its evening counterpart, the *Louisville Times*, also picked up Raskin's essay, and in a 1986 book that is three parts criticism and one part memoir, he recounts how eight days later, his Kentucky papers appointed the first newspaper ombudsman in the United States.[54]

Abe Rosenthal's summer 1972 innovation in the presentation of corrections did not go unnoticed, either in the press, internally at the *Times*, among fellow publishers, or among readers. Less than two months after corrections started appearing on the second front, *Newsweek*'s media column ran a piece on "a candid new trend . . . developing among U.S. newspapers."[55]

Internally, Rosenthal sent a memo to the *Times*'s publisher, Punch Sulzberger, on June 2,[56] though Sulzberger appears to have taken ten days to respond. Sulzberger had several reservations about the new policy, wondering "if we are not over-penalizing ourselves by always locating it within the Index." He was worried that running more than one or two corrections in a day would eat into the index space. But more than that, he seems to have been worried that perhaps the corrections were too noticeable: "let's not always stick it in one spot," he wrote to Rosenthal. "We will sure as fate be accused of something if we are obliged to relocate it in the future." To his credit, Rosenthal stuck by his policy, saying that if the editors had to cut items from the index, they would eliminate "those items which are really not very important, such as baseball games." More importantly, though, Rosenthal wrote that he had "heard so much favorable comment outside the office on its present position and on the idea that *The Times* was saying all the time to the reader that if we have a correction, you will know exactly where to find it, that it would hurt to shift so early in the game."[57]

There is no immediately apparent record of this public and industry response, at least in Rosenthal's papers. But he refers to it again in 1973, in another memo to his staff: "Our corrections policy is a good one, I think, and has attracted a lot of favorable comment in the business."[58] At least one note from a reader praising the corrections policy did make its way into Rosenthal's files, a handwritten note from someone named Ric Cox, of White Plains, New York:

> May I congratulate the *Times* on its policy to correct its errors in a
> prominent position in the paper. Far from reducing the paper's credi-
> bility, such display of fairness constantly restores my faith in America's
> press, the *Times* in particular.[59]

This note so completely echoes Rosenthal's reasoning for running corrections that it almost seems suspect (or at least explains why this note meant
so much to Rosenthal).

Despite Rosenthal's lofty aim of correcting all of the paper's errors in
order to improve reader trust, he was responsive to issues of aesthetics
(a too-crowded news index) and to Sulzberger's suggestion that publishing too many prominent corrections might be "over-penalizing." In a brief
1973 memo to Lewis Jordan, he wrote, "On corrections, I think that two is
enough for any one day. Three really looks rather heavy. Let's stick to two
unless there is a real pressing necessity for more."[60] He was obviously willing, at times, to compromise his ideals, though he stood by the policy for
years. In 1980, he defended the paper's policy to Richard Gelb, chairman
of the Bristol-Myers Company, who had written to complain that the *Times*
had buried a correction about the link between hair dye and cancer. "As a
matter of fact," Rosenthal wrote, "many readers, I have found, turn to the
second front to see what the corrections are for that day, almost before they
read anything else. I am one of these." Also, he wrote, "*The Times*'s emphasis on corrections was noted in the journalistic community and written
about. Since then, I believe that others have followed suit."

Others do seem to have followed suit. A 1973 study commissioned by
the American Newspaper Publishers Association found, "The practice of
printing corrections under a standing head is popular and promises to be
more so."[61] Of the thirty-eight newspapers with circulations of more than
100,000 that were surveyed, nine (24 percent) reported having a standing
head for corrections, though the numbers dropped quickly at smaller circulation papers.[62] But change often comes from the top papers first, so it is
not surprising that the practice had not yet filtered down from papers such
as the *Times*. Even in 1983, the practice was considered "new."[63] But the
Courier-Journal and the *Times* seem to have started something, with studies of corrections and their ethics proliferating after 1972.[64]

In 1986, Rosenthal brought out the Editors' Note for more complicated
clarifications. In May 2003, the *Times* published perhaps the longest and
most famous correction story, thoroughly investigating itself after the paper

learned that its reporter Jayson Blair had been fabricating stories. But, as Silverman points out in his book, newspaper corrections policies have basically been unchanged in the forty years since the *Times* began consolidating them in its news summary and index. The real innovation has been online, where technology allows for noting corrections in the text of an original story as well as consolidating corrections into a single column or even an RSS (Really Simple Syndication) feed. Writing for the *Columbia Journalism Review*'s website, Silverman singles out the online magazine *Slate* for being particularly inventive.[65]

So the tradition of earning reader trust through the regular, visible publication of corrections continues. It is a tradition that was most prominently started by Abe Rosenthal and the *New York Times*. But while Rosenthal should get credit for being a pioneer, he should not stand alone. Using Wendy Wyatt's model of press criticism, we can see that the ideas that influenced his decision filtered in from a critical public—in this case, Daniel Patrick Moynihan—through the critics at *(MORE)* and the *Columbia Journalism Review*, and into the institutional center of the *Times*. *(MORE)* itself might not have been enough of a force to nudge the *Times* toward a corrections policy, though, since the anti-institutional ideals of that publication were still too close to Daniel Hallin's sphere of deviance for the idea to take hold. It is only through the prodding of the more institutionally minded *Columbia Journalism Review* that the idea could attain legitimacy.

Richard Pollak, editor of *(MORE)*, put it in terms that were as feisty as any that Rosenthal himself might have used: "It's hard for me to believe that it was never discussed prior to 1971 in the halls of *The New York Times* by somebody," Pollak said of the idea of running regular corrections under a standing head and in a prominent place in the newspaper. "But I would hesitate to give Abe—I was never a big fan of Abe, and vice versa—but I would never just reflexively give credit to him for this. . . even if he's willing to take it."[66] Pollak is both right and wrong. Rosenthal deserves credit, though perhaps not as much as he was willing to give himself. Even on June 1, 1972, the idea for a fixed corrections box was part of a lineage of journalistic accountability that began at least as early as the Hutchins Commission report, and ran through Daniel Patrick Moynihan and then through two journalism reviews. The idea was already part of the culture of journalistic criticism and self-criticism. Sources of journalistic criticism at the fringes of what the *New York Times* found acceptable brought that idea into the professional conversation surrounding journalism. Then it took prodding from a source that Rosenthal knew and respected before the practice of correcting the record could make it into the newspaper of record.

The Accidental Press Critic

In his 1969 book *The Kingdom and the Power*, former *New York Times* reporter Gay Talese gave an insider's history of the goings-on in the newsroom of the newspaper that had become, by the mid-twentieth century, the newspaper of record for the United States. The *Times*, despite its insistence on openness and accountability among the other institutions of power in the United States, had always been a private, quiet place, at least when viewed from the outside. But *The Kingdom and the Power*, for the first time, gave an interested public a view of the petty jealousies, personal animosities, and structural barriers that affected the news that *Times* readers read every morning. From the point of view of a scholar, though, Talese's book is gossipy, with only glancing attribution for much of its sourcing, in the manner of the narrative-style New Journalism with which Talese was associated. However, at almost exactly the same time, a sober academic was lurking within the walls of the Gray Lady's 43rd Street offices, making tape recordings of meetings, interviewing several dozen of the paper's top executives and editors, and attempting—but failing—to rectify the ossified culture of the paper. And while this academic, the Harvard organizational scholar Chris Argyris, was unable to make direct interventions in the management structure of the *Times*, the book that resulted from his study (*Behind the Front Page: Organizational Self-Renewal at a Metropolitan Newspaper*) functioned as a sort of accidental press criticism, goading the paper into a kind of self-scrutiny that it may not otherwise have undertaken. At the request of the skittish and almost secretive *Times*, Argyris disguised the identity of the newspaper and of the editorial and business staff featured in the book. If the paper and its editors and business staff had remained confidential, the *Times* might very well have been able to sweep its conclusions under the plush rugs in the office of publisher Punch Sulzberger. However, *(MORE)*, which engaged in very intentional press criticism, decoded Argyris's book, publicly forcing the *Times* to confront its managerial shortcomings. Large institutional news organizations often operate under the sort of anti-intellectualism codified by Daniel Rigney as unreflective instrumentalism. This case study of the *Times* shows how *(MORE)* was able to pressure its largest and most frequent target of criticism into self-reflection.

Since as early as the 1950s and reaching a peak in the late 1970s, the practice of newsroom ethnography has provided valuable insights into the management structures of newspapers (and, later, other forms of news organization) and has helped to elucidate the unique culture of the participants in the field of journalism. Gaye Tuchman's *Making News: A Study in the Construction of Reality* and Herbert Gans's *Deciding What's News: A Study of CBS Evening News, NBC Nightly News,* Newsweek, *and* Time, two pillars of the genre from the late 1970s, have stayed in print for forty years and have informed the thinking of at least two generations of press scholars. Mark Fishman's *Manufacturing the News* was published in 1980, but was really also a product of the 1970s news culture. Recently, a new wave of scholars has taken up the practice of newsroom ethnography in order to explore the transition to digital publication and the organizational and cultural changes that have come with that transition,[67] while other scholars have theorized ways for newsroom ethnography to illuminate our understanding of the practices of newsmaking.[68]

In 1974, just as the 1970s wave of newsroom ethnography was about to crest, the publishing house Jossey-Bass released the latest work by a scholar of organizations named Chris Argyris. Argyris had set out to write about the management structure of a major American newspaper. Granted unprecedented access to editors and management at the *Times,* Argyris discovered a sclerotic, toxic management culture, based on tradition and the management's beliefs that what they were doing must be working.

In addition to the management lessons, *Behind the Front Page,* in its role as press criticism, demonstrates the ironic opacity of the *Times* as an institution of the press. While Argyris may have failed as a management consultant, he inadvertently succeeded as a press critic. Newspapers demand transparency from other institutions of power: governments, corporations, banks. But they have been particularly resistant to outside criticism themselves, and the *Times* was a particularly conservative paper in this regard. The editors struggled with their own politically and institutionally conservative impulses in 1972 when they chose to publish the Pentagon Papers, thinking that publication might destroy public confidence in not only the U.S. government, but in the newspaper as well. This second case study of the interactions between *(MORE)* and the *Times* shows the role of Chris Argyris as an outsider and accidental press critic in opening up the *Times* to criticism, through the intervention of an intentional organ of press criticism.

When Argyris published *Behind the Front Page*, he abided by his own sense of academic propriety and intense and repeated demands from editors and executives at the *Times* that he scrupulously maintain the paper's anonymity and that of its employees. As a result, his book reads as a slightly inscrutable roman à clef. It took the efforts of a New York University journalism professor, working for *(MORE)* to "decode" *Behind the Front Page*, to make some of its more sensational revelations accessible to a nonacademic reading public. Together, Argyris and *(MORE)* opened up the operations of the *New York Times* with a level of academic rigor that Gay Talese did not aspire to. Given the *Times*'s position as the newspaper of record and its influence on other newspapers around the United States, understanding the workings of its business and editorial processes provides insight into the operations of the papers that it influenced as well. Coverage in the popular press of the *Times*'s structural changes in 2017 also demonstrate the importance of its production processes to American journalism in a larger sense.[69]

This case study draws on Argyris's book, cross-referenced with the article from *(MORE)* that identified major publishing and editorial staff at the *Times,* as well as the institutional archives of the *Times*, particularly those of its top editor, Abe Rosenthal. Argyris secured access to the *Times* via its publisher, Punch Sulzberger, but Rosenthal's papers provide the most thorough portrait of the editorial staff's oppositional stance toward Argyris. The case study places Argyris's failure to effect change at the *Times* in the context of Wendy Wyatt's discursive theory of press criticism as well as theories of anti-intellectualism developed by sociologist Daniel Rigney out of the work of historian Richard Hofstadter.

Argyris had moved from a position at Yale University to one at Harvard's business school a few years before he published his study of the *Times*. His previous works had studied other kinds of organizations and the ways their management and workers interacted to get things done. His working style involved both study and intervention. He was not an entirely dispassionate academic who observed and wrote; instead he studied organizations and then diagnosed their problems before working to actively improve the organizational atmosphere within them. He had worked with IBM, Polaroid, General Electric, the U.S. State Department, the National Institutes of Health, and even the Cold War–era U.S. Defense Department, an organization that would seem to not be particularly amenable to an academic poking around in its business and telling them that their hierarchical system wasn't working.[70] Argyris had worked with some difficult organizations, but his new book proved to be about the most difficult organization he had ever worked with: a major metropolitan daily newspaper—the *New York Times*. Argyris wanted to understand the way its publishers and top editors interacted with each other and with the people they supervised. On the surface, that seems to be very much in line with his previous work and with the other books his publisher was putting out at the same time. It is also very much of a piece with the ethnographical studies of the late 1970s, and had Argyris not been a scholar working somewhat out of his field, *Behind the Front Page* might today be as much of a standard work as those have become.[71] But even though Argyris attempted to disguise the identities of the people he wrote about, and even though he referred to the paper as the *Daily Planet* (the fictional newspaper from the Superman comics), and even though he thought no one outside the academy or maybe some in the business world would be very interested in the book—despite all of that— his book really was about the *New York Times* and *(MORE)* figured that out. And when they did, they tried to make a big deal of it, in a way that probably brought more change to the organizational dysfunction at the *Times* than Argyris's study would have on its own.

Unlike the more traditional ethnographies, *Behind the Front Page* tried—and failed—at one additional step beyond participant observation and analysis. Because Argyris worked as a management consultant, not as a sociologist or anthropologist, he attempted to move his study of the *Times* into a second phase, in which he would have intervened in the paper's management structure in an attempt to effect change rather than simply studying the paper for purely academic reasons. Argyris brought an instrumental frame of mind to his work. But the business and editorial management of the paper were extremely resistant to that intervention, and he eventually threw up his hands. In addition, Argyris began his work as a study of management organization and institutional change but became overwhelmingly interested in ideas of objectivity and the best practices of the press after reading a report by a committee of the Twentieth Century Fund recommending the establishment of a national news council. Argyris tried to take advantage of his having an agreement to study the newspaper to switch his topic. The resulting book is as much about the researcher's struggle to persist in his original aim of changing the *Times*, and in his newfound obsession with objectivity. And the *New York Times* archives on which this case study draws show that from within the paper, the struggle was to maintain as much anonymity for the paper and its employees as possible. There is an irony in this, of course, given that newspapers pride themselves on uncovering important but uncomfortable information about powerful institutions. As the Argyris study shows, the newspaper was unwilling to treat itself in the same way. This intransigence serves as a demonstration of the underlying anti-intellectualism of major news institutions, an unwillingness to turn their critical eyes on themselves.

Anti-intellectualism, Criticism, and the Press

A renewed sense of intellectualism in American journalism manifested itself in the critical culture of 1970s newsrooms and in journalism reviews such as *(MORE)*. For this reason, a study of *(MORE)* illuminates not only the mores of journalists in the period, but also serves as a great starting point for an intellectual history of the seventies. While the ideas of academics, essayists, and public intellectuals are important, many more people engage with the popular press in forming their ideas. And *(MORE)* was the forum in which the best journalists of the 1970s engaged with each other's ideas.

At the same time, the 1970s were the beginning of the period that press critic Jack Shafer suggests are the closest thing to a golden age of American newspapers, by which he means not the quality of the product so much as the stability of their income: "from about 1970 to 2005 . . . consolidation of titles gave the surviving papers near monopoly power over mass market advertising in their markets."[72] David Halberstam's *The Powers That Be* serves as a sort of capstone to this period, having been published in 1979 and researched over the course of the tumultuous period that resulted in these newspapers' rise. Halberstam had come to prominence as a questioner of institutional authority, attempting to discover whether the narrative about the Vietnam War that government officials had been feeding him and other reporters was true. Of course he did this for one of the biggest institutions of the press in the mid-1960s, the *New York Times*. Halberstam eventually felt constrained by that institution and turned to books and magazines, just as his friend Tony Lukas and Gay Talese had before him. Both Halberstam and Talese were accused of painting unfair portraits of their subjects and even of getting their facts plain wrong, but the portraits have endured and their combined thesis—that these institutions of the press held immense power in shaping public thought—have endured, even if they are not rock-solid works of academic history. That *The Kingdom and the Power* and *The Powers That Be* both include the word "power" in their titles is no coincidence. Nor are their biblical resonances. By the end of the 1970s, Americans had learned that the "voice of God" tone of their journalism was manufactured by human beings, but they had also learned that the earthly kingdoms that controlled the media were no less powerful.

As noted in chapter 1, historians of the U.S. press have expended little effort examining its intellectual history. Journalism is a profession that traditionally has had critical examination of the public sphere as one of its core aims. It often concerns itself with public policy and the free flow of information in a democracy. Because of these factors and others, one could easily make the commonsense assumption that journalists, as a group, have adopted the probing, questing, questioning, and self-critical habits of mind that characterize intellectuals. Yet despite the near-continual presence of at least some intellectual journalism, the organized members of the U.S. mass media have on the whole been not merely a non-intellectual bunch, but rather an *anti*-intellectual group, actively fomenting a press that is populist, anti-elitist, and instrumentalist.

Those terms are derived from the work of the historian Richard Hofstadter, who wrote the key work on American anti-intellectualism.[73] Sociologist Daniel Rigney codified the three strains of anti-intellectualism that Hofstadter identified: religious anti-rationalism; populist anti-elitism; and unreflective instrumentalism.[74] The American press, largely, has been a rational enterprise, as a culture of skepticism and the doctrine of objectivity, roughly echoing the scientific method, has pushed journalists at least to claim that their work is based on the collection of fact as evidence of a larger truth. However, the other two strains of anti-intellectualism can be found in abundance in the history of the press. One-half of the journalistic aphorism suggests that to "afflict the comfortable" is a primary role of the press.

Some scholars have argued that the press is one of the elite institutions of American life, and that American journalism places the values of the elite over those of the general population—and therefore could not be anti-elitist in its orientation.[75] These arguments are largely persuasive, particularly in the era in which Argyris found himself studying the *New York Times*, one of the most elite of the nation's newspapers, as university-educated reporters began to replace the more working-class newsroom staff that preceded the baby boom generation. And the *Times* was a fundamentally conservative paper throughout most of the 1960s, reluctant to challenge the official sources who provided them with much of their news content. That conservatism began to crack with coverage of the Vietnam War, through the work of *Times* reporter David Halberstam, and also in the self-examination that came with the decision to publish the Pentagon Papers in 1971.[76] The *Times*'s choice to disregard the suggestions of Chris Argyris could itself be seen as a sort of anti-elitism in its rejection of an outsider attempting to reform the institution based on his own accumulated expertise. There is a paradox inherent in the elite press's acceptance of experts and objectively gathered evidence in the production of its news report, on the one hand, and the rapidity with which the institutions of the press reject the criticism of outsiders in reforming their own management practices, on the other. Certainly, there is an element of anti-elitism in the *Times*'s choice not to take the suggestions of a management consultant, though owing to the conflict between management practices and the news report, this phenomenon can be better understood through the third of the Hofstadter/Rigney classifications of anti-intellectualism, the newspaper's lack of reflexivity, or self-examination and self-understanding.

This section therefore examines the *New York Times* through the lens of unreflective instrumentalism and the newspaper's attendant lack of self-criticism, which is only one of the dimensions of anti-intellectualism identified by Rigney and Hofstadter. If things are working as they are, suggests the unreflective instrumentalist, why change? According to Rigney, it is "the devaluation of forms of thought that do not promise relatively immediate practical payoffs."[77] It is the philosophy of leaving well enough alone. This is not to say that anti-intellectualism means lack of intelligence. Unreflective instrumentalism just implies an unwillingness to turn those critical powers on oneself.

While the press may be slow to turn their critical eyes on themselves, there has been no shortage of people willing to criticize the performance of the press. History has not produced many professional press critics, but a wide variety of individuals and institutions have published both constructive advice for the institutional press and, of course, vicious attacks on its performance. In the same year that Argyris published his book about the *Times*, press scholar James Carey published an essay in which he argued that journalistic (as opposed to scholarly) press criticism was an "undeveloped profession," but one that was essential to the healthy functioning of the press as an institution of democracy.[78] Carey saw the press, in 1974, as having been ignored by scholars, who, he writes, "critically review the work of men in every field, devoting thousands of hours to the perceptions, methods and style of obscure 18th-century Romantic poets, yet never consider that journalists, who daily inform our lives, require, for their good and ours, at least the same critical attention." And journalists as a profession, he argued, were less self-critical than any other profession. Journalists, he wrote, "rarely gather to critically review one another's work, to expose its weaknesses, errors of commission and omission and its failure to live up to professional let alone public standards."[79]

Carey was correct in his assessment. Prior to the 1970s, very little regular critical work had appeared examining how news functioned in a democratic society. The *Columbia Journalism Review* had been publishing since the early 1960s, but this was more of a professional journal than a publication intended for a general audience. More recently, *(MORE)* had started its analysis of the press from an outsider point of view (and Carey briefly acknowledges it in his own essay). But this too was a publication consumed more by journalists than by a general public, even if the magazine's editors hoped for a broader readership. In this case study, both Argyris and *(MORE)* are examined as press critics. *(MORE)* would seem to be the more obvious model of criticism, as a journalism review, but Argyris can also be seen as a critic of the functioning of the press, both within its management structures and, once he was inspired by the Twentieth Century Fund report, as a critic of the newspaper's role in a democratic society.

James Carey's call for a profession of press criticism specifically addressed the lack of critics working at the middle level of Wyatt's model, where the concerns of the general public are transmitted to the working press and where the workings of the press, in turn, are explained to the general public.

Trying to place Argyris in Wyatt's model presents an interesting problem. *(MORE)* clearly functions in the role of intermediate critic (though many of its contributors were also members of the working press). But prior to undertaking his study of the *Times*, Argyris was mostly an interested outsider, working in an academic field largely unrelated to studies of the news and the institutions that produce it. In turning to the *Times,* and especially in attempting to analyze its functioning as a creator of ethical news, he thrust himself, a true outsider, into an unexpected and unaccustomed role of intermediary, perhaps jeopardizing any chance he had of effecting real change at an institution that was already unlikely to engage itself in any real self-criticism.

Wherever Argyris fits in Wyatt's model of criticism, he played an important role in opening the paper to external criticism and then to internal self-criticism as well. His interventions in the *Times*'s management structure and his inadvertent opening up of its inner workings began to leach some of the mystery out of the operation of the newspaper—and even more than Gay Talese's gossipy inside look at the paper, his more sober, rational analysis of the *Times* seems to have awakened the paper's executives to the idea that their lack of transparency in operations was precisely what led to the mounting public distrust in newspapers as institutions, represented by the *Times* as an archetype. As Carey put it in his 1974 essay on criticism,

> Perhaps herein lies the answer to those questions so quick to the lips of newspaper executives: Why do newspapers have a credibility gap? Why do all those polls show the public distrusting or at least lacking confidence in the newspaper? There are few modern institutions that engender much confidence in the public because they are so persistently remote from the public and because they mask their operation in the cloak of professional authority which effectively forestalls the critical involvement of the public.[80]

Argyris, in his book, managed to make himself an accidental press critic through the use of the well-established structure of the ethnographic study—a seemingly innocuous process that the *Times* was open to—but his interventions and the actions of *(MORE)* opened the paper to much more scrutiny than they had intended, and Argyris's book became a part of the critical culture surrounding the American press that Michael Schudson described in his "social history" of American news, published just a few years later.[81] Talese's report on the *Times* was no longer an anomaly, a single leak by a former employee. Argyris opened up Pandora's newsroom.

Argyris and the *Times*

Originally, the *Times* had invited Argyris to give some lectures on management, but Argyris declined, saying that he rarely found lectures to be effective. The study that resulted was his counteroffer to the *Times*.[82] According to the preface to *Behind the Front Page*, Argyris began his study with two objectives that were, he said, independent of each other. The second of those objectives "was to add to our knowledge of the processes needed to enhance organizational health and to create effective, on-going renewal activities within organizations." This was Argyris's life work, even in 1974 (he died in 2013 at age ninety), and for the purposes of a study of press criticism, there might be some interest in seeing how the theories of organizational communication can help critics of the press influence the large organizations that were increasingly constituting that press. But the real interest lies in Argyris's first objective: "to discover what must be done to create newspapers that are self-examining and self-regulating."[83]

Argyris had originally chosen the *Times* because he wanted to challenge himself and his previous findings. He writes that he had mostly studied healthy institutions and how they can best be designed and managed, and found that continual self-examination and self-renewal—hallmarks of an intellectual approach to professionalism—were the best guarantors of a healthy organization. But he had a suspicion that the press had little interest in those activities. "The *Planet*, I had been told by my informants, would be especially resistant to a behavioral science inquiry. 'To put it mildly,' said one informant, 'they would consider your views to be nonsense.'"[84] That challenge led Argyris to his second reason for studying the *Times*: he wanted to see what sort of effect his methods would have on an organization that wasn't receptive to them. Finally, he wanted to see whether the necrotic management attitudes at the paper would have any effect on the output—whether there was any relationship between thought and action at the paper. Argyris was inspired to examine what might make a newspaper self-examining not by his own professional interests but by a combination of civic-mindedness and the coincidence that had him in the midst of his study of the *Times* just as the Twentieth Century Fund released a report calling for a national press council to regulate the press, one of a series of book-length reports by a task force put together to examine the relationship between the press and the government.[85] It is not clear what about this particular report spurred Argyris to add an element of press criticism to his work of management consulting, except perhaps the fervor of the coincidence of being so deeply entrenched within the workings of a newspaper at a time of great excitement in the institutional press, with the publication of the Pentagon Papers in 1972 reviving the role of the press as government watchdog.[86]

Even though the Twentieth Century Fund report had identified the *Times* as one of the most credible newspapers in the country, Argyris had heard from his sources that it was still suffering from certain credibility problems. And by that time, he had spent enough time inside the newspaper to know that those problems were directly linked to internal issues of trust and competition:

Moreover, many members of the newspaper expressed a genuine sense of helplessness about changing these internal conditions, which included the win-lose dynamics among reporters and between reporters and copywriters, management by crisis and with hypocrisy, and the conception of advocacy journalism held by many of the top young reporters. If the public feels helpless in relation to newspapers, newspapermen themselves feel the same way. "Not you or anyone else will ever change this place" was a prediction I heard often at *The Daily Planet*—and it was backed up by serious offers to bet large sums of money on it.[87]

Tellingly, Argyris writes that unlike most of his studies of organizations, the bulk of this book would be devoted to detailing his process of winning cooperation from the management of the paper.[88]

Argyris spent several years on his study. The first phase alone lasted for a year. In this period, the *Times* granted him a spectacular amount of access. The top forty executives and editors at the paper granted him unlimited access for this period. He was free to tape record any meeting that occurred naturally and he interviewed all of these editors and executives for long sessions. He came and went as he pleased, and varied his visits so that he covered all days of the week.[89] Then he retreated in order to make his diagnosis, which he prepared and presented to the *Times*. The report ran to seventy-three typewritten pages, and he delivered it to the paper in June 1969.[90] This seems to be the moment when *Times* managing editor Abe Rosenthal first became concerned about the editorial activities of the paper being aired. He appears to have mentioned it to James Reston, either in a memo or just by speaking to him. Reston responded by memo:

> I think we had better leave bad enough alone on this one. The commitment is quite explicit, it seems to me, for not only "a study of the Times' top management" but also of its "news activities." If we try to raise the question of the original agreement, it seems to me that we can only get ourselves into an even more awkward situation.[91]

Rosenthal does seem to have left "bad enough alone" for a few years, since his file on Argyris falls silent, except for a collection of bills from Argyris. Though he does seem, in the same fit of pique, to have asked for a copy of the original agreement from the paper's publisher, Punch Sulzberger, who sent along the agreement and a letter from Argyris that clearly stated the terms: "Any written reports will be sent to you for examination, correction, and any editing appropriate to maintaining your institution's integrity and secrecy. However, in agreeing to cooperate there is also a commitment on the part of the Times not to veto a publication of some sort."[92] One can imagine Sulzberger grumbling at this news, but there is no documentary evidence of his reaction, except that the study continued. No one at the *Times* seems to have recorded any reaction, positive or negative, to the Argyris study again—until they received a draft of Argyris's manuscript for the book. That's when panic set in.

Behind the Front Page describes an institution comprising competing egos, and ensconced in fiefdoms that had long been established and that they defended with a sense that their fiefdoms were fragile and prone to collapse at any time. Argyris facilitated many meetings between these war-ring factions, none so intense as the rivalry between R, the newspaper's top editor, and the man variously known as Q and T, the editorial page editor. In mediating their interactions, Argyris sounds as much like a marriage counselor or a psychoanalyst as a management consultant. In one representative passage, Argyris describes T:

> I began to see an outline of a person who isolated himself from the main news activities, in the name of separating editorial matters from news and adminis-trative functions, yet really craved closer relationships with valued colleagues. This quality of wanting interpersonal closeness, but denying it or suppressing it by focusing on intellectual and rational issues, was characteristic of many of the top editors. It was as if the way they had learned to get close to people was to compete with them on an intellectual level. I mention this hypothesis because it would be incorrect to give the impression that T was unique in his need for closeness. The overwhelming majority of the news people showed the same need and the same ambivalence.[93]

Much of the book examines the often-contentious creation of the Op-Ed page, as Michael Socolow described in depth.[94] But large swaths of the book read like psychoanalysis of insecure but powerful men, who were of-ten quite openly fighting with each other—and, despite having their names disguised by single letters, were easily identifiable to anyone in the news-room, and maybe even outside of it. Even Talese's *The Kingdom and the Power* had not felt quite so intimate.

When Rosenthal, in 1973, read the draft manuscript that described all of this, he could only get halfway through before he felt compelled to write a letter to Argyris with his complaints.[95] But an executive actually put those complaints more eloquently, and despite the fractious atmosphere that *Behind the Front Page* described, the *Times* was able to put on a unified face in opposition to the book itself. The executive who wrote to Argyris on behalf of the paper was Harding Bancroft, who in 1973 was elevated from executive vice president to vice chairman of the paper. He told Argyris that of course they would abide by the agreement and not veto his right to publish a book based on his research. But he expressed the newspaper's concern that it was too closely identified in the book. In fact, Bancroft wrote, the *Times* was requesting that he not identify the newspaper as a newspaper at all, but maybe just as a media institution. Bancroft's letter to Argyris is worth quoting at length:

> I don't think we need here to elaborate on the reasons why identification of The Times as the subject of your study would be a most harmful disservice to the paper. We are already too much in the news and much too frequently analyzed. Hardly a week passes that some periodical does not have a piece that recounts some real or fancied internal event that has taken place within our organization, or that scrutinizes adversely or otherwise the generation of policy decisions or news judgments in terms of personalities on our staff. Your book would surely give momentum to this trend, excite further curiosity, generate more rumors, and unnecessarily provoke embarrassment or worse to The Times or members of its staff . . .
>
> Accordingly, our first and most imperative answer to the problem is to urge an adequate disguise; a disguise that hides our identity not only from scholars and students of organizational behavior and from the lay citizen, but also from the in-group of participants and close observers of journalism in this country.
>
> We don't know if such an adequate disguise is possible at all, but we are convinced that it is not possible if the subject of your publication is identified as a newspaper.
>
> Moreover, we don't see why for your purposes it need be.[96]

It seems willfully naïve for executives at the *New York Times* to not understand why identification of the *Times* as a newspaper was essential to the project that Argyris was undertaking. Perhaps the paper saw the original agreement between itself and Argyris as functioning something like a search warrant—where the *Times* had agreed that he could come into their premises and search for evidence of organizational inefficiencies, much as he had in his previous studies. But when he came, he found serious problems not only with management style but also with the ability to provide an accurate and comprehensive news report to its readers. However, the *Times* saw that as being outside the scope of the original warrant. The paper didn't make that argument to Argyris directly, though one later internal memo makes it clear that some people within the *Times's* hierarchy felt that Argyris had changed the terms of the agreement on them. After Argyris had responded to Bancroft, Rosenthal wrote to Bancroft, "I've read Argyris' letter and it seems to me designed, consciously or unconsciously, to rationalize the fact that a couple of years after he discussed the thrust of his book, he decided that it would take an entirely different direction."[97] More likely, though, Rosenthal and Bancroft and whichever other *Times* executives and editors were involved in discussions were particularly sensitized to criticism, since the last five years or so had opened the paper up to public scrutiny in a way that it never had been before. The publication of Talese's *The Kingdom and the Power* had opened the floodgates in 1969, and *(MORE)* had been a constant gadfly since 1971. Together, they had made it suddenly interesting and acceptable to write about the inner workings of the press, and the upper management at the *Times* had not yet gotten comfortable with that state of affairs. Even more so, the newspaper did not at all like the picture of itself that it found reflected in Argyris's book. Bancroft wrote to Argyris:

> Moreover, the picture that emerges of The Times is one of a childish, badly administered, and petty group who somehow, miraculously, puts out a good paper. The study naturally looks diagnostically at the things that are wrong and even pathological, tensions and immaturities of the "living style" and organizational and administrative ineptitudes. Given your own interests, we would not expect you to picture a happy band of editors, reporters and executives whistling on their way to work with their arms about each other's shoulders. But, if we are to be identified directly or inferentially, we think we have a right to have presented a balanced picture of our strengths and weaknesses, of the normal and sound relationships that exist, as well as the morbid.[98]

While Bancroft admitted that the *Times* could not exert its editorial control over Argyris's manuscript, he asked Argyris to make a better effort to disguise the paper. He closed with the request to obscure the fact that it was a newspaper at all.

Chapter 6

Argyris responded to Bancroft with a description of how he came to the main "thrusts" of his argument, a description that is very similar in its logic to the preface of the final published book. He also told Bancroft that he thought the *Times* may be overreacting: "I honestly believe that some of the Times people may be a bit more touchy than warranted." He may have been right about their reaction to being called "a childish, badly administered, and petty group who somehow, miraculously, puts out a good paper," though one can see why they may have been insulted. But Argyris turned out to be wrong if he thought that the executives at the *Times* were being too touchy about whether their paper could be identified.

Though Bancroft spoke on behalf of the *Times*, Rosenthal also sent along a letter of his own. He said that he didn't have much to add, but he did want to spend a few paragraphs, apparently, disparaging Argyris's work as a scholar of the press:

> I never would have given my time and confidence to a project such as yours if I had known the "thrust," because I do not believe that you can write about the whole issue of credibility and the council simply with the tools and information you had as a result of your particular method of inquiry.
>
> The issue of credibility goes far beyond questions of management and into the nature of the press, the nature of government, the nature of secrecy, the structure of our society and an infinite number of other things on which you do not even touch. As presented, I think that the issue of credibility is a distorted one.[99]

While Rosenthal is correct that the issue of press credibility is much more complex than the version that Argyris presents in his book, there is also certainly value in his criticisms. Institutional infighting certainly could lead to the kinds of credibility issues that Argyris describes, and his approach is a valid one, if not a complete one. Perhaps a media scholar covering the same material would have contextualized that material better, but Argyris's approach is sound and, from an ethnographic point of view, his conclusions are valid.

Argyris finally devised a system of obscuring the names of the *Times* editors and executives. It was not one that made the paper entirely happy, but it certainly makes the book difficult to read. Each editor or manager is identified by a single capital letter. So one person is X and one is A and one is C.

Argyris transcribes whole conversations that sometimes involve several of these unidentified people interacting with each other and even mentioning third parties who aren't present in the conversation. Each is identified with a different letter. To make matters worse, at least one of the editors, John Oakes, demanded that his letter be switched midway through the book, to further throw potential decoders off the trail.[100] On the one hand, it is easy to see why Argyris felt that he had adequately disguised the participants in the study. That's especially true given the limited and academic audience that he expected the book to have. On the other hand, David Rubin, who wrote a story about the Argyris book for *(MORE)*, said that *(MORE)* editor Dick Pollak, "asked me to decode the book, which wasn't all that hard to do, then put names to the people and the situations that had been in the book, which I did. And I interviewed Argyris, and he basically admitted that it was the New York Times that was his subject."[101] So Rosenthal was right to doubt the security of Argyris's system of concealment, especially when *(MORE)* got hold of the book and decoded it. At the time, Rubin was an assistant professor of journalism at New York University and was also one of *(MORE)*'s contributing editors.

In the lead to the piece he wrote for the cover of *(MORE)*'s November 1974 issue, Rubin lays out his justification for publishing the names associated with the book, breaching the confidentiality that the *Times* had negotiated with Argyris, saying that while it is clearly not a sequel to *The Kingdom and the Power*, it could have been, and might even have been a more powerful and revealing book about the way the *New York Times* operates than Talese's book was. But Argyris was his own worst enemy—especially because of his adherence to the standards of academic ethics:

> Argyris has vitiated his own material by cloaking the name of the paper and blurring the identities of his interviewees. In doing so, he has robbed the book both of cogency and impact. With a few names restored, however, his work becomes what it could have been: a laser beam on the considerable management problems at the *Times*.[102]

Rubin leaves the next logical step unspoken, but it is here that the power of the gadfly press critic really comes through: *(MORE)*, in "decoding" and publishing excerpts from Argyris's book, did as critics what Argyris as an academic felt was not within the realm of propriety. *(MORE)* took the information Argyris had hidden between the covers of a fairly dry academic book and turned it into a public critique of the paper. By publishing the piece, *(MORE)* forced the *Times* to confront this study in a way it might not have, had the paper's identity never been revealed. As the *Times* itself certainly understood, publicly confronting institutions with their shortcomings was a powerful way to induce change. By forcing the *Times* to confront the irony of its own lack of transparency, *(MORE)* pushed Argyris into the role of an intermediary press critic in Wyatt's discursive model of press criticism, enlisting him as an unwitting accomplice in the magazine's own mission to reform the *Times* and other institutions of the press.

To be sure, *(MORE)* sensationalized the coverage, perhaps overcorrecting from Argyris's tendency toward confidentiality and academic sobriety. The dust jacket of *Behind the Front Page* contains only the title, the author's name, and a geometric pattern that looks as if it is being turned back, like a page being turned. There is no jacket copy, except for a description of the book inside the flaps. No blurbs from authors. Not even a subtitle to give a bookstore browser any idea what might be inside. Though as Argyris told the *Times*, his book wouldn't be sold in bookstores anyway.[103] *(MORE)*, on the other hand, trumpeted the scoop on its cover, which had switched over from an all-text front page to an image-based cover one issue earlier. They called these "The *New York Times* Transcripts," and ran a few juicy excerpts right on the cover: A. M. Rosenthal telling editorial page editor John Oakes that his jibes make him "go home and get mean to my wife," and Oakes saying that he feels some reporters at the *Times* are becoming too much like editorial writers and that he "would fire some of those bastards."[104]

But the incidents Rubin picks out of *Behind the Front Page* for his examples are not just juicy insider gossip about the *Times*. He pinpoints the trouble (following from Argyris) in the gestation process for the newspaper's much-lauded Op-Ed page, the opinion page opposite the editorial page, which gives space for columnists and outside contributors' opinion pieces. Argyris revealed that debate over the page (which wasn't named in his book, of course, as that would reveal the true identity of the *Daily Planet*) had raged on for four full years. But when Argyris sat down the various parties and talked them through it, the specifics of the page's content and who would be in control of it were hashed out in thirty minutes of frank discussion. In addition, reporters and lower-level editors were afraid to speak out at open meetings. Staff members were afraid to criticize articles that had been praised by executives. Criticism was personalized, and every decision was portrayed as a win-lose proposition, which turned people against each other, creating fiefdoms and an air of defensiveness. Argyris also identified the insulation of the newsroom from the concerns of profit as a major impediment to improvement at the *Times*, which led, he believed, to the feeling of intractability felt by the staff he interviewed.

In the end, the excerpts that *(MORE)* chose to print were not particularly substantial (though perhaps this was for reasons of copyright). The text of the excerpts amounts to about a page and a half of *(MORE)*'s tabloid-size pages, a spread illustrated with a tongue-in-cheek antique portrait of some well-dressed swells out for a picnic in their suits and corseted dresses, labeled with a caption identifying them as *Times* executives on a management retreat. The first section *(MORE)* reprints is an argument between publisher Punch Sulzberger and editorial page editor John Oakes about the level of control the publisher should have in setting the topics for editorials. This is followed by a conversation between Oakes and Abe Rosenthal, in which they criticize each other's judgment and clash over the direction of the Op-Ed page. They finally find common ground in the problem of the leftward drift of the paper's news coverage and the rise of advocacy journalism, which they saw as pernicious. The final set of discussions is between Argyris, Sulzberger, and one or more executives to whom Rubin was unable to assign a name. They are discussing a problem that Argyris identified: the fact that Rosenthal was surrounded by a group of "yes men" who were unwilling to contradict him and also unwilling to talk to each other, preferring instead to meet with Rosenthal one on one. Sulzberger was able to see this as a problem, but was unable to solve it. In the end, though, he says that he is willing to dismantle the management structure of the newspaper and start over, if he has to.[105]

Rubin concludes his piece by saying that while the *Times* is notoriously resistant to the views of outsiders, something will need to change if the paper is going to succeed in matching the changes in media that are happening around it. He suggests that in the end, fear of competition—from cable television and from something Rubin calls "the home information utility," which in retrospect sounds awfully like the Internet—will force the paper to change.

The *Times* seems to have first heard that *(MORE)* was working on an article when Rubin contacted John Oakes for comment and confirmation. Oakes sent a memo to Harding Bancroft, who forwarded it along to several other editors and executives:

> It was quite evident from his questions that he knew that it was [i.e.,
> that Argyris's book was about the *Times*] and in fact he said to me
> he had had this point confirmed by other people he had talked to.
> However, I politely but adamantly refused to discuss this aspect of the
> Argyris book in any way, shape or form. I did not lie to him (particularly
> as he obviously knew what the facts were!) but I told him that I simply
> wouldn't discuss this matter, though I readily admitted that I was
> familiar with the book as I said anyone interested in current journalism
> would be.[106]

Though of course, that last bit was something of a lie. Anyone who was
interested in current journalism would not necessarily have heard of the
Argyris book, which was obscure from the point of view of mass circulation.
And even when *(MORE)* published its article, only twenty thousand or so
journalists would have seen the story and most of them were at the elite levels of the profession. It took some filtering for the *(MORE)* story to have an
effect even lower down the chain of newspaper editors. Ray Jenkins, editorial page editor of the Montgomery *Advertiser-Journal*, found out that the
Times's conversations with an outside researcher had been recorded when
he was later solicited to run a syndicated story about the transcripts. The
author of that story had clearly built on David Rubin's work in decoding the
book. Jenkins wrote to Rosenthal, enclosing the story and the syndicate's
pitch. Rosenthal did not retain the story for his files, but the pitch makes it
clear that it was the work of *(MORE)*:

> Enclosed is an article that reveals the bickering and jealousies among the
> Times management, with verbatim conversations.
>   The Times tried its best to suppress the identities of the principals involved,
> but a journalism professor has "decoded" them.[107]

In his response to Jenkins, Rosenthal admits that the book is about the *Times*
but dismisses Argyris, with whom he was clearly annoyed, calling his methods "tricky." But the second half of the letter shows that he had warmed to
Argyris's management consulting process, if not his academic publishing:

> I'm not at all sorry, though, that we went into the experiment, although
> it made us look a little silly in the end. There was a group of quite
> conscientious and dedicated and serious people trying to do what you

quite rightly say is so rarely done in our business—communicate with
each other. We certainly weren't entirely successful, but we certainly
did come to understand each other's minds better. Obviously, there was
a lot of intramural chit-chat, but the fact is that we did approach issues
of journalism that meant something to us.[108]

Rosenthal does not seem to be particularly disturbed by the *(MORE)* coverage so much as he is by Argyris. He takes a fatalistic approach to the
magazine, seeing the real violator here to be the management consultant
who overstepped the bounds of his role as an ethnographer. To Rosenthal's
thinking, the *(MORE)* intervention was almost inevitable. In other letters
he sent to friends and colleagues who assumed he must be sore about the
decoding, he seems to feel more and more that there is nothing embarrassing in what was said and that the *Times* had grown from the experience.[109]
Argyris, on the other hand, sent at least two additional defensive letters to
Rosenthal, one of them saying that he had asked Rubin for a retraction of
quotations that made it seem as if he had cooperated with Rubin in the
decoding, and saying that he was willing to take legal action if necessary.[110]
Rosenthal dismissed this as "a piece of unbecoming piety."[111]

Although Argyris knew that the *New York Times* would be resistant to
his brand of institutional criticism and reformation, he did not expect to
find an organization as difficult to remake as he did when he first came
into its newsroom. While his interventions failed from the point of view of
a management consultant owing to his status as an untrusted outsider, he
was much more successful by the less exacting standards of a press critic. In
Wendy Wyatt's conception of discursive press criticism, Argyris stirred up
conversations in the newsroom and publishers' offices that had been fester-
ing unspoken for years. His presence, the publication of *Behind the Front
Page*, and the subsequent goading by *(MORE)* did seem to have an effect
on the paper's self-regard. Over the decades since Argyris gave up on the
newspaper, it has become a more open and self-critical institution (though
it took another crisis, the lies published by reporter Jayson Blair, to force
the paper to install a public editor). While it is impossible to directly quantify the effects of one work of criticism on the subsequent development
of the management and editorial structures of a newspaper, Argyris found
himself becoming a part of the critical culture surrounding the American
press at the time.

One last letter that Argyris sent to Rosenthal resonates with his mission to force the *Times* to engage in self-scrutiny in the way that it engages in scrutiny of other institutions of power. In closing the letter, he writes, "Someday, we should sit down together with the article that you wrote on the corrosive impact of censorship in the White House and apply it to our relationship and the living system of the New York Times."[112] Rosenthal does not seem to have responded or to have taken Argyris up on his offer. On the other hand, the *Times* under Rosenthal did undertake some massive changes in the 1970s and early 1980s. The paper began running regular corrections on its second front page, and eventually on page A2. It consolidated its Sunday and daily editorial staffs into a single newsgathering organization. The paper began publishing in four separate sections. It introduced a Living section. The Business Day and Science Times sections debuted. The Op-Ed section began, as chronicled in *Behind the Front Page*. It was a time of huge changes at the *Times*. How much of that was a result of the goading and prodding of Chris Argyris and David Rubin and *(MORE)*? It's impossible to quantify. But these gadflies did force the *Times* to re-examine itself and its practices, and that is, to a large extent, the role of press criticism.

These two cases—*(MORE)*'s first issue pushing the *New York Times* to begin a new daily corrections section, and its translation of Chris Argyris's amateur press criticism into something more public and, for the *Times*, more embarrassing—demonstrate the layers of the power structure that press criticism must traverse in order to have real-world effects. These efforts each took years to manifest in the *Times*, but they were more tangible, and even at that temporal distance, more immediate, than almost anything else that *(MORE)* achieved. Criticism as a social force is vital for shaping the development of intellectual life and public discourse, but rarely are the effects so visible as they are in the eight-year relationship between the chief public watchdog in the United States (the *Times*) and *(MORE)*, its primary gadfly in that period.

7. How the Press Became the Media

More Becomes a "Media Magazine"

When *More* returned to its subscribers' mailboxes and showed up on newsstands in the late summer of 1976, it certainly *looked* like a different publication. The cheap newsprint and the tabloid sized pages were gone, replaced by glossy magazine stock in a traditional magazine size—about eight inches by eleven inches. The iconic squared parentheses were gone from the logo as well. And more importantly than that, the subtitle of the magazine had changed. No longer would *(MORE)* be a journalism review. Now it was *More: The Media Magazine*. That change alone says as much about the magazine's new direction as did the physical redesign.

The redesign was done by Milton Glaser and Walter Bernard. Glaser was a cofounder of *New York* magazine with the editor Clay Felker, and would achieve his most-lasting fame when he designed the "I ♥ NY" logo for New York City's tourism office. Bernard was his design partner. Since Michael Kramer was a *New York* columnist, Felker agreed to "loan" Glaser to *More* for its redesign.[1] Glaser and Bernard did not become regular staff members, but remained on the masthead of the magazine as "design consultants." Kramer says that he took advantage of that consultant status, and took mock-ups of every month's cover to Glaser for his criticism. According to Kramer, Glaser thoroughly reworked almost every cover, in one case practically ordering Kramer to arrange a photo shoot for a brand-new cover idea.[2]

Despite the physical overhaul, the masthead of the new *More* did not look as different from the old one as fans of the old *(MORE)* might have feared. Kramer was editor and publisher, of course, but his executive editor was journalist Ron Rosenbaum, who had been working for the previous incarnation of *(MORE)* as well. Claudia Cohen was promoted to managing editor. Longtime contributors Philip Nobile and David Rubin got space on the masthead as senior editors. And even though Kramer had, at one point, said that Richard Pollak would stay on as editor, Pollak was apparently willing to move a few slots down and remain on staff as associate editor. Malcolm Frouman stayed on as art director. Quite a few other familiar names stayed on as contributing editors too, including David Halberstam, Bob Kuttner, J. Anthony Lukas, and cartoonist Marty Norman. Kramer also added seven editorial assistants, who functioned mostly like interns—young, eager journalists who were willing to work for nothing, or almost nothing, in exchange for being able to work with people like those listed above them on the masthead. Perhaps the most significant change, though, was the expansion of the business side of the magazine. In addition to Kramer, who straddled both sides, there was now an associate publisher, a business manager, an advertising salesperson, and a publishing assistant.

But did the content change? In his introductory letter, Kramer outlined what he was trying to do in revamping the magazine. He's not changing *More*'s focus on print journalism, he writes, just expanding it. Instead of covering only the press, the new *More* would cover "the other kingdoms in the media realm: television, film, radio, advertising, publishing, public relations, design and marketing."[3] Of course, not all of this was new. The old *(MORE)* had devoted an entire issue to publishing and a steady trickle of articles afterward. It had looked at advertising and public relations from the point of view of the journalist—a somewhat adversarial point of view, to be sure. And Kramer was being somewhat disingenuous when he said that the old version of *(MORE)* had focused entirely on print journalism; surely he knew that it had done fairly extensive coverage of broadcast journalism as well. A house ad in the second Kramer-edited issue, in September 1976, doubled down on the idea that the magazine had broadened its scope to encompass coverage of the media more generally:

No longer will *MORE* be content to read between the lines in newspapers and magazines.

The fact is that what an AP radio wire says about an event can be as important as what *The New York Times* says. Or doesn't say.

And Hollywood's portrayal of life in America might be a lot closer to reality than *Time* magazine's.

What's more, as hard as it might be to admit, Mr. Whipple could just play a larger part in the life of many Americans than Mr. Reston.[4]

Figure 6. When *(MORE)* was sold to the former *New York* magazine editor Michael Kramer in 1976, Kramer hired designer Milton Glaser to redesign the newly renamed *More: The Media Magazine*, as a glossy magazine (Courtesy of Columbia Journalism Review).

That last assertion—that a fictional shopkeeper spokesman for Charmin toilet paper (the one who scolded his customers when they squeezed the product) might be more influential than a trusted political columnist for the *New York Times*—could very well have been true. But while there is value in analyzing Hollywood movies and Madison Avenue advertising and their effects on the public at large, this new focus (or lack of focus) must have rankled many of the magazine's longtime subscribers. This new incarnation of *More* never exactly conflated journalism—the practice of gathering and disseminating news that is vital to the perpetuation of a representative democracy—with media more broadly, but it did fold journalism into a larger field, and those who came to *More* with an eye toward that first, often

193

very serious practice, may have been dismayed at the turn toward attempting to reach a general audience.

The first issue reflected some of Kramer's added portfolio. For one thing, the Big Apple department, focusing on New York City media, was gone, but Hellbox remained, and eight or nine new departments made their debut (depending on whether one counts Rosebud, which had previously been a part of Hellbox). Those departments were Language, Advertising (which got two stories the first month, perhaps signaling a particular interest), Sports, Television, Timeswatch (focused entirely on *More*'s old bête noir, the *New York Times*, and written by Dick Pollak), Foreign Desk, Nuts & Bolts, and Publishing. There were also nine major feature stories, a significant increase over the average issue in the era of the founders.

The Michael Kramer era of *More* started with a splash. The cover story examined Spiro Agnew's accusation that the media was run by a "Jewish cabal." The piece is an interesting and nuanced one, given the delicacy of the subject matter. The author, Stephen Birmingham, begins with an exploration of the different social strata of Jewish society in New York City—the differences between German and Eastern European Jewish descendants, the separation between observant and secular Jews. He does this by way of dispelling the "cabal" part of Agnew's accusation. But, as a sidebar called "25 Jews in the News" attests, there was a large number of Jewish journalists and publishers in 1976, and Birmingham turns to Stephen Isaacs's book *Jews and American Politics* for some of the historical reasons Jewish people were attracted to media careers—a history Agnew had ignored. Isaacs points to a history of support for intellectualism as a route out of ghettos and into mainstream society, as well as an emphasis on education in general. He also notes that many Jews in the media consider themselves journalists first and Jews second, and he lists three staffers on the *New York Times* alone who used initials in their bylines in order to avoid revealing that their first name was Abraham.

The magazine also had profiles of the well-known *New York Times* writer R. W. Apple and of the *New Yorker*'s John McPhee, a writer it called "one of the least-known and best writers we have."[5] Critic John Leonard wrote a guide for those who planned to watch the political conventions on television—what to watch and what not to. Regular contributor Nick von Hoffman contributed a piece too. The debut sports column was about New York Yankees broadcaster Mel Allen, and the first television column was written by Frank Rich, who would go on to be the *New York Times* theater critic and columnist and then a columnist for *New York*. Dick Pollak inaugurated the column about the *Times*. The Nuts & Bolts column, written by a science writer, literally described how a television works. And there was a Language piece that called William Safire stiff and old-fashioned. Safire had recently started a column about language in the *Times*.

It was an ambitious relaunch issue, and it was supported by significantly more ads than ever appeared in the Rosebud era. There was one for Mobil, one for International Paper, one for the book publishing arm of the *New Republic*, one for *New York* (which was likely a gift from Clay Felker to his protégé), one for a biography of Nelson Rockefeller (cowritten, not coincidentally, by Michael Kramer), one for the *Progressive* magazine, one for Seagram's 7 whiskey, and a back-cover ad for Marlboro cigarettes. Those were all full-page ads, and there was a smattering of smaller ads in the magazine too. It's unclear how many of them were paid, but eight full ad pages was still far short of the number Kramer had calculated the magazine needed to turn a profit.

By the second issue under Kramer's leadership, Malcolm Frouman was gone—off to a job at the *New York Review of Books*.[6] Rudy Hoglund replaced him as art director. The issue itself was thinner, perhaps because the debut issue was meant to be a double issue. Advertising topics had moved to the cover for the first time too. The cover story of the September 1976 issue was about the outcome of a talent search for the perfect child to star in a new campaign for breakfast cakes that Hostess was going to begin marketing. Three other stories recalled the *(MORE)* of old—two about the *Washington Post* and one that was a collection of memories about starting out a journalistic career on the police beat. In October, the cover story returned to politics, with a story by Ken Auletta about how the Democratic presidential candidate Jimmy Carter dealt with the press. But that serious story was followed immediately in the issue by a bit of frivolity about Hollywood actors who write poetry.[7]

Kramer says that one of the pieces he is proudest of in his time as editor of *More* was one of a pair of articles about criticism that ran in the July/August 1977 issue. The first piece, by Gerald Nachman, a critic for the *New York Daily News*, critiqued the critics of the New York papers.[8] But it was the second piece that Kramer was really proud of: a study of the power of critics, conducted by two New York University professors with help from a University of Rochester researcher. The study took six months—half the time that Kramer owned *More*—and looked at the theater reviews of five critics over a ten-year period, assigning a numerical value from 1.0 (for a pan) to 5.0 (for a rave). The study concluded that critics did have the power to close a show. There was a strong correlation between critics writing pans and the show closing within fifty performances. Of course, the shows may also have closed because they were terrible. While academics had long written for *More*, this article was the only instance of the magazine commissioning its own academic study.

The Michael Kramer era of *More* had a wider variety of story types than the Rosebud Associates era. There was a transition from a more essayistic, *New York Review of Books* style to one that reflected the new format and emphasized reported stories more than "think pieces," a shift from deep thinking to verification of fact. One style is not necessarily better than the other, but the distinction between the two eras is clear. This can be illustrated by a *More* cover story that, as it turned out, may have had particular resonance for the demise of *More* itself in the summer of 1978.

The Profile of Rupert Murdoch That Rupert Murdoch Killed

Rupert Murdoch had already been living in New York for three years before most of the city's journalism establishment cared much about who he was. Sure, he owned a few papers around the country, and he was known for having turned the U.K.'s *News of the World* from a winkingly naughty paper that hid behind a screen of Victorian propriety into the screaming scandal sheet that it remained until its closure in 2011. And of course he was also known for being an Australian press lord. But in New York, he was quiet, a one-man sleeper cell getting the feel for a new place—making friends with Clay Felker, the man who bought *New York* magazine from the ashes of the *New York Herald-Tribune* and turned it into the first city magazine, and then, through Felker, making the acquaintance of Dorothy Schiff, the longtime Roosevelt liberal (and rumored Roosevelt paramour) who had turned America's oldest newspaper into a tabloid aimed at a diminishing, mostly Jewish, educated middle-class readership.

And then Murdoch struck, buying the *Post* from his New York social scene acquaintance. She was a cantankerous, capricious publisher, to be sure, and even those writers who respected her and were loyal to her didn't seem to like her much. But still, the sale of the *Post* to the Australian press lord? That was a *story* (one, it seems, that the *Post* itself was scooped on).

Felker wasn't going to let this story get away, though. He too was unpredictable as an editor, but most of the time, people threw in words like "extremely talented" or even "genius." The man had more or less invented a category of media, and had nurtured the careers of New Journalists like Tom Wolfe, Jimmy Breslin, and Gail Sheehy (who was also Felker's wife). So Felker jumped into action when the *Post*/Murdoch news broke. He commissioned cover art from illustrator David Levine, known for his *New York Review of Books* caricatures. Levine came back with a portrait of Rupert as a killer bee, his stinger pointed toward the base of the new World Trade Center towers.

For the profile itself, Felker enlisted a pair of writers, showing in his choices some of the editorial acumen he was known for. Presumably to handle the New York angle, but also with knowledge of Britain, Felker chose Jon Bradshaw, a *New York* contributing editor who had written a book about backgammon, of all things, and had worked as a writer in England (at the Sunday *Times*, long before Murdoch bought that too). To get the Australian side of things, Felker turned to Richard Neville, cofounder of an Australian satirical magazine called *Oz*, a magazine that, between its Australian and English versions, got Neville involved in no fewer than three obscenity trials (and earned him the honor of being played in movies by both Hugh Grant and Cillian Murphy).

And then, before they went to press, the story and the illustration were killed. Rupert Murdoch had bought *New York*.

A January 1977 article in *Time* claimed that "Felker thought better of it," though it also implied that the illustration was a reaction to the news that Murdoch had wrested *New York* away from Felker, which seems bizarre, unless it was commissioned in the period when Murdoch was still wresting and Felker was still clinging to his beloved creation. What seems more likely is that the story and cover illustration were commissioned in that brief period (less than two months, from Thanksgiving to New Year's) between Murdoch's purchase of the *Post* and his takeover of *New York*. And if Rupert Murdoch owned *New York*, there was no way that it would be running a comprehensive cover story about the boss's past.

The story did eventually run, just not in *New York*. Instead, *More* continued its tradition of swiping up stories that had, in one way or another, been too hot for their original publications. According to the italicized blurb that introduced the article in the February 1977 issue, the article and illustration (which *More* ran on its own cover) "were commissioned before Rupert Murdoch acquired control of that publication."

More had already run a pretty extensive package on Murdoch's *Post* coup, just the month before. The January number featured an article on how Murdoch's takeover of the *Post* might result in "old-fashioned newspaper war," especially if the *Daily News* dared to enter the evening newspaper market (though of course it was the *Post* that switched to mornings).[9] There was a collection of memoirs of Dolly Schiff by former *Post* people Pete Hamill and Nora Ephron and by independent muckraker and proto-blogger I. F. Stone.[10] Doug Ireland, a veteran of the *Post*—as well as of *New York* and the *Village Voice,* a third publication that wound up under Murdoch in the *New York* deal—wrote the main story, as well as a sidebar on how the Newspaper Guild would handle Murdoch if he tried to fire their unionized employees. "He ain't gettin' rid of nobody in Guild jurisdiction," Ireland quoted the executive vice president of the guild as saying. "We don't exist as a severance paying mechanism." As Rich pointed out in his piece, Murdoch didn't have to fire them. He just drove them away (most of them, anyway).[11]

The January 1977 issue also marked the first glossy, staged photograph to appear on *More*'s cover, after six years of cartoons. The image illustrated a story called "Kiss & Tell Journalism" by Ron Rosenbaum, and it was the cover Milton Glaser came up with and told Michael Kramer to redo. Kramer had come to Glaser with a cover done entirely in type, and according to Kramer, Glaser said, "Are you crazy? Are you out of your minds? This is the one thing you've done that could mildly be considered salacious. You need to get some journalists in bed together!"[12] The final version of the cover shows a shirtless Rudy Hoglund, the art director, in a brass bed with a woman model. He is tape-recording something; she is typing on an electric typewriter.

But even with all of this prior coverage, how could *More* turn down the opportunity to run a profile of Rupert Murdoch that might have been inspired by Murdoch's looming takeover of the magazine that commissioned it, and that was doomed by the fact that Murdoch conquered that magazine, leaving story and illustration unceremoniously impaled on a spike?

Given what we now know about Murdoch, the profile isn't shocking (though it is slightly odd that Neville quotes himself in the third person). We learn about his Charles Foster Kane–like beginnings in Australia, redeeming his father's lost newspaper career. We learn about his first attempt to own a "respectable" paper when he founds the *Australian*. We learn about the takeover of *News of the World*. There's even a seven-column spread of twenty-one covers of the *Daily Mirror* from 1976, most of which have pretty prosaic headlines, given the "Headless Body in Topless Bar" excesses that were to come at the *Post*.[13]

One story that seems to have largely been forgotten is the shocking story of Digby Bamford. Here is Bradshaw and Neville's version (and given the kicker, likely more Neville's than Bradshaw's):

> One day in March 1964, a bewildered migrant walked into the offices of Murdoch's *Daily Mirror*, clutching his daughter's diary in his hand. Appalled by what he had read, he sought advice from the seemingly omnipotent arbiters of community taste. For other reasons, the *Mirror* shared the migrant's concerns and decided to print the contents of the little red book on its front page: "Sex Outrage in School Lunchbreak," the *Mirror* blared. Reproduced passages of the girl's diary spoke of secret rendezvous and sexual encounters with schoolmates. As a result of the publicity, the 14-year-old girl and her "boyfriend," Digby Bamford, were expelled from school. And for Murdoch's readers, that is where the story ended. It was never reported that the following day, young Digby Bamford was found hanging from a clothesline in his backyard; nor was it ever reported that a pathologist from the children's welfare department filed a report of the incident in which he stated that the 14-year-old girl was still a virgin.
>
> Only Richard Neville's "obscene" publication, *Oz*, printed the whole story at the time.[14]

What this 1977 profile shows is that we knew who Rupert Murdoch was long before the 2011 *News of the World* phone hacking scandal. And even then it was old news, as Bradshaw and Neville saw:

> Since 1952 he has built his bordello of newspapers across three continents. For 25 years, his papers have been purveyors of cheap thrills, inciters of death and false alarms, advocates of obsolete prejudices, saboteurs of taste, hawkers of back seats and second fiddles, of cocks and bulls.[15]

So the contemporary assessment of Murdoch isn't hindsight. We've seen it all along. It's just that until now, we've played along. The subhead to the *More* story asks, "Is this the future?" And the answer, of course, is yes. Yes, it was.

Ironically, though, publishers buying publications in order to kill troublesome stories may also have played a role in *More*'s own end. But first came one last Liebling Convention.

Chapter 7

Liebling V

There is even less information about the final A. J. Liebling Convention, held in the fall of 1976, than about Liebling IV, in 1975. This was the only Liebling Convention held in the era of Michael Kramer. By the time of the fifth iteration, the conventions had become enough of an institution as to not interest the press—mainstream or alternative—enough to send reporters to cover it. *More* placed an ad in *New York* that gave the names of some participants including Seymour Hersh, Nora Ephron, *Hustler* publisher Larry Flynt, *New Yorker* critic Brendan Gill, Nat Hentoff, Liz Smith, and New York local TV newsman Gabe Pressman.[16] One house ad in *More* didn't give much more information, except to say that the conference had been scaled back to a single day and its price ramped up again, now to thirty dollars. It had also been pushed back to the fall of 1976, likely since the sale of the magazine was being negotiated the previous spring, when the Liebling Convention would normally have been held. There were only six panels in three concurrent sessions. There was one on sources and the effect of Woodward and Bernstein's "Deep Throat" anonymous source. There was a reprise of "The Art of the Interview" from the previous year (with new panelists, of course). There was a panel about gossip. There was one about obscenity. One panel had private investigators giving tips to reporters. And then the A. J. Liebling Award would be given to the staff of *60 Minutes*: producer Don Hewitt and correspondents Dan Rather, Morley Safer, and Mike Wallace. This last was a change on two fronts: this was the first network news show that would be given the award, and it was the first time the recipient of the award was announced in advance.[17] Even so, Kramer had trouble getting the award made in time, and Hewitt ribbed him about it for years, asking him where his award statue was every time the two talked afterward.[18] James Aronson, who wrote the only substantial story about the 1976 conference, was offended by the conference in general—he said that he wished Liebling could rise up and reclaim his good name—but especially by the Liebling Award. It was accepted, he said "by Mike Wallace, who a few months earlier on 'Sixty Minutes' had helped dig a grave at CBS for Daniel Schorr in an interview marked by calculated baiting and, according to Schorr, calculated editing. The award should have gone to Schorr."[19]

Over the years, the Liebling Award was given out to five recipients:

- 1972: Independent investigative journalist I. F. "Izzy" Stone
- 1973: *New York Times* reporter Homer Bigart

- 1974: *Washington Post* investigative reporter Morton Mintz
- 1975: Oral historian Studs Terkel
- 1976: The staff of *60 Minutes*

While there is no denying that *60 Minutes*, known for its muckraking, brought a new level of seriousness to television journalism, there was still a subtle move toward populism in Kramer's choice for the Liebling Award, though to be fair, it is one that had been ongoing since the very first counter-convention in 1972. Izzy Stone was a reporter most famous for producing a newsletter out of his own home. From there, the award progressed to reporters for major national newspapers, then to a very popular author and broadcaster in Studs Terkel. This move toward the mainstream cannot be ascribed completely to Michael Kramer's reimagining of *More*.

Afterwards, *More* didn't even run a substantial recap of the goings-on of this convention. There was a two-page photo spread instead, with a photo caption that referred to the panel about interviews as "controversial" but gave no hint as to why. And so the counter-conventions ended with a bit of a shrug, lost in the shifting management of the last two years of the magazine and in the shifting priorities of its publishers and editors. The A. J. Liebling Counter-Convention got the worst of it, getting bumped unceremoniously from spring to fall, and then being abandoned altogether.

But the Liebling conventions did have a legacy and they lived on in the "Hello Sweetheart" posters that young journalists brought home and used as inspiration. Bob Stepno, who recently retired as a journalism and media professor at Radford University, remembered the conferences as "a chance for young reporters from the boonies, who hadn't been to a big journalism school, to connect with the stars of the profession." He and some friends came down to at least a couple of the conferences from Hartford, where he was then working for the *Courant*, and he had what sounds like typical counter-convention experiences, looking up at his journalistic heroes, but also meeting the author of a book on polyamorous relationships at a bar across the street. It was, he said,

a very romantic time to be a young journalist, even if you were far from the New York excitement. We subscribed to New York Magazine and CJR and [MORE], and we had the New York mag issue that launched "Ms." and the one with a (Sorel?) cartoon showing Superman in a phone booth putting ON his Clark Kent clothes and saying "This is a job for a Mild Mannered Reporter!" under a headline something like "Investigative reporters, the new American heroes."[20]

(MORE) may have hit on the timing of the romantic side of journalism by accident, the side that turned journalists into celebrities and heroes. But it also had a hand in the mythology—and of course led the fight to make the institutional press think more critically about itself, at least in the magazine's early days. The counter-conventions undoubtedly changed from their origins at the Martin Luther King Jr. Labor Center in 1972.

The Last Six Months of Kramer's *More*

The month after *More* published the long profile of Murdoch, Dick Pollak and Tony Lukas disappeared from the masthead for the first time in the magazine's publication history. It's not clear what happened. Neither Kramer nor Pollak remembers, and Lukas died in 1997. Meanwhile, the magazine was getting thinner again. The sixty-four-page issue that Kramer had hoped to produce every month had fallen to fifty-four pages. The April 1977 issue had only four feature stories and four departments, plus the Hellbox. In May, that fell to only two feature stories and three departments, plus Hellbox. But that month Kramer added a young freelance writer named Robert Friedman to the masthead as a senior editor. Friedman had begun writing for the magazine when Pollak was still the editor, but even though the first and second editors were feuding over the direction *More* should go in, Friedman had maintained relationships with both of them, and Kramer invited him on board as a staff member. Friedman readily agreed, not having had a regular job since he had graduated from college several years earlier.[21] It is probably not a coincidence that Friedman moved onto the masthead when Claudia Cohen left the magazine. He took her spot, and within a few months he had her title too: managing editor.

Intimations of the End

In the last year of *More*, some of the covers begin to feel prophetic, or even as if there is an intended double meaning. The September 1977 issue devotes the cover to an article about obituaries. The cover photo has five mourners surrounding an open casket. All five mourners—and the man in the casket—are reading the newspaper. Only the dead man seems unsurprised by what he's reading; everyone else has their mouth agape. Perhaps they're reading some deathbed revelation about which the corpse himself was well aware. Or perhaps he's only unperturbed because he's dead.

That issue was the last one produced by Michael Kramer as editor and publisher. News of the sale came just as the September issue would have been hitting the newsstands, so there was less lead time before the next owners took over than there was when Kramer bought the magazine from Rosebud Associates. Kramer told the *New York Times* that the magazine had been losing too much money to sustain it. He claimed that the circulation had doubled from ten thousand to twenty thousand, but said that the magazine had lost about $400,000 since he had bought it the previous summer, and it was currently $100,000 in debt. Despite the new, broader focus on media, Kramer's more populist approach to editing had not elicited huge circulation gains as he had wanted. The Audit Bureau of Circulations report that *More* filed showed that subscriptions had actually dropped. The average number of paid subscriptions in the preceding year had been 14,626. By the end of 1976, that number had dropped to 11,958. Newsstand sales were up slightly, but not nearly enough to counteract the drop-off in subscriptions. Kramer's new vision for the magazine was struggling, as it was unable to find a general audience.

Even during this period of circulation decline, however, the *type* of person who remained a loyal *More* subscriber speaks to the influence the magazine had, both in its original incarnation and potentially even in its newer, broader incarnation. After Kramer agreed to sell the magazine to its third and final owner, founding editor Dick Pollak scoured the magazine's subscription list to compile what he called his list of "heavies." Pollak hoped that by targeting these subscribers, *More* could build circulation through a direct mail campaign—and maybe even get some of them to donate to keep the magazine going. Going through the subscription list numerically by ZIP Code, Pollak compiled an eleven-page, handwritten list of subscribers on a legal pad. These subscribers included:

- Pete Miller, editor of the *Berkshire Eagle*
- Tom Winship, editor of the *Boston Globe*
- Robert Manning, editor of the *Atlantic*
- author Justin Kaplan
- Garry Trudeau, the author and cartoonist who created *Doonesbury*
- writer Linda Greenhouse, who would be appointed the following year to cover the Supreme Court for the *New York Times* for the next three decades

- conservative writer, *Firing Line* host, and *National Review* founder William F. Buckley Jr.
- advice columnist and psychologist Joyce Brothers
- S. I. Newhouse, publisher of the *Staten Island Advance* and owner of *Condé Nast* magazines
- *Village Voice* writer Nat Hentoff
- Robert L. Bartley, editorial page editor of the *Wall Street Journal*
- Albert Shanker, president of the United Federation of Teachers
- *Forbes* publisher Malcolm Forbes
- Al Goldstein, publisher of the pornographic newspaper *Screw*
- *New Yorker* writer Calvin Trillin
- attorney and journalist Steven Brill, who would found the media criticism magazine *Brill's Content* more than twenty years later
- gossip columnist Liz Smith
- the New York bureau of Japanese newspaper *Asahi Shimbun*
- Harold Evans, editor of the *Sunday Times* of London
- publisher Alfred Knopf Jr.
- ABC news reporter Barbara Walters
- more than twenty separate subscriptions at the headquarters of CBS
- conservative writer Irving Kristol
- more than a dozen subscriptions at the offices of NBC
- editor and publisher Nan Talese
- the Russian news agency Tass
- author David Halberstam
- literary agent Sterling Lord
- *Paris Review* cofounder George Plimpton
- *60 Minutes* correspondent Mike Wallace
- author Theodore White
- *Commentary*'s Norman Podhoretz
- writers Ken Auletta and Judith Crist
- critic Vincent Canby
- cartoonist Jules Feiffer
- NBC journalist Tom Brokaw
- *New Yorker* editor William Shawn
- *Cosmopolitan* editor Helen Gurley Brown
- Seymour Topping, managing editor of the *New York Times*, who would go on to administer the Pulitzer Prizes
- author Robert Caro

- the Washington, DC, bureau of the *Baltimore Sun*
- Westinghouse Broadcasting
- journalist James Fallows
- Carl Bernstein of the *Washington Post*
- consumer advocate Ralph Nader
- journalist and author Sanford Ungar
- *New York Times* reporter Neil Sheehan
- Jimmy Carter's speechwriter Hendrik Hertzberg, who would go on to edit the *New Republic* and serve as managing editor at the *New Yorker*
- television reporter Lesley Stahl
- *Washington Post* editor Ben Bradlee
- two subscriptions at the offices of the Federal Communications Commission
- writer Garry Wills
- John Seigenthaler, then the editor of the *Nashville Tennessean*
- the *Antioch Review*
- Stuart Loory, managing editor of the *Chicago Sun-Times*
- Will Jarrett, managing editor of the *Dallas Times Herald*
- LGBT newsmagazine the *Advocate*
- at least a dozen subscriptions at the *Los Angeles Times*
- television personality Dinah Shore
- press critic and author Ben Bagdikian
- Frank Fasi, mayor of Honolulu
- the *Seattle Post-Intelligencer*
- *Stars and Stripes*
- the *Vancouver Sun*
- four copies to the Canadian Broadcasting Corporation
- the *Toronto Star*
- the *Toronto Globe and Mail*
- the *Washington Post* Cairo bureau
- R. W. Apple of the *New York Times*, in London
- the *Washington Post* London bureau
- *Time*'s Helsinki correspondent
- the *New York Times* in New Delhi
- *Newsweek* in Tokyo
- *Newsweek* in Cape Town
- the Associated Press and the *New York Times* in Rio de Janeiro
- CBS News in Mexico City[22]

This is just a partial list of what Pollak included. These journalists and news institutions collectively had enormous influence across both journalism and public life more broadly, and brought the revolutionary ideas of *More* across the country and around the world. These are pacesetters for American journalism, and they were all reading—or at least subscribing to—*More* as of 1977.

Pollak addressed this list to new owner James Adler, who had made a personal fortune by founding the Congressional Information Service, a company that turned congressional documents into microfilm and made then accessible. He would take over control of the magazine by assuming its liabilities. Robert Friedman would become editor.[23] Friedman had maintained relationships with Kramer and with both Dick Pollak and Tony Lukas, which worked out well, since Adler, the new publisher, had brought Pollak and Lukas back as advisers. Friedman says that during his time as editor, from the time Adler bought the magazine until it folded less than a year later, he did not know Adler well at all and could never speak to his motivations for buying the magazine, even when they were ostensibly working together.[24] The *Washington Post* article about the sale calls Adler "a loyal subscriber" to *More*, and notes that Adler and Lukas had worked together at the *Harvard Crimson* when they were in college. So it is entirely possible that Pollak and Lukas knew that *More* was in financial trouble and actively recruited Adler as publisher, hoping he would set the magazine's finances right again and allow Friedman to set a clear editorial course that was in line with the one the two cofounders had established in 1971. The *Post* quoted Pollak, who expressed a tentative enthusiasm about the new publisher. "I want to feel enthusiastic," he said. He said it was the first time that someone who owned the magazine would have real business experience.[25]

The *Post* article also reveals that the investors group Kramer had led had called themselves Namequoit, Inc. Lukas, Pollak, and Woodward had called their group Rosebud Associates in a sly reference to the childhood sled of the newspaper magnate Charles Foster Kane in the film *Citizen Kane*. Namequoit was named for "the summer sailing camp on Cape Cod that Kramer and his fellow investors attended as children."[26] Given Woodward's immense family wealth, perhaps it is unfair to see resonance in that difference, but one name clearly calls to a mythical history of journalism and the other seems to indicate a stronger interest in money.

8. Further *(MORE)*

The Demise of *(MORE)*, and Its Legacy for Press Criticism

It is not entirely clear how *More* was sold from Michael Kramer to James B. Adler, owner of the Congressional Information Service, but either it was engineered, in part, by the original Rosebud Associates or they used the opportunity of Kramer's departure to reassert some influence over the magazine. Though Adler did not take over as publisher until the fall of 1977, it seems that the transition might have been planned as early as February of that year. The letter from Pollak to Adler mentioned in chapter 7 is dated February 25. That part of the date is typewritten. Pollak seems to have added "1978" in handwriting, then crossed it out and changed it to "1977." This was clearly done much later—so either Pollak had been collaborating with Adler for months by the time Adler took over with editor Robert Friedman in October, or he was sending along his advice a few months after the regime change.

Either way, Pollak had some suggestions for how the magazine might proceed under its new ownership, and he used the word "our" to describe the ownership of *More*, as in "our initial thrust to build circulation." Pollak suggested that they concentrate on New York and Washington, trying to double circulation in just those areas, since those were the primary circulation zones for the magazine. He suggested Los Angeles as a possible third target area. They should buy mailing lists of *Village Voice* subscribers, members of the Newspaper Guild, or public relations people in those cities, and target them. Pollak also suggested tailoring the pitch to specific audiences. "I'm thinking particularly of politicians," Pollak wrote, "who are always getting it in the neck from the press and might like to get a magazine that does unto the press what the press does to them." He also proposed an ad asking each subscriber to bring in one new subscriber, and slip the ad under the doors of places such as the National Press Building. "As you know," Pollak told Adler, "we drafted such a letter once and got Pauline

Kael, Mike Wallace, Edwin Newman and Jules Feiffer (all subscribers) to sign it." *More* could also pursue subscriptions at journalism schools, Pollak wrote, and should focus on schools where they know they already have subscribers. Finally, Pollak nods to the kind of popular culture credibility that the magazine had already built up:

> Our poster is clearly visible on the wall of the city room of the *Lou Grant Show*. Can't we get a still of that, or have a photographer take a shot, and use it for promotion in some way[?][1]

Robert Friedman Takes *More* to the End

The October 1977 issue feels like something of a reunion of the old *(MORE)* staff, even though the magazine has a new editor and a new publisher. James Adler, in his note from the publisher, seems to be saying the same thing: the old magazine you knew is in good hands again:

> My job as publisher is to provide *MORE* with the kind of stability, support, and solid management it has always needed. Given this firm foundation, *MORE* will become a better magazine than it has ever been before. And every reader knows that *MORE* at its best has been very good indeed.[2]

Adler promises to expand the magazine's Washington coverage—since he is going to remain in Washington himself—and to refocus the magazine on strong, independent press criticism. He also announces that both Pollak and Lukas have returned as associate editors, as has David Rubin.

The first cover story under Friedman (though given the lead time for magazine articles, it's possible that it was commissioned earlier) looked at a growing and important issue in the late 1970s: media monopolies. *More* ran three stories in the package. One examined the recent Washington, DC, Court of Appeals decision that ordered all companies that owned a newspaper and a broadcast station in the same market to sell the broadcast station unless it could prove that the cross-media ownership was in the public interest.[3] The second was a case study of a man named John Johnson, who owned the only newspaper, the only television station, and two local radio stations in Watertown, New York. He was also a powerful political figure in the area.[4] The third story was a review of research on the effects of cross-media ownership.[5] It was as thorough a package as *More* had ever put together on a single subject, and one that was very much representative of the sort of media consolidation that was going on all over the country in 1977. *More* would run a similar package of stories a few months later, looking at press freedom in South Africa. The other major stories in the October issue are a profile of the owner of *Variety*, a story about an American reporter who was kicked out of the United Kingdom for violating the Official Secrets Act, and a story by Pollak about the developing sex discrimination lawsuit brought by a group of women against the *New York Times*.

The next month, *More* returned to coverage of Rupert Murdoch, but this time Friedman and writer Rinker Buck got Murdoch to talk. Friedman remembered how difficult Murdoch was to deal with. Murdoch would not talk to *More* unless he was able to see the story beforehand and approve his quotes. Friedman told him journalism did not work that way. Eventually, he was able to get Murdoch to agree to a compromise: he could see the story before publication, but could not make any changes.[6] Murdoch agreed to quite a long interview and answered questions about the tabloid's coverage of the Son of Sam murders (Murdoch directed much of the coverage himself), about press monopolies (he claimed he had no ambition to grow, but admitted that there was a lot of room for growth), and about accusations that the *Post*'s news coverage blatantly favored candidate Ed Koch against Bella Abzug in the recent New York City mayoral election (he denied it). But *More*, in keeping with its tradition of independence, analyzed the actual coverage and found that Murdoch was either lying, uninformed, or just wrong. The analysis found zero unfavorable articles about Koch after the day the *Post* endorsed him.[7]

The departments covering advertising, television, and all of the various other media are notably missing from the first few issues under Friedman. Only Hellbox, Rosebud, and a catch-all essay department called Furthermore remain. The other media are still covered—they have not disappeared completely—but they aren't the focus that they used to be.

More continued to attract big-name authors in its last few issues. Roy Blount Jr. contributed a piece about weathercasters in April 1978,[8] and Christopher Hitchens also wrote a piece that month, about an editor who became a terrorist target after accompanying Egypt's Anwar Sadat on a trip to Israel.[9] Todd Gitlin and Michael Arlen were contributors to the same issue. But in the unintentional tradition of prophetic cover lines, the May 1978 issue declared, "And Then There Was One." *More* would go out of business after the June issue.

It's possible that the editorial staff was living in dread of the end, because James Adler had been shopping the magazine around since at least April. Adler had been sick, hospitalized for a month. He claimed that he had fielded several offers, though he didn't tell the *Washington Post* whom those offers were from.[10] The editors were equally desperate to find a new owner to keep the magazine in business, and they were happy to talk to the press. Pollak, Friedman, Rubin, and senior editor Robert Manoff told the *New York Times* that *More* had lost $1.3 million in its existence and probably needed $750,000 over three years to be saved.[11] Adler put the number at between $300,000 and $600,000.[12] But while Adler and the editors looked for more than a month to find a savior, they were unable to find anyone willing to take on the project without compromising *More*'s principles, and at a price that wouldn't lose too much money for Adler.

More put out its June issue, featuring a cover story by Nicholas von Hoffman previewing the Supreme Court case in which WBAI, the New York City Pacifica Radio station, was challenging FCC sanctions. WBAI had aired some of the comedian George Carlin's "Seven Dirty Words," and the type and quantity of the "dirty" words had offended a few listeners. In the same issue, Noam Chomsky looked back on the Tet Offensive, ten years later. But there was lighthearted material too—a piece about how the *New York Times* covered animals, and a bit of black humor about how media outlets in New York City would respond to a neutron bomb going off in Midtown.

The ad hoc office atmosphere of the early days of *(MORE)* had faded somewhat, and by the end, the magazine had four full-time editors, a designer, a business manager, and "a whole flock" of interns, in the words of Steve Robinson, who began working at *More* as an intern himself before becoming the magazine's last managing editor. The offices were a small suite in an office building at 40 West 57th Street in New York, with three glassed-in individual offices for editor Robert Friedman, senior editor Robert Manoff and the art director, Paul Richer. Everyone else—Robinson, assistant editor Kathleen Hughes, the business manager, and the flock of interns, sat "shoulder to shoulder" in a common space. Tony Lukas, Dick Pollak, and David Rubin stayed on the masthead until the end as associate editors, and Robinson says that Pollak, at least, came into the office fairly regularly. "He always had this grim demeanor," Robinson said. "I always pictured him sitting hunched over like a vulture on a tree branch." Robinson said that despite his threatening appearance, he was a great teacher to the younger editors and to the interns. "He said one thing to me and I took it with me for the next forty years," Robinson said. "I had done a Hellbox piece and I ended it with a quote, and he handed it back to me and told me. 'That's *Time-Newsweek* stuff. If you can't figure out how to wind up a piece in your own words, it's not worth doing.'"[13] According to Robinson, the other editors were also very generous in teaching the younger staff— though even the oldest editors were no older than their mid-thirties. Claudia Cohen mentored him when he started. Rob Manoff was opinionated, passionate, and very funny. And David Rubin was responsible for bring in the "flock" of NYU interns in the first place.

Brian Beker was an intern at the time of *More*'s demise, and a student at Vassar College, about seventy-five miles north of New York City, in 1977 and 1978. Like many students aspiring to a career in journalism at the time, he knew and admired the work that *More* was doing. When he saw a poster on a Vassar bulletin board advertising an internship at *More*, he knew immediately that he had to apply. When he got it, he ended up spending as much time in *More*'s 57th Street offices in New York City as he did on campus. "That internship," he says, "became my full-time job." He had a small desk in the open part of the offices, which he said were probably no more than 1,500 square feet, including the private offices.[14]

Manoff would occasionally assign Beker to track down some facts for a story that someone else was working on, or to initially confirm a tip that had come in. One particularly interesting rumor came into the office—Beker did not know where from—that members of various subcommittees of the Pulitzer Prizes were griping that their recommendations were being ignored by the Pulitzer committee so that those members could give the prizes to their own newspapers instead. It would have been a scandal if it were true, and a perfect story for *More*. According to Beker, Manoff asked him to start tracking down the story, and slowly, over months, the story began to check out. The details were confirmed. The Pulitzers were rigged— with the rules of the Pulitzers, but still in a way that felt seamy. Manoff and Friedman considered giving the story to a more experienced reporter at this point, but they let Beker continue with it. At this point, he had to contact the editors and publishers who may have conspired to give themselves and each other Pulitzers. Beker vividly remembers the phone conversation he had with Ben Bradlee, editor of the *Washington Post*, who had just been portrayed memorably on screen by actor Jason Robards. "I won't take up much of your time," Beker told Bradlee, who responded, "You're goddam right you won't, you little pissant."[15]

According to Beker, the editors of *More* told him that they were giving him the cover for his Pulitzer story. "Here I was, nineteen years old, and I was going to be on the cover of *More*," he said. On the day the finished magazines were supposed to be delivered to the offices, Beker came down from Poughkeepsie and waited for the hand truck with the boxes to be wheeled in. He eagerly ripped one open and when he saw the front cover, he began to realize that his story was not only not on the cover, but it wasn't in the magazine at all. "There was no mention of the Pulitzer story," he said. "None at all. Manoff and Friedman saw me and they came out of their offices, sheepishly, and said they needed to talk to me." Something had happened, they told Beker. *More* had been sold to the *Columbia Journalism Review*.[16]

To Beker, the implication was clear: *CJR* was owned by Columbia University. The Pulitzer Prizes were administered by Columbia. Columbia, Beker deduced, had bought *More* to kill the Pulitzer logrolling story. "*More* was my life," Beker said. "Truth. Ethics. These guys at *More* were drilling that into my head all the time, and then, for this to happen, without even giving me a warning, it felt like they lacked the courage or the integrity to tell me." Beker says he had no idea that *More* might be nearing the end. He remembers the issue that didn't include his Pulitzer story as *More*'s last. A sudden ending, one that echoed the profile of Rupert Murdoch that *New York* magazine spiked when Murdoch bought the magazine—and which *More* ran. Only this time, it was *More* that was purchased to kill a story.[17]

Beker says that he kept his notes until Steve Robinson, who went on to work for *Life* magazine, called him and said that he wanted to run the story, and asked if he could see Beker's notes. Beker trusted Robinson and said that he sent them all, but Robinson never did anything with the notes. Beker thinks it's possible that Robinson legitimately wanted to pursue the story, but he also thinks it's possible that this was one last attempt to silence it.[18]

Robert Friedman said he had a vague recollection of someone working on a story about corruption at the Pulitzer Prizes, but that Beker's version of the story was almost certainly misremembered. He said that as editor he would have known about any stories that would have been killed, especially if they were cover stories, and he had no recollection of the events occurring in the way that Beker remembered them.[19] Steve Robinson also said that he had no recollection of these events. "I don't remember anything about this," he said. "Does it mean we didn't ask him to report a story about the politics behind the Pulitzers? No, that's exactly the kind of story that we would have pursued. But the idea that Columbia would buy the magazine as a way to short-stop a story is just ludicrous." Robinson also said that he doesn't remember asking Beker for his notes on the Pulitzer story, and adds that it seemed implausible to him because he was an entry-level reporter for *Life* at the time, and even if it had been a year or two later, after Robinson had become *Life*'s news editor, it was unlikely that the magazine would even have been interested in that kind of story. "The last thing in the world that that magazine would have done back in '78, '79, '80 is one that would have been an exposé of the Pulitzer Prizes," he said.[20]

Without documentary evidence, it will remain unclear what exactly happened in the last days of *More*. Perhaps Columbia University did get wind of an investigation that would tarnish the most illustrious journalism prizes, and either started or sped up its efforts to obtain control of *More*. Maybe James Adler and Columbia reached an agreement and *then* Columbia asked *More* not to run the story. Or maybe the story was pulled for other reasons—a lack of solid sourcing, or getting bumped forward into a month when, as it happened, *More* no longer published. And it is almost certain that four decades have dimmed memories of those who were involved.

Whether or not *More* was taken down by its institutionally minded rival, the *Columbia Journalism Review*, or merely sold to it in ignominy, the obituaries came. On July 22, 1978, both the *Washington Post* and *More*'s longtime nemesis the *New York Times* reported that *More* would be ending publication and selling its subscription list to the stodgy older review. Edward Barrett, the publisher of *CJR*, said that there would be no editorial changes as a result of the merger.[21] The *Post* wrote the more perceptive article, noting the "touch of irony" that left some staff members bitter about the sale, since *(MORE)* was originally meant to be an alternative to the *Columbia Journalism Review*. Adler chose *CJR* because he had lost $400,000 and Columbia University is a tax-exempt institution. That would allow him to take a tax exemption for the donation. Though Adler and the editors had been looking for a buyer since April, only two real offers had emerged. Adler turned down one from a commercial publisher that had sought to turn *More* into a sort of gossip magazine. The other had come from the liberal opinion magazine the *Nation*, which wanted to turn *More* into a press section of the magazine. Adler had turned down that offer because they had not offered enough money.[22]

Chapter 8

The document deeding what Dick Pollak called "the carrion" of *More* to Columbia University mostly reads like a standard legal document. There is no sign of motive in turning over the remains of the magazine to its rival. But the document does give everything to Columbia:

> The trade names "MORE" and "MORE Magazine," any and all trademarks and copyrights, the complete inventory of back issues, all accounts receivable from subscribers, the complete list of all current subscribers and all expired subscriptions on record, all editorial and business files and records (including the documentation of past promotional efforts), and the right to receive the net proceeds of all rentals of the subscriber list accruing after the date of this gift.[23]

It is signed July 18, 1978.

Adler sent a letter to subscribers explaining the end of *More*. He blamed expenses and his own illness for the end, and said it was a service to readers and society that they went on even as long as they did. Most of the letter discusses how *More*'s monthly subscription would translate into *CJR*'s six-times-a-year subscription (monthly subscriptions that didn't match directly would be rounded up). But one paragraph in particular addressed the poignancy and irony of the manner of *More*'s death:

> In some ways this development is ironic; MORE and CJR have been rivals in terms of content, advertising, and, of course, readers. But each has had a basic respect for the other's outlook and editorial principles and, of course, a shared purpose. Adding our readership and other strengths to those of CJR will make for a stronger publication dedicated to helping raise standards in American journalism. CJR has invited me to play an advisory role in the months ahead. We also hope that some of your favorite writers, whose works have enlivened MORE's pages, will come on board with CJR.[24]

Tony Lukas was bitter about the donation of *More* to *CJR*. He called *CJR* stodgy and out of touch with younger journalists, and had a special contempt for Adler: "For Adler to not only destroy the magazine, but then hand it to the magazine to which it was supposed to be an alternative, is the ultimate irony and the ultimate obscenity," Lukas told the *Post*. He said that in ten months, Adler had done nothing to support the business side of the magazine. He called asking Adler to take over "the single biggest mistake" that the editorial staff of *More* had ever made. But the magazine was probably never commercially viable and its end was probably inevitable, even if it had not come at the hands of James Adler. The *Post* article mentioned that the *Columbia Journalism Review* was in talks with at least one *More* staff member to come on board.[25]

And with that irony, *More* came to an end. There had been fifty-eight issues under the original ownership. Michael Kramer had overseen thirteen issues. Robert Friedman had put out nine issues under the ownership of James Adler. There had been six conventions: four in New York, one in Washington, DC, and one in San Francisco. Circulation had peaked at a little more than twenty thousand. Thousands more had attended the conventions. And maybe the magazine had influenced the press it covered. Certainly, it had managed to annoy the media, the primary role of a gadfly.

Gawker, Content, Bloggers, *Spy*: The Legacy of *(MORE)*

(MORE) was a part of the intellectual world of working journalists in the 1970s. Particularly at the most elite levels of journalism, it would have been nearly impossible to avoid the magazine's existence. If you were working as a journalist in New York or Washington, and in many of the other cosmopolitan urban centers of the United States between 1971 and 1978, *(MORE)* would have been one of the primary ways you connected to your profession, whether it was through reading the monthly issues you subscribed to, or borrowing a copy that had been floating around your newsroom, or attending one or more of the A. J. Liebling Counter-Conventions to meet your journalistic idols or just hang out with your friends in the industry. At its peak of circulation, *(MORE)* reached somewhere between twenty and twenty-five thousand paid issues, with a pass-along rate that was likely significantly higher than that. For a magazine, twenty thousand is a small circulation number (the smallest circulation category for the National Magazine Awards is "under 100,000"), but twenty thousand journalists is still a lot of journalists. If *(MORE)* was able to influence only those twenty thousand, and those journalists brought some of the ideas of *(MORE)* to their newsrooms and to their own work, which was read by millions more, then it is very possible that the reach of *(MORE)*'s ideas was much wider than those raw circulation numbers indicate. *(MORE)* started a conversation in the nation's press, and the nation's press leads the conversation of the nation.

The three editors who led *(MORE)* has each assessed the magazine's legacy. Dick Pollak believes that *(MORE)* was part of an important moment in the self-regard of the press:

I think over the long haul we were influential, because we helped start
a movement that has taken hold, and the press is better for it. I think
the movement toward self-criticism, which has become established
throughout journalism today was basically started by the early journalism reviews.[26]

Dick Pollak and his cofounder Tony Lukas started the magazine to counter what they saw as the rampant anti-intellectualism in the press, an entrenched belief among publishers and editors that the press operated in
a certain way and had always operated in a certain way, and that the press
existed to sell newspapers, not to raise questions about how the institutions
that determined American life functioned. And certainly not for the press
to raise questions about itself. They knew that they could not change the
entire ecosystem of the American press, that the vast majority of newspapers existed to deliver baseball box scores and comic strips and community
news. But they set out to change the attitudes of the highest levels of the
press, hoping that at least those who operated the most serious "thought
leader" publications felt a responsibility to keep the public as well-informed
as possible, and to operate as a check on the power of authoritative institutions of government and big business. It was an attitude that was firmly
rooted in the anti-institutionalism of the late 1960s, but it was also an attitude that stemmed from the personal experiences of the founding editors.
Certainly Pollak's own experience validated that attitude:

> I was the editor of the *Honolulu Star-Bulletin*, and I sent myself to
> Vietnam during the Tet Offensive, and I wrote ten or twelve pieces
> from there and then I wrote a full op-ed page piece, titled "My Country
> Is Wrong." And I got some feedback on that, but nowhere *near* the
> feedback I got when we ran the [same] answers to the Jumble two days
> in a row. The whole island lit up to tell us we made that mistake. And
> that was a lesson to me. And that's demoralizing. Because if you want to
> do really first-rate work, you can't do it in most places.[27]

His cofounder Tony Lukas saw that even at the best of newspapers—for
him, it was the *New York Times*—there were limits to the kind of work good
reporters could do. They were constrained by the editorial policies of their
publications and forced into restrictive definitions of acceptable journalistic objectivity. Pollak described the experience of three former *Times*men,

including his friend Lukas, *(MORE)* contributor David Halberstam, and Gay Talese, author of *The Kingdom and the Power*, the book about the inner workings of the *Times* in the 1960s:

> The combination of the staff not having any real intellectual depth and the management not having any real intellectual depth, or at least not feeling any demand for it, is why a lot of people leave the profession. It's why Halberstam and Lukas and Talese leave. They can't do the long form. They hit a ceiling beyond which you can't go—I don't mean in terms of money or promotion—I mean in terms of intellectual elbow room. You just can't do it at a magazine or a newspaper, and I think that happens to anybody who has any real intellectual curiosity.[28]

For Pollak, then, the effect of *(MORE)* was at those highest levels. He believes the *New York Times* did learn from its management issues in the 1970s, and is a better place for good reporters to do their best work than it was when he was running *(MORE)*, the primary gadfly to the *Times* in that period. *(MORE)* was able to open up some "intellectual elbow room" at the elite publications, and start a conversation that led to self-criticism at these publications. And self-criticism is a hallmark of intellectualism.

For Michael Kramer, the second editor of *(MORE)*, the matter was a simple one of the magazine fulfilling the same watchdog function toward the press that the press had toward other institutions of power, as well as building a community among journalists. "I think it gives people the impression that their profession is a profession and that people are watching. And maybe it made people a little bit more careful," he said.[29] So if for Pollak, *(MORE)* was a gadfly to the watchdogs of powerful institutions, constantly pushing the *Times* and other news organizations of its ilk toward better standards of performance, then for Kramer, *(MORE)* was more of a watchdog to the watchdogs, making sure they *maintained* certain levels of performance, rather than pushing for progress. It is still a valuable approach to the role of the press critic, if a more conservative one. Perhaps in some ways that is a product of the individuals who were running the magazine, but it is also likely a reaction to the time. Pollak ran *(MORE)* when it was building on the anti-institutional attitudes of the 1960s. Kramer took over after the successes of Watergate, when the press was feeling proud of its accomplishments and basking in a new celebrity. The institutional press felt as if it could hardly get any better, so a journalism review bent on maintaining performance standards fit the ethos of the year or so in the mid 1970s when Kramer was in charge.

Robert Friedman sees the effects of *(MORE)* on the professional press to be a part of changes were taking place in journalism in the 1970s, not necessarily driving them, but participating in them, and perhaps helping to propel those changes forward. Like Kramer, Freidman ran the magazine in the post-Watergate era. But rather than just using *(MORE)* as a way to try to keep the press honest, Friedman saw that Watergate and its aftermath opened journalism up as an alluring career path for young people with an idealistic and intellectual tendency:

> With the popularity engendered by *All the President's Men*, I think that's the first time I can think of that reporters sort of became popular heroes, and what did they do? They brought down a president, so that was significant. It's not just that they wrote some good stories or covered a war well, but they actually had a huge impact. And I think that changed the attractiveness of journalism as a profession and lured a lot of people into the business who might not have gone into it earlier. And I think that new blood that came into the business helped make it better and more in tune with the kind of journalism that *(MORE)* magazine supported and thought should be done. Now, across the nation, newspapers still tended to be owned by conservative owners; editorial pages continued to support the war until the bitter end. But in certain mainstream institutions, I think there was a sea change that happened in the mid '70s. What role did *(MORE)* play in that? Probably less than more, but some. And I think it served as a good adjunct to those changes that were happening and helped push them and propel them, and that's great.[30]

Some of the changes in the way the press talked about itself were already under way even before *(MORE)* began publishing in 1971. The ombudsman movement had started. The regional journalism review movement was under way. The underground and alternative press had been seeking ways to report the stories the mainstream press was not adequately representing, in their opinion—stories about minority experience, stories about women, stories questioning the received wisdom that American capitalism was an unquestionable good and that the government was a benign institution that always worked for the good of individual Americans. But many of these ideas were too radical for the mainstream press. *(MORE)* served as a bridge to bring some of these fresh ideas to the mainstream.

As the 1970s ended and *(MORE)* finally disappeared, Friedman (like both Pollak and Kramer before him) felt that the magazine did have a lasting influence on the way the media are discussed in the press. Prior to *(MORE)*'s existence, there was very little writing about how publications or broadcasts were assembled and delivered to their readers or viewers. There were a few critical studies and a smattering of in-house ombudsmen, but the 1970s saw the quantity of this sort of writing skyrocket. "I think *(MORE)* did change the dialogue about media coverage, how people think and talk about the media," Friedman says. "And I think a lot of it got absorbed into the media, so that you've got people who, only after that period of time, were hired to write about the media as a beat, who were hired as ombudsmen, to think about the foibles of the publication and to write critically about the media."[31]

Wendy Wyatt's Discursive Press Criticism and Intellectual Self-Scrutiny

Wendy Wyatt argues that true press criticism can only come from outside the press, from critics who are not situated in the knowledge of the operations of the institutional press. For Wyatt, press criticism functions when discourse exists between a peripheral "critical public," a self-appointed group of critics outside the press, in conversation with that critical public, and with the institutional press at the core of her model.[32]

In Wyatt's model, the writing in *(MORE)* would exist almost exclusively at what Wyatt calls "third level criticism." In third-level criticism, ideas for reform are introduced by the press itself, and discussed within the profession, what could be called self-criticism. Wyatt's model requires that these ideas then be shared with the critical public at the periphery of her model. One shortcoming of this model is that it fails to account for the fluidity with which people move from one level to another of her model in American society. As there is no licensing or regulatory system for who can and cannot work as a journalist in the United States, people are simultaneously journalists and concerned citizens. And from the standpoint of individual press institutions, *(MORE)* made sure that its writers were outsiders at least to those institutions about which they were writing. They may have been journalists, by and large, but they were not journalists for the particular institutions that they were covering. Their intent, in most cases, was to induce the sort of self-criticism that Richard Hofstadter saw as central to intellectualism.

So while *(MORE)* did function as third-level critical discourse, facilitating the conversation among members of the working press, it also served to encourage the sort of searching and quest for self-betterment that Hofstadter describes. The difficulty would be in trying to create the public that would be interested enough in the operations of the press to engage with the same ideas that concerned these self-examining reporters. The incarnation of *More* that Michael Kramer created attempted to reach this audience, aiming its coverage and criticisms of the press not just at the press itself but also at an imagined interested public. However, it quickly found that no such public existed, or at least not enough of one to make a general-interest media magazine a profitable enterprise. The popularity of journalism and journalists at the height of the *All the President's Men* era might have been the best opportunity to foster that sort of public. But given the lack of interest by the general public, *(MORE)*'s attempts to foster discussion within the profession seems to be as strong an effort as could have been made in the 1970s. At least it was able to spur self-criticism and to help incorporate whatever little outside criticism (such as Moynihan's analysis of the press) into that discussion. Wyatt also sees press criticism as a form of regulation for the press, but one that the press would find more palatable than outside regulation from bodies such as press councils, which journalists tend to find as reprehensible as government regulation. The discursive critical process allows journalists to have a discussion about the values they want to support and how they can best serve the public interest.[33] Given Dick Pollak's repeated arguments against the idea of a national press council, he would likely agree with Wyatt's assessment.

Arthur S. Hayes's Criteria for Judging Press Criticism

Arthur S. Hayes proposed a nine-part test of the effectiveness of a press critic.[34] This section will address those questions, as applied to *(MORE)*, one by one.

1. Has the critique led to the dismissal, resignation, or reassignment of a reporter, broadcast public affairs personality, editor, or news executive?

(MORE) certainly got people fired in the course of its existence, though it was rarely for the reasons the magazine intended. A reporter was fired from the *Philadelphia Inquirer* in part for her having attended the first A. J. Liebling Counter-Convention (see chapter 4), and another was fired

from the *New York Times* for supplying a copy of a rejected manuscript to *(MORE)* via *Rolling Stone*. But there are few, if any, examples of *(MORE)* demonstrating the incompetence or malfeasance of someone in the press, and that person's employer firing him or her for the offense.

2. Has the critique led to content or programming changes consistent with widely acknowledged journalism ethical standards?

3. Has the critique led to a reform of a news organization's standards and practices?

(MORE) had substantial, if indirect, effects on its primary target, the *New York Times*. Whether or not that change can be directly attributed to the call to action that *(MORE)* published in its first issue, the *Times* certainly changed its policy on corrections in the 1970s. The direct mover may have been the *Columbia Journalism Review*, but *(MORE)* initiated the idea. To some extent, that offers an answer to Hayes's question 3 more than it does question 2. But *(MORE)* was less concerned with forcing individual institutions to adhere to "widely acknowledged journalism ethical standards" and more concerned with establishing those standards in the first place.

4. Has the critique spurred public debate in public forums and in the news media about news media performance or the business of mass media, helping to shape public opinion on the issue?

(MORE) found itself covered by general-interest news media on several occasions, though most consistently for the A. J. Liebling Counter-Conventions. *(MORE)* likely had little direct influence on the way the public at large viewed issues of ethical standards for the press, but most of that is attributable to the fact that the public had little interest in establishing ethical standards for the press. Perhaps through a sort of two- or three-step process, *(MORE)* did have some effect on how the press was viewed by the public at large, but that would have been filtered through changes in the behavior of the press, either from direct agitation from *(MORE)* or through following the lead of national news outlets such as the *New York Times*.

5. Do news media outlets quote the individual or organization as an authority on news media ethics and performance?

Nearly every reference to *(MORE)* in the press identifies the magazine as an influential voice of press criticism.

6. Does the individual or organization have a longtime and substantial following, measured in viewers, books [sic] *sales or Web-site hits?*

(MORE) reached a circulation of more than twenty thousand at its peak, which is a substantial number for such a niche publication. And the attendance at its annual conventions indicated that the magazine had a very devoted following, if not a large one by the standards of general-interest publications. Though the magazine lasted for only eight years, that can be seen as a surprisingly long time, given the publication's narrow content and the lack of advertising support for most of its history.

7. Has the individual or organization inspired a movement?

This is a difficult question to answer, since during *(MORE)*'s run there was certainly a change in the way journalists thought about themselves and about the institutional press that employed them. It is very hard to say how much of that is attributable to *(MORE)* and how much *(MORE)* was just chronicling a movement that was already under way. *(MORE)* was not the first journalism review, though it was the one within the movement that had the broadest mandate and the most nationwide appeal. Robert Friedman, the magazine's final editor, argued that *(MORE)* was a part of the reason that the 1970s saw an influx of talented young journalists who helped shape the journalism of the forty years that followed, but without survey evidence, it would be difficult to substantiate that claim.

8. Has the individual or organization established standards of inquiry, analysis, or proposals used by other critics?

9. Have the individual's critiques gained currency among other critics and scholars who point to the individual as a groundbreaking activist or thinker in news media criticism?[235]

(MORE) has had a broad influence in the ecosystem of press criticism that has persisted in its wake. The remainder of this chapter looks at some of the organizations and individuals that have followed in *(MORE)*'s footsteps, whether consciously or not. The development of reportorial coverage of the press as well as press criticism owe much to the example set by *(MORE)* from 1971 to 1978.

The Inheritors of the *(MORE)* Legacy

Only a few of the journalism reviews that sprang up around the country before or during *(MORE)*'s run are still published today. The *Columbia*

Journalism Review is the most prominent of these. Even though the founders of *(MORE)* saw a bitter irony in having their subscription list donated to *CJR* when their own magazine went out of business in 1978, the *(MORE)* approach to press criticism has eventually come to influence the more conservative, institutionally minded magazine to which they saw themselves as an alternative. When *(MORE)*'s subscription list was being sold to *CJR*, the *Washington Post* reported that the Columbia review was in talks with one of *(MORE)*'s staff members to join its own staff. That staffer was *(MORE)*'s final senior editor, Robert Manoff, who did in fact take a job at *CJR* and eventually served as editor. Later, Victor Navasky, who had been a friend of *(MORE)* and an occasional contributor, became the chairman of *CJR*. Manoff and Navasky (as well as other *(MORE)* contributors who eventually wrote for *CJR*) helped to bring some of the *(MORE)* approach to press criticism—a more freewheeling, impish, and critical way of looking at the media—to *(MORE)*'s former rival.

As of 2019, thirty-six years after it absorbed *(MORE)*, *CJR* illustrates some of those changes. Cover stories from the last five years include the very *(MORE)*-like "How Can We Improve American Media's Coverage of Race, Class, and Social Mobility?"[36] an article about the serious dangers of bad personal health reporting,[37] and a survey of journalists and academics that attempted to come to an answer (or a range of answers) on what the true purpose of journalism is.[38] The cover for the last of those articles also contained a very *(MORE)*-like gesture in that it reprinted one reporter's answer to the title question: "What Is Journalism For?" That answer was "It's not fucking rocket science." The word "fucking" was placed just above the UPC code on the cover, not far from where the address label would be placed. It is reminiscent of *(MORE)*'s coverage of obscenity regulation, and the early headline that contained the playfully "censored" word "b——shit." In 2018, *CJR* acknowledged the debt it owes to *(MORE)* directly, publishing an article calling for the spirit of *(MORE)* to be revived.[39] And the day after publication, *CJR*'s editor, Kyle Pope, tweeted,

> Thrilled to (finally) publish this profile of *MORE*, a journalism magazine from the '70s with a ton of attitude and swagger. Now seems like the perfect time to reconsider it, and maybe resurrect its counter-convention. Anyone interested in joining @CJR in the effort? @jackshafer?

So perhaps the idea of the Liebling Counter-Conventions may be revived in a time when the crisis of confidence in American journalism seems to have revived too.

A few of the regional journalism reviews remain as well. And at the national level, the *Washington Journalism Review* eventually became the *American Journalism Review*, published by the Philip Merrill College of Journalism at the University of Maryland. In 2013, the magazine ceased print publication, and stopped publishing new content in 2015. Perhaps *(MORE)* could have made a similar transition to online publication, saving itself the tremendous cost of printing, if the Internet had existed in 1978.

Columbia Journalism Review and the regional *Gateway Journalism Review* are the only publications devoted to coverage and criticism of the press that have published consistently since *(MORE)*'s demise. But there have been other attempts to launch similar publications. In fact, in 1990, several of the journalists involved with *(MORE)* at various stages, as well as a few other like-minded journalists, attempted to launch a new magazine that would very much have continued *(MORE)*'s legacy. The magazine would have been called *Mercury*, though according to a *New York Times* article about the project, no one involved really loved the name (others that had been floated included *Tell*, *Media Watch*, and *Gadfly*). The "inner circle" of the nascent magazine was Ken Auletta, who had written for *(MORE)*, J. Anthony Lukas, Frances Fitzgerald, and venture capitalist Arthur Dubow. Other *(MORE)* alumni and friends of the magazine, including Richard Pollak, David Halberstam, Bill Kovach, Robert Caro, and Bill Moyers, became involved. The idea had come from a public relations person named John Scanlon, who had told Auletta that there was a need to revive a magazine like *(MORE)*, but with a broader appeal and focus. Perhaps it would have been more like the late-era *(MORE)* that attempted to cover more of the media than just the news. At that early stage, though, the main players in this magazine were not optimistic that the $6 million they needed to launch the magazine could be raised in what was then a very weak magazine market.[40] Nothing ever came of the proposal, though it was the closest attempt to reviving *(MORE)* that has happened in the more than thirty-five years since it went out of business.

The attorney and journalist Steven Brill had made a splash with his creation of the *American Lawyer* and the Court TV network when he decided that the country was ready for another general-interest magazine about the media. That magazine was *Brill's Content*, which debuted in the summer of 1998 and ran until fall of 2001. Brill wrote the cover story himself, a twenty-five-thousand-word opus indicting the media's coverage of the Bill Clinton/Monica Lewinsky sex scandal. But he also hired veteran reporters to work for him, including *(MORE)* alumni such as former editor Michael Kramer and contributor Calvin Trillin. Brill spent lavishly to promote the magazine too, reportedly spending about $1 million to attract attention to the first issue.[41] Brill intended to market the magazine to a general audience, in much the same way that Kramer had hoped to do when he took over *(MORE)*. But Kramer had hoped to reach thirty thousand subscribers; Brill was aiming for half a million.[42] *Brill's Content* did approach a circulation of nearly three hundred thousand, but as Arthur Hayes argues, Brill ran up against the same two problems that face all publications devoted to coverage and criticism of the media: an overestimation of public interest in the subject and a lack of desire to advertise to whatever that market is. "Nevertheless," Hayes writes, "reform-minded media professionals cannot seem to part with the idea that there is a substantial readership beyond those who subscribe to trade publications willing to spend money to read about how the sausage gets made in the news media business or to read critiques of press performance."[43] No one has attempted such a publication since, but that does not mean that press criticism or coverage of the press have languished because of this.

In the 1980s and 1990s, *Spy* magazine, a satirical monthly founded by Kurt Anderson and Graydon Carter, ran a column under the pseudonym J. J. Hunsecker, which was the name of the press agent character in the movie *Sweet Smell of Success*. Whoever was writing the articles was, appropriately, a spy inside the *New York Times*, and while most of the Hunsecker columns were not really press criticism intended to prod the paper into better coverage, the puckish stories are reminiscent of some of the more sophomoric pranks that *(MORE)* undertook. Hunsecker and *Spy* were mostly interested in the romantic life of Abe Rosenthal, who was still in charge of the news division of the *Times* in 1987. So even though the aim was not at all high-minded in *Spy*, that magazine's editors obviously took some of the same delight in prodding Rosenthal that *(MORE)*'s did. And Rosenthal apparently expressed as little interest in *Spy* as he did in *(MORE)*.[44]

In somewhat the same snarky, sophomoric vein, but also with what seems to be a real, if occasional, intent to better the media through criticism, the blog *Gawker* began mixing outrage, gossip, and real news about Manhattan media in 2003. Mostly, *Gawker* was nothing like *(MORE)*, except that it was a New York City publication that claimed to focus on media news and gossip. *Gawker* mostly interested itself in its later years with posts that would drive web traffic, but also addressed real issues of press coverage from time to time. In 2012, for instance, *Gawker* ran a series of insider articles written by a then-anonymous employee of Fox News Channel who called himself the Fox News Mole. Fox quickly identified him as a producer named Joe Muto, but his dispatches describing the working atmosphere inside the most successful national cable news network created a brief stir and are a direct descendent of *Spy's* J. J. Hunsecker.[45] Very little of *Gawker's* content addressed the media toward the end, but it was a part of the ecosystem of media coverage and criticism that has evolved online and was an early and vociferous participant in the social media conversation about the press. *Gawker* eventually met its end as a result of a lawsuit brought by entrepreneur and venture capitalist Peter Thiel, who bankrolled lawsuits against the publication in retaliation for its public outing of him as gay.[46]

Perhaps the most visible form of press criticism in the last two decades has been on television. While shows such as *The Daily Show*, *The Colbert Report*, and *Last Week Tonight* have been widely discussed as satire of the content of the news, less attention has been paid to their role as critics of the news media. Jon Stewart, the second and best-known host of *The Daily Show* not only parodied the format of television news, but also frequently commented on how insipid cable news had become, and he focused much of his ire on Fox News, though he famously appeared on the CNN show *Crossfire* and attacked the hosts for poisoning American discourse.

While it was perhaps inevitable that a specialized publication such as *(MORE)* could not have survived in an era of expensive printing and distribution costs without finding either foundation support or a steady stream of advertisers, technological change and new advertising models have allowed the beginnings of a new golden age of press criticism. Jack Shafer, writing at the time for Reuters, called it "our national pastime."

Like an algae bloom, press criticism has seeped into every inhabitable niche. Rare is the cable news talk show, magazine feature story, or blog post that reaches its midpoint without some sort of examination and excoriation of the press. The current level of scrutiny would startle the savvy news consumer of the 1970s, even a reader of Alexander Cockburn's *Village Voice* "Press Clips" column. Readers from the 1960s would overdose on the saturation coverage. People tend not to recall that Liebling, who died in December 1963, worked only part-time at press criticism while at the *New Yorker* and was most active between 1945 and 1953.[47]

Shafer was correct in 2013, and his own press criticism has been a part of the current flowering of press criticism, one that has continued for at least five years past when he wrote that column.

General-interest publications have picked up some of this, particularly in the wake of the divisive 2016 presidential election, which caused no end of navel gazing, soul searching, and genuine constructive criticism from journalists, scholars, and an interested public in the vein of what Wendy Wyatt proposed in her model of discursive press criticism. Data journalist Nate Silver's eleven-part 2017 mea culpa and apologia for the press and polling[48] exhibits this, and even before the election, *New York* magazine's "The Case Against the Media, by the Media" assembled interviews with 113 members of "the media" to compile what amounts to a collective work of press self-criticism, and ran the story on the cover.

Much of the conversation about the press now takes place now over Twitter, where a significant community has been built up. That community is an ideal version of the sort of community of journalists that coalesced around *(MORE)* in the 1970s, except that instead of being able to meet and discuss ideas with each other once a year at the A. J. Liebling Counter-Conventions, press critics, press junkies, members of the press, and journalism and media professors can all interact with each other, share ideas and articles, and instantly react to the latest developments in media news. On a typical day, one might find New York University professor and press critic Jay Rosen linking to a long essay about the role of the press on his *PressThink* blog or discussing his role as an adviser to the new publication being started by eBay founder Pierre Omidyar and journalist Glenn Greenwald, who helped bring to light the revelations of National Security Agency leaker Edward Snowden. Or perhaps City University of New York journalism professor Jeff Jarvis is discussing his reaction to a published conversation between Greenwald and former *New York Times* editor Bill Keller over whether the *Times* paradigm of objectivity or Greenwald's preferred advocacy journalism is a better model for the future of journalism.[49] Or maybe it is Jack Shafer, the press critic who writes for *Politico*, engaging with the late David Carr, who was a media columnist for the *New York Times*. The *Times* also had a series of six people serve as a "public editor," their version of an ombudsman, from 2003 to 2017, and while the quality of their work was variable, the penultimate public editor, Margaret Sullivan, was an active and inquisitive writer and critic, often forcing the *Times* to be more introspective. She went on to become a well-respected media columnist for the *Washington Post*. The decision to end the public editor position was controversial, demonstrating that people began to care about holding the press responsible for its performance. And the "Reader Center," a moderated forum for airing questions and complaints about the paper's coverage, has been ineffective at filling the gap left by the Public Editor's absence, as evidenced during the uproar in 2017 over the *Times*'s decision to run an uncritical profile of a white nationalist who lived in the suburbs and ate at chain restaurants.[50]

The Internet has opened up a realm of debate and discussion that was never really available in the days of *(MORE)*, when journalists had to subscribe to a thirty-two-page newsprint tabloid to see what the latest news of their profession was, or had to travel to a hotel in New York City in order to hear the most thoughtful and provocative journalists of their day have a heated debate about the issues they were facing in their work. The diffusion of press criticism has allowed it to survive too. Unlike *(MORE)* or *Brill's Content*, which relied on expensive printing and distribution, the Internet allows for press critics to work anywhere and for the discussion to continue without the pressures of filling a monthly magazine. The world of press criticism is as robust now as it was in the heyday of *(MORE)*, with as many interesting topics in flux as journalism works through another huge moment of transition, much as it did in the 1970s. The media ecosystem that exists four decades after the demise of *(MORE)* allows for more discussion of the press than ever before. On any given day, press criticism that is in some way a direct descendant of *(MORE)* can be found in a variety of places:

- *On the Media*, a weekly radio show and podcast about the press
- *Columbia Journalism Review*, now a much more general audience-oriented publication than it was in 1974
- *PressThink*, a blog about the media written by New York University journalism professor Jay Rosen
- critic Jack Shafer's column in *Politico*
- critics Margaret Sullivan and Erik Wemple, both of the *Washington Post*
- NPR media reporter and commentator David Folkenflik
- reporter and essayist David Uberti
- *MediaFile*, a student-founded (in 2016) and student-staffed national press criticism site at George Washington University

- comments sections appended to many publications' online stories
- criticism and commentary in online message forums such as those at Reddit, as well as in other social media such as the comments below a news organization's posts on Facebook, as well as Twitter, perhaps the most open of the Internet forums for criticism
- CNN's weekly press commentary show *Reliable Sources*
- satirical television programs such as *The Daily Show* and *Last Week Tonight* and satirical websites including *The Onion* and *McSweeney's*

And that's a good thing. The rise of fake news prior to the 2016 election, followed almost immediately by President Donald Trump leading attacks on the press, led to a crisis of confidence in the American press that has distinct echoes of the one that *(MORE)* confronted in the wake of the Vietnam War, the Pentagon Papers, the Nixon administration's attacks on the press and the Watergate investigation, and the general lack of confidence in institutions. Criticism, done properly, can have a spectacularly salutary effect on the trust that the public puts in its institutions of news and information. *(MORE)* provided that for eight years in the 1970s. Something like it could help end the crisis that emerged forty years after it died. Founding editor Dick Pollak said that *(MORE)* faded away because it was no longer necessary. And that may briefly have been true. But more criticism—and even *(MORE)*'s criticism—can only improve the public discourse necessary for the perpetuation of representative democracy. The current model of journalism is again struggling to adequately describe the world it is trying to cover. The best minds in journalism can find each other easily now, but another *(MORE)* needs to finish the job it started—to make the press more self-aware, more self-critical, more flexible, and better able to rethink its best practices in the face of its own failure.

Coda: What Happened to the Staff of *(MORE)*?

Robert Friedman, the last editor of *(MORE)*, went on to edit the *Village Voice* and later worked as an editor at *Life* and *Fortune* before he became an editor at Bloomberg News, where he manages and edits long-term, in-depth coverage of global finance.[51]

Michael Kramer, who preceded Friedman as editor, went back to writing political commentary after he sold the magazine. After working at *Time*, he turned to being a playwright, having his play *Divine Rivalry*, about Leonardo da Vinci and Niccolò Macchiavelli, produced by the Hartford Stage.[52]

Malcolm Frouman, *(MORE)*'s second art director, left the magazine to work for the *New York Review of Books*, which had been designed by his predecessor at *(MORE)*, Samuel Antupit. Frouman went on to be the longtime art director of *BusinessWeek* magazine until it was sold to Bloomberg.[53]

Longtime contributor and senior editor David Rubin continued to teach at New York University, until he left to become the dean of Syracuse University's S. I. Newhouse School of Public Communication. He retired as dean in 2008.[54]

(MORE)'s first Washington editor, Brit Hume, spent more than two decades at ABC News, where he eventually became the network's chief White House correspondent. He eventually left to become a correspondent and editor at the conservative Fox News.

Claudia Cohen, *(MORE)*'s second assistant editor, left the magazine to pursue a career as a gossip columnist, first with the *New York Post*'s Page Six, beginning in 1977, and eventually moving on to being a broadcast entertainment reporter. She was a regular on WABC, and then on the syndicated talk show *Live with Regis and Kathie Lee*. She married and divorced Ronald O. Perelman, chairman of the cosmetics company Revlon. When Cohen died of ovarian cancer in 2007, Perelman donated a large sum of money to have a building named in her honor at the University of Pennsylvania, her alma mater.[55]

Cohen's predecessor as assistant editor, Terry Pristin, worked for more than a decade at the *Los Angeles Times*, where she covered Hollywood, among other topics. She eventually moved to the *New York Times*, where she covers commercial real estate and continues to write for other publications as well.[56]

Kathy Jones, who arranged several of the A. J. Liebling Counter-Conventions, left *(MORE)* to work for the *New York Review of Books*, where she rose to be associate publisher and advertising director. She surprised herself by marrying a journalist, *New York Times* reporter Clyde Haberman. She is now director of special projects for Human Rights First, where she manages relations with donors and, true to her counter-convention experience, arranges major events for the non-profit organization.[57]

Of the three members of Rosebud Associates, the founders of *(MORE)*, only Richard Pollak is still alive. William "Woody" Woodward added to the trail of tragedy in his family in 1999. His mother had shot and killed his father, by accident, she claimed; she killed herself after being portrayed as guilty by Truman Capote, even though she had been officially exonerated. Woodward's younger brother, Jimmy, killed himself by jumping from a hotel window. Woodward ran for public office, seeking the support of his old mentor Dolly Schiff, and later worked as a bureaucrat for New York State, supervising the banking system. But at age fifty-four, he jumped from the window of his apartment on the Upper East Side of Manhattan and fell fourteen stories to his death.[58]

J. Anthony Lukas continued to write as a freelancer and book author, achieving his highest level of fame—and his second Pulitzer Prize—for the book *Common Ground*, which chronicled the stories of several Boston families in their struggle over their city's government-imposed school busing. Shortly after he finished his last book, *Big Trouble*, however, Lukas, who had been battling depression, killed himself at home, tying a cord around his neck and strangling himself. Kathy Jones's husband, Clyde Haberman, wrote Lukas's obituary for the *Times*.[59] The Columbia University Graduate School of Journalism gives two annual prizes named in his honor.[60]

Richard Pollak served as a literary editor and executive editor at the *Nation*, and wrote several books, including an account of an around-the-world trip on a container ship after the 9/11 attacks, and *The Creation of Dr. B: A Biography of Bruno Bettelheim*. He published a memoir about the death of his brother when they were children, and a book about traveling the world on a cargo ship. He lived for many years on the Upper West Side of Manhattan, and moved to Portland, Maine, with his wife, Diane Walsh, a concert pianist.[61]

Notes

Introduction

1. W. Joseph Campbell has been a tireless corrector of myths of American journalism, and provides a good explanation of where Cronkite's "most trusted man" reputation came from. See Campbell, "Cronkite 'the most-trusted'? Where's the evidence?"

2. See Lerner, "Abe Rosenthal's Project X."

3. Argyris, *Behind the Front Page*.

Chapter 1 A Culture of Criticism

1. Carey, "Journalism and Criticism," 227–49, 235.

2. Ibid., 227.

3. Ibid., 236.

4. Ibid.

5. For one explanation of the early development of objectivity, see Tucher, *Froth and Scum*.

6. Carey, "Journalism and Criticism," 245.

7. *(MORE)*, June 1971, 2.

8. *(MORE)* would also award its second ever Liebling Prize to Bigart.

9. Carey, "Journalism and Criticism," 235.

10. Thomas Jefferson to John Norvell, June 14, 1807, in *The Founders' Constitution*, vol. 5.

11. Daly, *Covering America*, 53–54.

12. Wilmer, *Our Press Gang*.

13. Ibid., 13.

14. Ibid.

15. Marzolf, *Civilizing Voices*.

16. Ibid., 2.

17. Ibid.

18. Ibid., 121.

19. Dabbous, "'Blessed Be the Critics of Newspapers'"; and Dicken-Garcia, *Journalistic Standards in Nineteenth-Century America*.

20. Goldstein, *Killing the Messenger*.

21. On journalism and professionalism, see Reese and Cohen, "Educating for Journalism"; and Schudson and Anderson, "Objectivity, Professionalism, and Truth Seeking in Journalism."

22. Vos and Finneman, "Early Historical Construction of Journalism's Gate-keeping Role."

23. Wyatt, *Critical Conversations*, 7.

24. Wyatt, "Press Criticism."

25. McChesney and Scott, *Our Unfree Press*.

26. Irwin, *American Newspaper*.

27. McChesney and Scott, "Introduction" to *The Brass Check*, by Upton Sinclair.

28. Lippman, *Liberty and the News* (1920); Lippman, *Public Opinion* (1922); and Lippman, *The Phantom Public* (1925).

29. Daly, *Covering America*, 225–26.

30. Lippmann and Merz, "A Test of the News."

31. Ibid.

32. Lippmann, *Public Opinion*.

33. Seldes, *Freedom of the Press*.

34. Marzolf, *Civilizing Voices*, 141.

35. Ibid., 141–42.

36. Midura, "A .J. Liebling: The Wayward Pressman as Critic."

37. Sokolov, *Wayward Reporter*, 52; and Harrison, "'The Wayward Press' Revisited."

38. Shafer, "Church of Liebling."

39. Liebling, "The Wayward Press: Do You Belong in Journalism?"

40. Tebbel, *Open Letter to Newspaper Readers*, 11.

41. Hayes, *Press Critics Are the Fifth Estate*, 53–63.

42. Bagdikian, "The American Newspaper Is Neither Record. . .."

43. Isaacs, *Untended Gates*, 107–109.

44. Bagdikian, *Information Machines*.

45. Efron, *News Twisters*.

46. Accuracy in Media, Our Mission.

47. See Campbell, *Getting It Wrong*, 128–29.

48. McChesney and Scott, *Our Unfree Press*, 7.

49. Brown, *Reluctant Reformation*.

50. Ibid., 70.

51. For an extended examination of the way liberal values suffused the news-room, see Pressman, *On Press*.

52. In a study of reporters-turned-writers, from Walt Whitman and Mark Twain to Ernest Hemingway, Shelley Fisher Fishkin wrote that nineteenth- and early twentieth-century reporters chafed under "the limits of conventional

journalism as they knew it—the subjects that were excluded, the superficial, formulaic treatment of subjects that were discussed, the lack of connection to any time but the present, the extravagant claims to authoritativeness, the failure to challenge the reader to think for himself—were apparent to them . . .”; Fishkin, *From Fact to Fiction*, 8. For a longer discussion of the evolution of reporters' attitudes toward their work, see Schudson, *Discovering the News*.

53. Schudson, *Discovering the News*, 181.

54. For an account of the biggest women's uprising in a newsroom, see Povich, *Good Girls Revolt*.

55. Pauly, "Finding Ourselves in the New Journalism," 135.

56. See Addis, "Study of the Surface Accuracy of *The Columbia Journalism Review* and *MORE*"; and Northington, "Media Criticism as Professional Self-Regulation."

57. DeZutter, "The Trial: You had to be there."

58. "Need Help?"

59. Diamond, "Cabal at the 'New York Times'" 42.

60. Ibid., 43.

61. Ibid., 45.

62. Talese, *Kingdom and the Power*.

63. Halberstam, *Powers That Be*.

64. Gitlin, *Whole World Is Watching:*.

65. Rodgers, *Age of Fracture*.

66. Wolfe, *New Journalism*.

67. Christopher B. Daly's *Covering America* does a particularly good job of describing the changes in the American newsroom in chapters 11 and 12.

68. Killen, *1973 Nervous Breakdown*.

69. Schulman, *The Seventies*.

70. Kluger, *The Paper*.

71. Draper, Rolling Stone Magazine: *Uncensored History*.

72. Nobile, *Intellectual Skywriting*.

73. Hynds, *American Newspapers in the 1970s*.

74. Tifft and Jones, *The Trust*.

Chapter 2 Rosebud Associates

1. David Halberstam to Clifton Daniel, NY Times Records: Daniel Papers, box 6, folder 6.

2. Lukas, "Two Worlds of Linda Fitzpatrick," *New York Times*, Oct. 16, 1967.

3. A. M. Rosenthal to Clifton Daniel, Nov. 28, 1967, NY Times Records: Rosenthal Papers, box 27, folder 41: Lukas, J. Anthony.

4. Lukas, *Barnyard Epithet*, 2.

5. Lukas, *Barnyard Epithet*, vii.

6. Lukas, "Disorder Erupts at Chicago Trial," *New York Times*, Feb. 5, 1970.

7. Lukas, *Barnyard Epithet*, viii.
8. Pollak, interview with the author, Sept. 8, 2011.
9. Ibid.
10. Dorfman, "Truth, Justice and the American Way"; and Dorfman, "Journalists' Movement."
11. Emery, Emery, and Roberts, *Press and America*; Mott, *American Journalism*; Pöttker, "News and Its Communicative Quality"; Salcetti, "Emergence of the Reporter"; Starr, *Creation of the Media*; and Stephens, *History of News*.
12. Solomon, "Site of Newsroom Labor," 116.
13. Seldes, *Lords of the Press*.
14. Salcetti, "Emergence of the Reporter."
15. Solomon, "Site of Newsroom Labor."
16. Haskell, *Emergence of Professional Social Science*.
17. Banning, "Professionalization of Journalism"; Kovach and Rosenstiel, *Elements of Journalism;* and Schudson, *Discovering the News*.
18. Kovach and Rosenstiel, *Elements of Journalism*, 72.
19. Lippmann, *Liberty and the News*.
20. Schudson, *Discovering the News*.
21. Porwancher, "Objectivity's Prophet."
22. Gans, *Deciding What's News*, 101.
23. Hallin, *Uncensored War*.
24. Schudson, *Discovering the News*, 179.
25. Ibid., 180.
26. Ibid., 184.
27. Ibid.
28. Ibid., 185.
29. Wolfe, *New Journalism*.
30. This analysis is based on a panel discussion held at the first A. J. Liebling Counter-Convention, sponsored by *(MORE)* in 1972.
31. Brick, *Age of Contradiction*, 37–39.
32. Pauly, "Finding Ourselves in the New Journalism."
33. McMillian, *Smoking Typewriters*; and Peck, *Uncovering the Sixties*.
34. Trillin, "U.S. Journal: Seattle, Wash.: Alternatives," *New Yorker*, Apr. 10, 1978, 118–25.
35. Hale, *Nation of Outsiders*.
36. See Mindich, *Just the Facts*; Schudson, *Discovering the News*; and Zelizer, "When Facts, Truth, and Reality Are God-Terms."
37. Trillin, Telephone interview with the author, June 21, 2012.
38. Dorfman, Interview with the author, Aug. 10, 2012.
39. "The Media: Promising More," *Newsweek*, June 14, 1971, 64.
40. The sensational story of the Woodward murder and subsequent suicide is told by Susan Braudy in her pulpy but well-researched book *This Crazy*

Thing Called Love: The Golden World and Fatal Marriage of Ann and Billy Woodward.

41. *Life* magazine, quoted in Yardley, "Heir to a Fortune, and to Tragedy; Suicide Ends the Life of a Wealthy, and Haunted, Man," *New York Times*, May 8, 1999.

42. Ibid.

43. Diamond, "Cabal at the 'New York Times,'" *New York*, May 18, 1970, 45.

44. Braudy, *Crazy Thing Called Love*, 373.

45. Diamond, "Cabal at the 'New York Times,'" *New York*, May 18, 1970, 45.

46. Pollak, Interview with the author, Sept. 8, 2011.

47. The reference to the request for a leave of absence appears in a memo from Jean Gilette to Paul Sann, dated May 13, 1971; Schiff Papers, box 38, folder: *(MORE)* 1971, May 4–1977, May 23.

48. Ibid.

49. Dorothy Schiff memo to file, May 20, 1971, Schiff Papers, box 38, folder: *(MORE)* 1971, May 4–1977, May 23.

50. Nobile, *Intellectual Skywriting*, 27.

51. MORE A JOURNALISM REVIEW Trademark Details, serial number 72398753, accessed via Justia Trademarks.

52. Memorandum from Henry Erbach to Arthur Brody, June 3, 1971, Schiff Papers, box 38, folder: *(MORE)* 1971, May 4–1977, May 23.

53. Memo from Paul Sann to Dorothy Schiff, Schiff Papers, box 38, folder: *(MORE)* 1971, May 4–1977, May 23.

54. "Review of Press in Bow," *New York Post*, May 18, 1971, 10.

55. "Literati: 'More' Deserves Encore," *Variety*, May 26, 1971, 54.

56. "The Media: Promising More," *Newsweek*, June 14, 1971, 64.

57. Advertisement for *(MORE)*, *New York Times Book Review*, May 30, 1971, BR12.

58. "The Media: Promising More," *Newsweek*, June 14, 1971, 64.

59. Ibid.

60. MacDougall, *The Press*.

61. MacDougall, "Boring from within the Bourgeois Press: Part I," and "Boring from within the Bourgeois Press: Part II."

62. *(MORE)*, June 1971, 2.

63. Ibid.

64. Hellbox, *(MORE)*, June 1971, 2.

65. Cowan, "Slicking Over the Oil Industry," *(MORE)*, June 1971, 9.

66. Dorfman, "Battling the Myths in Chicago," *(MORE)*, June 1971, 18.

67. Pollock, "An Intra-Family Sort of Thing,' *(MORE)*, Oct. 1971, 3.

68. Pollak, Interview with the author, Sept. 8, 2011.

69. Reedy, "Moynihan's Scholarly Tantrum," *(MORE)*, June 1971, 7.

70. "New York City Catches Up: Has a Journalism Review," *Wall Street Journal*, May 19, 1971, 16.

71. "Best Bets," *New York*, May 24, 1971, 52.
72. "News-Media Review Begins Publication," *New York Times*, May 19, 1971, 45.
73. Hentoff, "Broyard & *(MORE)*," *Village Voice*, May 13, 1971, 19–20.
74. "Literati: 'More' Deserves Encore," *Variety*, May 26, 1971, 54.
75. "The Media: Promising More," *Newsweek*, June 14, 1971, 64.

Chapter 3 The Marble Admonition

1. Richardson, *Bomb in Every Issue*.
2. Pristin, discussion with the author, Dec. 17, 2011.
3. Pristin, "Is Anybody Downtown Listening?" *(MORE)*, Oct. 1971, 6–8.
4. Pristin, discussion with the author, Dec. 17, 2011.
5. Ibid.
6. Lukas, "Life in These United States," *(MORE)*, June 1971, 3–4.
7. Cowan, "Slicking Over the Oil Industry," *(MORE)*, June 1971, 7–9.
8. Welles, "Soft Times for Wall Street," *(MORE)*, Dec. 1971, 1, 10–13.
9. Norman, conversation with the author, Dec. 14, 2011.
10. von Hoffman, "Where Not to Find Your New Car," *(MORE)*, Nov. 1971, 1, 14.
11. MacDougall, "For Kraft Cheese, How About a Cow?" *(MORE)*, Nov. 1971, 8–9.
12. Hentoff, ". . . and on the Printed Page," *(MORE)*, Jan. 1972, 9–11.
13. Asher, "Smoking Out Smokey the Bear," *(MORE)*, Mar. 1972, 12–14.
14. Cassidy, "Stripping Out the Facts," *(MORE)*, Apr. 1972, 3–5.
15. Ridgeway, "Exploits of 'The New Adventurers,'" *(MORE)*, July 1972, 1, 18–20.
16. Navasky, "Substantiating the 'Permissible Lie,'" *(MORE)*, Dec. 1972, 5–7.
17. Green, "Talking Back to the Hucksters," *(MORE)*, Oct. 1973, 6–9.
18. McCartney, "How IBM Spindles the Media," *(MORE)*, Sept. 1973, 1, 19–21.
19. *(MORE)* Advertising Rates advertisement, *(MORE)*, Mar. 1973, 17.
20. Woodward, Column Two, *(MORE)*, Mar. 1973, 2.
21. Hume, *Inside Story*.
22. Lukas, "Say It Ain't So, Scotty," *(MORE)*, May 1973, 1, 17–22.
23. Pinsky, "Riding the Airwaves to Washington," *(MORE)*, Mar. 1973, 4–6.
24. Aronson, "On Assignment with WFBI," *(MORE)*, Feb. 1972.
25. Diamond, "Fishing in Ellsberg's Wake," *(MORE)*, Jan. 1972, 1, 13–16.
26. Pollak, "Trying to Remember Vietnam," *(MORE)*, Mar. 1973, 8–9.
27. Ibid., 8.
28. Ibid., 9.
29. Price, "How to Become a Reliable Source," *(MORE)*, May 1973, 11, 14–15.

30. Ibid., 11.

31. Ibid., 15.

32. Kuttner, "Politics of Leaksmanship," *(MORE)*, Nov. 1973, 1, 14–16.

33. Ibid., 16.

34. Jacqueney, "Nibbling at the Bureaucracy," *(MORE)*, Oct. 1973, 15–17.

35. Whittemore, "Plugging of the President," *(MORE)*, Feb. 1972, 4–6.

36. Harris, "Strange Love of Dr. Kissinger," *(MORE)*, Mar. 1972, 1, 14–16.

37. Nolan, "Ron among the Plastic Alligators," *(MORE)*, Sept. 1972, 11–13.

38. Kaplan, "Preserving Dignity on 43rd Street," Big Apple, *(MORE)*, Dec. 1973, 12.

39. Roddy, Column Two, *(MORE)*, Oct. 1973, 2, 20–21.

40. Kuttner, "Television Turns on Nixon," *(MORE)*, Dec. 1973, 5–6.

41. Sayre et al., "Underneath the Nixon Landslide," *(MORE)*, Dec. 1972, 1, 15–17.

42. Hellbox, *(MORE)*, Aug. 1973, 2.

43. Sherman, "Long Good-Bye," *Vanity Fair*, Nov. 30, 2012.

44. If the *Times* was the most influential paper in the profession of journalism, then obviously influencing the influencer would allow *(MORE)* to have its most powerful impact on the profession and the industry.

45. Roddy, "Notes from a Bargain Typewriter," *(MORE)*, Nov. 1971, 3–5.

46. Ibid., 3.

47. Howard, "No. 3274 Looks Back," *(MORE)*, Jan. 1973, 4.

48. Ibid., 5.

49. Pristin, "Singles Set," *(MORE)*, July 1973, 12–13.

50. "Cupid, Changes at Newsday, and That Penthouse Boy," Big Apple, *(MORE)*, Jan. 1973, 8–9.

51. Kutik, "Competition for the Post?" *(MORE)*, Jan. 1973, 7, 10.

52. Kempton, "Effort to Break with Tradition," *(MORE)*, Apr. 1972, 6–7, 17–20.

53. Ibid., 6.

54. Kilday, "Short, Unhappy Life of L.A.," *(MORE)*, Feb. 1973, 7–9, 16.

55. Pristin, Column Two, *(MORE)*, Aug. 1973, 2.

56. Roddy, "New Intellectuals," *(MORE)*, July 1973, 16–17.

57. Pristin, "Up with People," Big Apple, *(MORE)*, Aug. 1973, 13.

58. Cohen, "Top Secret," Big Apple, *(MORE)*, Oct. 1973, 12–13.

59. Kovach, "Fighting over Boston's *Phoenix*," *(MORE)*, July 1972, 8.

60. "*The Phoenix* (cont'd)," Hellbox, *(MORE)*, Aug. 1972, 2, 16

61. "(Still) Fighting over *The Phoenix*," *(MORE)*, Sept. 1972, 2.

62. MacDougall, "Up Against *The Wall Street Journal*," *(MORE)*, Oct. 1972, 1, 12–18.

63. MacDougall, "Boring from within the Bourgeois Press," Part I," and "Boring from within the Bourgeois Press: Part II"; and MacDougall, "Memoirs

of a Radical in the Mainstream Press." For a longer discussion of the MacDougall incident, see Reese, "News Paradigm and the Ideology of Objectivity."

64. Fisher, "La Participation," *(MORE)*, Oct. 1972, 8–11.

65. *Branzburg v. Hayes*, 408 U.S. 665 (1972).

66. Goodman, "On 44 Hours in Civil Jail," *(MORE)*, Apr. 1972, 12–14.

67. Graham, "Will Earl Caldwell Go to Jail?" *(MORE)*, June 1972, 1, 14–16.

68. Ibid., 1.

69. Bridge, "In Defense of Newsmen's Rights," *(MORE)*, Nov. 1972, 3–4; Landau, "Harassing the Press," and Lewis, "Bad Time for Civil Liberties," *(MORE)*, Dec. 1972, 8–11.

70. Strainchamps, "Why We Can't Say B——shit," *(MORE)*, July 1972, 8.

71. Roddy, "Judge Tyler's New Mature Courtroom," *(MORE)*, Apr. 1973, 13–15.

72. McIntyre, "Muting Megaphone Mark," *(MORE)*, July 1973, 5–6.

73. Hentoff, ". . . and on the Printed Page," *(MORE)*, Jan. 1972, 9–10.

74. "'Are We Sure They're Just Eating with Their Hands, Bernie?'" Big Apple, *(MORE)*, Nov. 1973, 12–13.

75. Volz, "Post-Ombudsman," *(MORE)*, Jan. 1972, 3–5.

76. Lukas, "Limits of Self-Criticism," *(MORE)*, Sept. 1972, 3, 15, 17.

77. Pollak, "Case against Press Councils," *(MORE)*, Feb. 1973, 3.

78. Ibid.

79. Smith, "Why So Little Investigative Reporting?" *(MORE)*, Nov. 1973, 7–9.

80. Kaplan, "'Literature of Exposure,'" *(MORE)*, Sept. 1973, 3–6.

81. Potts, "Surviving the TV Newsroom," *(MORE)*, Mar. 1972, 6–8.

82. Reisig, "'Biggest Freeloaders Around'" *(MORE)*, May 1972, 5–8.

83. McCormally, "Who Cares about the Pulitzer Prize?" *(MORE)*, May 1972, 9–11.

84. Lukas, "Prince of Gonzo," *(MORE)*, Nov. 1972, 4–7.

85. Trillin, "Further More: On Using Newspapers," *(MORE)*, Dec. 1973, 24, 22.

86. Rubin, "You Are What You Eat," *(MORE)*, Dec. 1973, 7–9.

87. Kaplan, "Baptism," Big Apple, *(MORE)*, Oct. 1973, 13.

88. Accounting books of Marty Norman, Private collection.

89. Van Gelder, "Passionate Parvenu: A Guide," *(MORE)*, Oct. 1971, 5–6.

90. Sherr, "Some *Mad* Predictions," *(MORE)*, Apr. 1972, 8–9.

91. Thompson, "Lindsay Tosses Aurelio in Ring," *(MORE)*, Feb. 1972, 12–13.

92. "Games *Times*men Play?" Big Apple, *(MORE)*, Nov. 1972, 10.

93. Shafer, "Rise and Fall of the 'Bus Plunge' Story," *Slate*, Nov. 13, 2006.

94. Brownmiller, "Brownmiller Reviews Mailer . . . Almost," *(MORE)*, Oct. 1971, 1, 16.

95. Ibid., 1.

96. Mailer, letter to the editor, *(MORE)*, Nov. 1971, 16, 18.

97. Howard, "Watch Your Language, Men," *(MORE)*, Feb. 1972, 3.
98. Ibid., 4.
99. Siegel, "'He'll Think You Baked All Day,'" *(MORE)*, May 1972, 14.
100. "Good News, Bad News," Big Apple, *(MORE)*, Feb. 1973, 11.
101. Pristin, "Progress Report," Big Apple, *(MORE)*, Aug. 1973, 12.
102. Ibid., 13.
103. Pristin, Column Two, *(MORE)*, Aug. 1973, 2.
104. Dunbar, "Notes from the Belly of the Whale," *(MORE)*, Apr. 1972, 1.
105. Ibid., 1.
106. Pristin, "*Esquire's* Black Pointy-Heads," *(MORE)*, Jan. 1973, 6–7.
107. "Blackout?" Hellbox, *(MORE)*, Jan. 1973, 18.

Chapter 4 The Gathering of the Gothamedia

1. Letter from William Woodward III to Abe Rosenthal, February 25, 1972, NY Times Records: Rosenthal Papers, box 87, folder 8.
2. See Lerner, "Abe Rosenthal's Project X."
3. Letter from A. M. Rosenthal to William Woodward III, March 1, 1972, NY Times Records: Rosenthal Papers, box 87, folder 8.
4. Schudson, "Objectivity, News Management, and the Critical Culture," in *Discovering the News*, 160–94.
5. Lukas, "Taking Our Cue from Joe," *(MORE)*, May 1972, 1.
6. Ibid., 18.
7. It is worth pointing out, however, that Agnew did not use the famous phrase "nattering nabobs of negativism" to refer to the press. That coinage, attributed to speechwriter and future *New York Times* columnist William Safire, was directed at politicians who criticized President Nixon. He seems never to have used the term "Gothamedia" in public. See Lewis, "Myth of Spiro Agnew's 'Nattering Nabobs of Negativism.'"
8. Crouse, *Boys on the Bus*.
9. Zelizer, "Journalists as Interpretive Communities."
10. Hofstadter, *Anti-Intellectualism in American Life*, 25.
11. See Gans, *Deciding What's News*; and Tuchman, *Making News*.
12. Pristin, Interview with the author, Dec. 17, 2011.
13. "Why a Counter-Convention," *(MORE)*, May 1972.
14. Letter from Woody Woodward to Abe Rosenthal, NY Times Records: Rosenthal Papers, box 87, folder 8.
15. "Nathan's Employes [*sic*] End Their Strike; Agree to Arbitrate," *New York Times*, May 19, 1972, 57.
16. "A. J. Liebling Counter-Convention," *Chicago Journalism Review*, May 1972.
17. Quinn, "Journalism's New Nation: New Journalism's Counter-Convention: Egos and Insult," *Washington Post*, Apr. 26, 1972, D1–D2.

18. Long, "A. J. Liebling Counter-Convention Colossus," *Quill*, June 1972, 34.

19. Meehan, "The Time Renata Adler Didn't Dump Soup on Tom Wolfe's Head," *Saturday Review*, June 3, 1972, 22–24.

20. Charles Long, in "A. J. Liebling Counter-Convention Colossus" (*Quill*, June 1972), says 1,500 crowded into the room for the New Journalism panel alone; in her article for the *Philadelphia Journalism Review*, "Seeds of Revolution," Patricia McBroom hedged with "several hundred"; the *Chicago Journalism Review* ("A. J. Liebling Counter-Convention") had it at between two thousand and three thousand; Sally Quinn in the *Washington Post* said "nearly 2,000 attended each day's sessions" ("Journalism's New Nation . . ."); *Time* had "some 2,000" ("Journalism's Woodstock"), as did *The Progressive* (Erwin Knoll, "New Journalists, Old Journalism"); *Newsweek* said "more than 1,500" ("The Enemy Within"); Nora Sayre, in her chapter on the convention in *Sixties Going on Seventies*, is the most optimistic, putting the number at three thousand, which is the same number that *(MORE)* itself later reported (Richard Pollak, "After the Counter-Convention," *(MORE)*, June 1972, 3).

21. Letter from J. Anthony Lukas and Nora Ephron, co-chairmen to "Colleagues," NY Times Records: Rosenthal Papers, box 87, folder 8.

22. A. J. Liebling Counter-Convention Draft Program, NY Times Records: Rosenthal Papers, box 87, folder 8

23. "Best Bets: The Press Gang," ed. Stock, *New York*, Apr. 24, 1972.

24. *WBAI Folio* 13, no. 4 (April 1972(: 26–27 (April Listings).

25. " A. J. Liebling Counter-Convention," *Chicago Journalism Review*, May 1972, 4.

26. McBroom, telephone interview with the author, Mar. 30, 2013.

27. "Journalism's Woodstock," *Newsweek*, May 8, 1972, 96.

28. "Enemy Within," *Newsweek*, May 8, 1972, 62; and Quinn, "Journalism's New Nation," *Washington Post*, Apr. 26, 1972, D2.

29. Quinn, "Journalism's New Nation," *Washington Post*, Apr. 26, 1972, D2.

30. See Wolfe, "Birth of 'The New Journalism,'" *New York Magazine*, Feb. 14, 1972.

31. "Tom Wolfe and His Dirigible," *(MORE)*, July 1972, 11, 16.

32. Meehan, "Time Renata Adler Didn't Dump Soup," *Saturday Review*, June 3, 1972, 22–24; " A. J. Liebling Counter-Convention," *Chicago Journalism Review*, May 1972, 4.

33. Handwritten notes from first A. J. Liebling Counter-Convention, Sayre Papers, box 40, folder 6.

34. Meehan, "Time Renata Adler Didn't Dump Soup," *Saturday Review*, June 3, 1972,," 22–23.

35. Carr and Parker, "House of Cards: What Happens When a Reporter Becomes an Army of One?" *New York Times* Media Decoder blog, Feb. 28 2013.

36. Diamond, "Cabal at the New York Times: Which Way to the Revolution?" New York, May 18, 1970.

37. Dorfman, "Truth, Justice and the American Way."

38. Long, "A. J. Liebling Counter-Convention Colossus," *Quill*, June 1972, 36.

39. "A. J. Liebling Counter-Convention," *Chicago Journalism Review*, May 1972, 4.

40. A. J. Liebling Counter-Convention program, Sayre Papers, box 40, folder 6.

41. "Enemy Within," *Newsweek*, May 8, 1972, 61.

42. Quinn, "Countering the Publishers," *Washington Post*, Apr. 24, 1972, B3.

43. Quinn, "Journalism's New Nation," *Washington Post*, Apr. 26, 1972, D2.

44. Folsom, *Mad Ones*, 5.

45. Quinn, "Journalism's New Nation," *Washington Post*, Apr. 26, 1972, D2.

46. Knoll, "New Journalists, Old Journalism," Progressive, June 1972, 39.

47. Quinn, "Journalism's New Nation," *Washington Post*, Apr. 26, 1972, D2.

48. Handwritten note from Claudia Dreifus to Nora Sayre, Sayre Papers, box 40, folder 6.

49. Quinn, "Journalism's New Nation," *Washington Post*, Apr. 26, 1972, D2.

50. Handwritten notes from first A. J. Liebling Counter-Convention, Sayre Papers, box 40, folder 6.

51. Quinn, "Journalism's New Nation," *Washington Post*, Apr. 26, 1972, D2.

52. Ibid.

53. Handwritten notes from first A. J. Liebling Counter-Convention, Sayre Papers, box 40, folder 6.

54. McBroom, Telephone interview with the author, Mar. 30, 2013.

55. "A. J. Liebling Counter-Convention," *Chicago Journalism Review*, May 1972, 3.

56. J. Anthony Lukas Oral History Memoir.

57. Memo from "A.M.R." to Mr. Sulzberger, March 15, 1972, NY Times Records: Rosenthal Papers, box 87, folder 8.

58. Greenwald, *Woman of the* Times.

59. Memo from Charlotte Curtis to Mr. Sulzberger, March 23, 1972, NY Times Records: Rosenthal Papers, box 87, folder 8.

60. Memo from "A.M.R." to Seymour Topping, April 6, 1972, NY Times Records: Rosenthal Papers, box 87, folder 8.

61. Letter from "A.M.R." to Michael Kramer, October 6, 1976, NY Times Records: Rosenthal Papers, box 87, folder 8.

62. Draft of letter to the editor of *(MORE)* by Dorothy Schiff, September 22, 1971, Schiff Papers, box 38.

63. Memo from "Bob" [Spitzler] to "Paul" [Sann], September 23, 1971, Schiff Papers, box 38.

64. Annotated transcript of WBAI broadcast of "What Kind of P.M. Paper Should New York Have?" Schiff Papers, box 38.

65. Memo from Bill Hanway to Floyd Barger and M. J. O'Neill, April 26, 1972, Schiff Papers, box 38.

66. McBroom, "Seeds of Revolution," *Philadelphia Journalism Review*, June 1972.

67. Ibid.

68. A. J. Liebling Counter-Convention program, 1972, Sayre Papers, box 40, folder 6.

69. "As Soon as You Want Something . . ." *(MORE)*, June 1972, 4.

70. "A. J. Liebling Counter-Convention," *Chicago Journalism Review*, May 1972, 6.

71. McBroom, "Seeds of Revolution," *Philadelphia Journalism Review*, June 1972, 3.

72. Handwritten notes from first A. J. Liebling Counter-Convention, Sayre Papers, box 40, folder 6.

73. Quinn, "Journalism's New Nation," *Washington Post*, Apr. 26, 1972, D2.

74. McBroom, "Seeds of Revolution," *Philadelphia Journalism Review*, June 1972, 3.

75. McBroom, Telephone interview with the author, Mar. 30, 2013.

76. "Counter-Convention (cont'd)," *(MORE)*, July 1972, 21.

77. Kilday, "Meet the Press."

78. "Darts and Laurels," *Columbia Journalism Review*, July/Aug. 1972, 7.

79. See Herman and Chomsky, *Manufacturing Consent*; and Alterman, *What Liberal Media?*.

Chapter 5 Get Me Rewrite

1. Program of The Second A. J. Liebling Counter-Convention, Sayre Papers, box 40, folder 6.

2. United States Bureau of Labor Statistics CPI Inflation Calculator.

3. Quinn, "*(MORE)* Party," *Washington Post*, May 4, 1973, B1.

4. "Things to Do," *D.C. Gazette*, Apr. 25, 1973, 9.

5. von Hoffman, "Pardon . . . Me," *Washington Post*, May 7, 1972, 3–5.

6. "NPR Special: Journalistic Lessons of Vietnam War."

7. Ibid.

8. Quinn, "*(MORE)* Party," *Washington Post*, May 4, 1973, B2.

9. "Convention Discriminates, NOW Says," *Washington Post*, May 5, 1973, C3.

10. MacPherson, "Meet the Press," *Washington Post*, May 7, 1973, B3.

11. Quinn, "*(MORE)* Party," *Washington Post*, May 4, 1973, B2.

12. Woodward, Column Two, *(MORE)*, Mar. 1973, 2.

13. Jones, Interview with the author, Nov. 14, 2011.

14. Program of The Second A. J. Liebling Counter-Convention, Sayre Papers, box 40, folder 6.

15. Handwritten notes from second A. J. Liebling Counter-Convention, Sayre Papers, box 40, folder 6.

16. Krassner, *D.C. Gazette*, July 1973, 22.

17. MacPherson, "Meet the Press," *Washington Post*, May 7, 1973, B3.

18. Ibid.

19. Pollak, Column Two, *(MORE)*, June 1973, 2, 14–15.

20. Ibid., 14.

21. Jones, Interview with the author, Nov. 14, 2011.

22. Friedman, interview with the author, Jan. 17, 2014.

23. This portrait of the office was compiled from interviews with Richard Pollak (Sept. 8, 2011, and Feb. 21, 2012), Kathy Jones (Nov. 14, 2011), David Lusterman (Oct. 31, 2011, via telephone), and Malcolm Frouman (Oct. 27, 2011).

24. Nelson, "Money Makes the Press Go 'Round," *(MORE)*, Mar. 1974, 1.

25. Ridgeway, "Trying to Catch the Energy Crisis," *(MORE)*, Jan. 1974, 1.

26. Perry, "'I See a Big White House . . .'" *(MORE)*, Apr. 1974, 1.

27. Schickel, "Truth Went Thataway," *(MORE)*, Feb. 1974, 1.

28. Cockburn, "How to Earn Your Trench Coat," *(MORE)*, May 1974, 24.

29. Ibid.

30. Cockburn, "Death Rampant! Readers Rejoice," *(MORE)*, Dec. 1973, 1.

31. "10 Worst," *(MORE)*, May 1974, 16–17.

32. Pollak, interview with the author, Sept. 8, 2011.

33. Lusterman, telephone interview with the author, Oct. 31, 2011.

34. Advertisement for Mobil, *(MORE)*, July 1974, 15.

35. Pollak, "Firing of Denny Walsh," Column Two, *(MORE)*, Sept. 1974, 2.

36. Hume, "Mayor, *The Times*, and the Lawyers," *(MORE)*, Aug. 1974, 1, 16–18.

37. Rubin, "Perils of Muckraking," *(MORE)*, Sept. 1974, 5–9.

38. Howard, "'Stay Right Where You Are, Geraldo Is Coming!'" *(MORE)*, Sept. 1974, 11.

39. Cockburn, "Here's to Old Blue Eyes (59)," *(MORE)*, Sept. 1974, 17.

40. Epstein, "Furthermore: The Media as Villain." *(MORE)*, Sept. 1974, 24.

41. Jones, interview with the author, Nov. 14, 2011.

42. Program of *(MORE)*'s Third A. J. Liebling Counter-Convention, *(MORE)*, May 1974, 32.

43. Barhrach, "Countering: [MORE] than a Convention," *Washington Post*, May 13, 1974, B4.

44. Ibid.

45. "Good, the Bad & the Boring," *Village Voice*, May 16, 1974, 25.

46. Jones, interview with the author, Nov. 14, 2011.

47. MacPherson, "Meet the Press," *Washington Post*, May 7, 1973, B3.

48. Advertisement for *(MORE)*'s Third A. J. Liebling Counter-Convention, *(MORE)*, May 1974, 30.

49. Barhrach, "Countering: [MORE] than a Convention," *Washington Post*, May 13, 1974, B4.

50. Reisig, "Is Journalism an Air-Brushed Profession?" *Village Voice*, May 16, 1974, 24.

51. Cockburn, "Press Clips," *Village Voice*, May 16, 1974.

52. Jones, interview with the author, Nov. 14, 2011.

53. Barhrach, "Countering: [MORE] than a Convention," *Washington Post*, May 13, 1974, B4.

54. Cockburn, "Press Clips," *Village Voice*, May 16, 1974.

55. Trillin, "Weekend in a Panel Colony," *(MORE)*, June 1974, 15.

56. Jones, interview with the author, Nov. 14, 2011.

57. Trillin, "Weekend in a Penal Colony," *(MORE)*, June 1974, 18.

58. Jones, interview with the author, Nov. 14, 2011.

59. "For [MORE] Information . . .," produced by Anita Frankel, February 1975, Pacifica Radio.

60. Jones, interview with the author, Nov. 14, 2011.

61. Random Notes, *Rolling Stone*, Apr. 10, 1974, 14.

62. MacDougall, telephone interview with the author, Aug. 18, 2012.

63. Norman, interview with the author, Dec. 13, 2011.

64. *Washington Journalism Review*, Dec. 1981.

65. Advertisement for Liebling IV, *(MORE)*, Apr. 1975, 11.

66. Pollak, "Liebling IV," *(MORE)*, July 1975, 14.

67. Witcover, "Media in the Mirror," *Progressive*, July 1975, 28–29.

68. Durbin, "Journalists at Play: The *(MORE)* the Merrier?" *Village Voice*, May 19, 1975, 7–9.

69. Ibid., 9.

70. Pollak, *Stop the Presses, I Want to Get Off!*, back cover (Talese and Rather), ix–xiii (Pollak).

71. Friedman, Review of *Stop the Presses, I Want to Get Off!*

72. Dennis, Review of *Stop the Presses, I Want to Get Off!*

73. Wills, "What's Wrong with This Magazine?" *(MORE)*, June 1975, 6–8.

74. "Sale of More Magazine Being Negotiated," *New York Times*, Mar. 4, 1976.

75. Pollak, interview with the author, Sept. 8, 2011.

76. "First Annual Anchorman Face-Off," *(MORE)*, Apr. 1976, 16–17.

77. "Reflections on Hollywoodstein," *(MORE)*, Apr. 1976, 7–9.

78. Astor, "Gospel According to Mobil," *(MORE)*, Apr. 1976, 12–15.

Chapter 6 The Gadfly

1. Dorothy Schiff, Letter to the Editor of *(MORE)* (Draft), Sept. 22, 1971, Schiff Papers, box 38.

2. Memorandum from Jean Gillette to Dorothy Schiff, Sept. 28, 1971, Schiff Papers, box 38.

3. Transcript of telephone conversation between Dorothy Schiff and Richard Pollak, Sept. 22, 1971, Schiff Papers, box 38.

4. Dorothy Schiff, Letter to Hellbox (Draft), Oct. 4, 1971, Schiff Papers, box 38.

5. Dorothy Schiff, Memorandum to Paul Sann and James Wechsler, Oct. 4, 1971, Schiff Papers, box 38.

6. Missed phone call memorandum to Dorothy Schiff, Oct. 29, 1971, Schiff Papers, box 38.

7. *Newsweek* gives credit to Norman Isaacs's two Louisville papers for being the first, with a feature called "Beg Your Pardon" that began in 1969. According to *Newsweek* (Aug. 28, 1972), "Some 50 other U.S. newspapers have already approached the *Courier-Journal* for advice about starting a similar feature."

8. Moynihan, "Presidency & the Press."

9. Pollak, interview with the author, Feb. 21, 2012.

10. Hellbox item, *(MORE)*, June 1971, 23.

11. Hellbox item, *(MORE)*, July 1972, 21.

12. Pollak, interview with the author, Sept. 8, 2011.

13. Moynihan, "Presidency & The Press," 51.

14. Ibid., 46–47.

15. Max Frankel to Daniel Patrick Moynihan, Mar. 5, 1971, NY Times Records: Rosenthal Papers, box 30, folder 42.

16. Note from Max Frankel to Abe Rosenthal Mar. 15, 1971, NY Times Records: Rosenthal Papers, box 30, folder 42.

17. Memorandum from A. M. Rosenthal to Mr. Topping; Bullpen; Mr. Greenfield; Mr. Gelb; Mr. Roberts; Mr. Mullaney; Miss Curtis; Mr. Roach; Mr. Shepard, Dec. 21, 1970, Rosenthal Papers, box 4, vol. 1.

18. Siegal, e-mail to the author, Mar. 14, 2012.

19. A. M. Rosenthal to Daniel Patrick Moynihan, June 24, 1971, NY Times Records: Rosenthal Papers, box 30, folder 42.

20. Allan M. Siegal, email to the author, Mar. 14, 2012.

21. Pollak, interview with author, Sept. 8, 2011.

22. Program for the A .J. Liebling Counter-Convention, *(MORE)*, Apr. 1972, 23.

23. A. M. Rosenthal to Michael Kramer, Oct. 6, 1976, NY Times Records: Rosenthal Papers, box 87, folder 8.

24. Whitney, "Begging Your Pardon," 4.

25. Silverman, *Regret the Error*, 229.

26. Sanders, "What Are Daily Newspapers Doing to Be Responsive to Readers' Criticisms?," 151.

27. Barkin and Levy, "All the News That's Fit to Correct."

28. Whitney, "Begging Your Pardon," 3.

29. Hess, "Corrections: When the News Media Make Mistakes."

30. Nemeth and Sanders, "Meaningful Discussion of Performance Missing."

31. Maier, "Accuracy Matters."

32. Maier, "Setting the Record Straight."

33. Garfield, "Regret the Error 2014."

34. Bugeja and Peterson, "How Complete Are Newspaper Corrections?"

35. Bugeja, "Making Whole."

36. Wyatt, *Critical Conversations*.

37. Ibid., 148.

38. Hallin, *Uncensored War*.

39. Correction, *New York Times*, June 2, 1972.

40. *New York Times*, Mar. 9, 1972. *N.b.*: this is the British actress Helen Haye, not the better-known American actress Helen Hayes.

41. *New York Times*, Jan. 15, 1972.

42. Siegal, "Introduction," in *Kill Duck before Serving*, xiv.

43. Memorandum from A. M. Rosenthal to Mr. Topping; Bullpen; Mr. Greenfield; Mr. Gelb; Mr. Roberts; Mr. Mullaney; Miss Curtis; Mr. Roach; Mr. Shepard, Dec. 21, 1970, Rosenthal Papers, box 4, vol. 1.

44. Memorandum from A. M. Rosenthal to Bullpen; Mr. Gelb; Mr. Greenfield; Mr. Roberts; Mr. Alden; Miss Curtis; Mr. Frankel; Mr. Lieberman; Mr. Morris; Mr. Mullaney; Mr. Roach; Mr. Shepard; Mr. Witkin, Mar. 31, 1971, Rosenthal Papers, box 4, vol. 1.

45. A. M. Rosenthal to Edward W. Barrett, Director of the Communications Institute, June 1, 1972, NY Times Records: Rosenthal Papers, box 73, folder 3.

46. Memorandum from A. M. Rosenthal to Mr. Topping, Mr. Jordan, Mr. Hauck, and Mr. Butsikares, June 1, 1972. Private collection of Allan M. Siegal.

47. Memorandum from Lewis Jordan to ALL Desks and Summary—Thomas Ennis; Index—Martin Drucker; Composing Room, June 2, 1972, Rosenthal Papers, box 4, vol. 2.

48. *New York Times*, June 1, 1972.

49. Barrett, "Self-Coddling on Corrections."

50. Barrett, "Editorial Notebook: Department of Correction."

51. Raskin, "What's Wrong with American Newspapers?"

52. Wyatt, *Critical Conversations*, 148.

53. *Free and Responsible Press*.

54. Isaacs, *Untended Gates*.

55. "Beg Pardon," *Newsweek*, Aug. 28, 1972.

56. Memorandum from A. M. Rosenthal to Mr. Sulzberger, June 2, 1972, Rosenthal Papers, box 4, vol. 2.

57. Memorandum from A. O. Sulzberger to Mr. Rosenthal, June 12, 1972, Rosenthal Papers, box 4, vol. 2.

58. Memorandum from A. M. Rosenthal to Mr. Gelb; Mr. Jones; Mr. Greenfield; Miss Curtis; Mr. Mullaney, Apr. 4, 1973, NY Times Records: Rosenthal Papers, box 73, folder 3.

59. Postcard from Ric Cox to A. M. Rosenthal, Jan. 21, 1973, NY Times Records: Rosenthal Papers, box 73, folder 3.

60. Memo from AMR to Mr. Jordan, Apr. 2, 1973, NY Times Records: Rosenthal Papers, box 73, folder 3.

61. Sanders, "What Are Daily Newspapers Doing to Be Responsive to Readers' Criticisms?" 167.

62. Ibid., 151.

63. Barkin and Levy, "All the News That's Fit to Correct."

64. See, for example ibid.; Whitney, "Begging Your Pardon"; Hess, "Corrections: When the News Media Make Mistakes"; and Bugeja, "Making Whole."

65. Silverman, "Slate Shuts the Window."

66. Pollak, interview with the author, Feb. 21, 2012.

67. See, for two prime examples, Anderson, *Rebuilding the News*; and Usher, *Making News at the New York Times*.

68. Cottle, "New(s) Times"; and Willig, "Newsroom Ethnography in a Field Perspective."

69. See, for example, Schmidt, "Why hundreds of New York Times employees staged a walkout," *Washington Post*, June 30, 2017; Horowitz, "New York Times staffers stage walkout in support of copy editors," *CNN Money*, June 29, 2017; Kelly, "'Death panels' to break pink-slip news to dozens of NY Times copy editors," *New York Post*, July 11, 2017; and Pompeo, "Agony and Anxiety of The New York Times," *Vanity Fair*, July 24, 2017.

70. Rubin, "'Behind the Front Page,'" *(MORE)*, Nov. 1974, 7.

71. To be sure, though, the book has not been completely ignored. It was, for example, a major source for Michael Socolow in his history of the creation of the *New York Times* Op-Ed page. The editorial struggles over that "new feature's" inception occupy, in a coded manner, a large piece of Argyris's book; Socolow, "Profitable Public Sphere." Susan E. Tifft and Alex S. Jones also briefly tell the story of Argyris's newsroom intervention as a part of their history of the *Times*, *The Trust: The Private and Powerful Family behind The New York Times*.

72. Shafer, "Move over Bezos, ESPN can do news better than you," *Reuters*, Oct. 23, 2013.

73. Hofstadter, *Anti-Intellectualism in American Life*.

74. Rigney, "Three Kinds of Anti-Intellectualism: Rethinking Hofstadter."

75. For example, see Sigal, *Reporters and Officials*; Rachlin, *News as Hegemonic Reality*; and Tuchman, *Making News*.

76. Lerner, "Abe Rosenthal's Project X."

77. Rigney, "Three Kinds of Anti-Intellectualism: Rethinking Hofstadter," 444.

78. Carey, "Journalism and Criticism."

79. Ibid, 245.

80. Ibid., 234.

81. Schudson, *Discovering the News*.

82. Ibid, 7.

83. Argyris, *Behind the Front Page*, ix.

84. Ibid., x.

85. Balk, *Free and Responsive Press*.

86. Lerner, "Abe Rosenthal's Project X."

87. Ibid., xi.

88. Ibid., x.

89. Ibid., xiv.

90. Preliminary report of *New York Times* study by Chris Argyris. NY Times Records: Rosenthal Papers, box 2, folder 19.

91. Memo from James Reston to A. M. Rosenthal, Sept. 19, 1969, NY Times Records: Rosenthal Papers, box 2, folder 19.

92. Letter from Chris Argyris to A. O. Sulzberger. Nov. 6, 1968, NY Times Records: Rosenthal Papers, box 2, folder 19.

93. Argyris, *Behind the Front Page*, 177.

94. Socolow, "Profitable Public Sphere."

95. Letter from A. M. Rosenthal to Chris Argyris, May 15, 1973, NY Times Records: Rosenthal Papers, box 2, folder 19.

96. Letter from Harding Bancroft to Chris Argyris, June 13, 1973, NY Times Records: Rosenthal Papers, box 2, folder 19.

97. Memo from A. M. Rosenthal to Harding Bancroft, July 16, 1973, NY Times Records: Rosenthal Papers, box 2, folder 19.

98. Bancroft to Argyris, June 13, 1973, NY Times Records: Rosenthal Papers, box 2, folder 19.

99. Letter from A. M. Rosenthal to Chris Argyris, July 23, 1973, NY Times Records: Rosenthal Papers, box 2, folder 19.

100. Rubin, "Behind the Front Page," 7.

101. Rubin, interview with the author, Oct. 19, 2011.

102. Rubin, "Behind the Front Page," 7.

103. Memo from Harding Bancroft to Sulzberger, Oakes, Rosenthal, Veit, Dec. 4, 1973, NY Times Records: Rosenthal Papers, box 2, folder 19.

104. Cover, *(MORE)*, Nov. 1974.

105. Rubin, "Behind the Front Page," 8–9.

106. Memo from John B. Oakes to Harding Bancroft, Oct. 8, 1974, NY Times Records: Rosenthal Papers, box 2, folder 19.

107. Letter from Ray Jenkins to A. M. Rosenthal and enclosures, undated, NY Times Records: Rosenthal Papers, box 2, folder 19.

108. Letter from A. M. Rosenthal to Ray Jenkins, Nov. 8, 1974, NY Times Records: Rosenthal Papers, box 2, folder 19.

109. Letter from AMR to Andy Fisher, Jan. 3, 1975, NY Times Records: Rosenthal Papers, box 2, folder 19.

110. Letter from Argyris to AMR, Arthur Ochs Sulzberger, Chairman and President, James Reston, Vice President, Sydney Gruson, Executive Vice President, Harding F. Bancroft, Vice Chairman, John Oakes, Editor, Editorial Page, Nov. 6, 1974, NY Times Records: Rosenthal Papers, box 2, folder 19.

111. Letter from AMR to Chris Argyris (Bcc: Sulzberger, Reston, Gruson, Bancroft, Oakes), Nov. 12, 1974, NY Times Records: Rosenthal Papers, box 2, folder 19.

112. Letter from Chris Argyris to A. M. Rosenthal, Nov. 20, 1974, NY Times Records: Rosenthal Papers, box 2, folder 19.

Chapter 7 How the Press Became the Media

1. Kramer, interview with the author, Jan. 23, 2013.

2. Ibid.

3. Kramer, "New Lead," *More*, July/Aug. 1976, 2.

4. "Now More has a nose for more than just the news" (advertisement). *More*, Sept. 1976, 13.

5. Schwartz, "Establishing the Levels of the Game," *More*, July/Aug. 1976, 38.

6. Frouman, interview with the author, Oct. 27, 2011.

7. Levenstein, "ITT's Big Gamble on a Ten-Year-Old Kid," *More*, Sept. 1976, 22; Auletta, "How Carter Plays the Press," *More*, Oct. 1976, 12–22; and Stillman, "Make Way for the Show Biz Bards," *More*, Oct. 1976, 23–31.

8. Nachman, "Who's Afraid of the Broadway Critic?" *More*, July/Aug. 1977, 18–22.

9. Kramer, "Great New York Newspaper War," *More*, Jan. 1977, 12–13.

10. "We Remember Dolly," *More*, Jan. 1977, 14–17.

11. Ireland, "Rupert Murdoch Comes to Town," *More*, Jan. 1977, 18.

12. Kramer, interview with the author, Jan. 23, 2013.

13. Bradshaw and Neville, "Killer Bee Reaches New York," *More*, Feb. 1977, 12–23.

14. Ibid., 14.

15. Ibid., 23.

16. Ad for the 5th Liebling Counter-Convention, *More*, Nov. 1976, 36–37.

17. Ibid.

18. Kramer, interview with the author, Jan. 23, 2013.
19. Aronson, "On the Banquet Trail of the Failure of American Journalism."
20. Stepno, email to the author, June 28, 2012.
21. Friedman, interview with the author, Jan. 17, 2014.
22. Pollak, Handwritten list. Facsimile provided by Richard Pollak.
23. "*More*, the Review of Journalism, Being Sold to Washington Group," *New York Times*, Aug. 30, 1977.
24. Friedman, interview with the author, Jan. 17, 2014.
25. White, "*More* Changing Hands and Changing Goals," *Washington Post*, September 1, 1977, B1.
26. Ibid., B12.

Chapter 8 Further *(MORE)*

1. Letter from Richard Pollak to James Adler, Feb. 25, 1977 or 1978. Facsimile provided by Pollak.
2. Adler, "Under New Management," *More*, Oct. 1977, 2.
3. Masters, "Media Monopolies: Busting Up a Cozy Marriage," *More*, Oct. 1977, 12–13.
4. Buck, "Watertown, N.Y.: Suitable Grounds for Divorce?" *More*, Oct. 1977, 14–20.
5. Sandman, "Cross-Ownership on the Scales," *More*, Oct. 1977, 21–26.
6. Friedman, interview with the author, Jan. 17, 2014.
7. Buck, "Can The 'Post' Survive Rupert Murdoch?" *More*, Nov. 1977, 11–23.
8. Blount, "Weathercasters: Getting to Snow You," *More*, Apr. 1978, 30–35.
9. Hitchens, "Assassination in Nicosia," *More*, Apr. 1978, 22–23.
10. Collins, "*More* Magazine for Sale," *Washington Post*, Apr. 25, 1978.
11. Dougherty, "Backer for *More* Sought," *New York Times*, May 8, 1978.
12. "Publisher of *More* Seeking to Sell His Monthly Review of Journalism," *New York Times*, May 24, 1978.
13. Robinson, telephone interview with the author, Oct. 3, 2018.
14. Beker, telephone interview with the author, May 11, 2018.
15. Ibid.
16. Ibid.
17. Ibid.
18. Ibid.
19. Friedman, telephone interview with the author, Sept. 25, 2018.
20. Robinson, telephone interview with the author, Oct. 3, 2018.
21. "*More* Magazine Ends Publication to Join Journal at Columbia," *New York Times*, July 22, 1978.
22. Kramer, "[MORE] Journalism Review Donated to Publisher of Its Rival," *Washington Post*, July 22, 1978.
23. Deed of Gift of MORE Magazine to The Trustees of Columbia University, July 18, 1978. Copy provided by Richard Pollak.

24. Letter from James B. Adler to subscribers, July 27, 1978. Copy provided by Richard Pollak.

25. Ibid.

26. Pollak, interview with the author, Sept. 8, 2011.

27. Ibid.

28. Ibid.

29. Kramer, interview with the author, Jan. 23, 2013.

30. Friedman, interview with the author, Jan. 17, 2014.

31. Ibid.

32. Wyatt, *Critical Conversations*.

33. Ibid., 149–50.

34. Hayes, *Press Critics Are the Fifth Estate*, 4.

35. Ibid.

36. *Columbia Journalism Review*, Mar./Apr. 2013.

37. Freedman, "Survival of the Wrongest," *Columbia Journalism Review*, Jan./Feb. 2013.

38. "What Is Journalism For?" *Columbia Journalism Review*, Sept./Oct. 2013.

39. Lerner, "*(MORE)* guided journalists," *Columbia Journalism Review*, May 10, 2018.

40. Jones, "Media Business," *New York Times*, July 2, 1990.

41. Hayes, *Press Critics Are the Fifth Estate*, 86–87.

42. Ibid., 87.

43. Ibid., 93.

44. Alexander, "Modern Striking; Spies in the Press," *Chicago Reader*, Aug. 6, 1987.

45. Cook, "'Fox Mole' to Plead Guilty to Misdemeanor Charges over Gawker Posts," *Gawker*, May 9, 2013.

46. Holiday, *Conspiracy*.

47. Shafer, "Our National Pastime: Press Criticism," *Reuters*, Oct. 23, 2013.

48. Silver, "Real Story of 2016," *FiveThirtyEight*, Jan. 19, 2017.

49. Keller, "Is Glenn Greenwald the Future of News?" *New York Times*, Oct. 27, 2013.

50. Lerner, "Assessing James W. Carey's Culture of Journalism Criticism Four Decades Later."

51. "Bloomberg Link: Robert Friedman."

52. Gates, "Two Artistic Giants, and the Man Who Manipulated Them," *New York Times*, Mar. 12, 2011.

53. Frouman, interview with the author, Oct. 27, 2011.

54. Newhouse Faculty: David Rubin.

55. Fox, "Claudia Cohen, 56, Socialite and a Reporter of Gossip, Is Dead," *New York Times*, June 16, 2007.

56. Pristin, interview with the author, Dec. 17, 2011.

57. Jones, interview with the author, Nov. 14, 2011.

58. Yardley, "Heir to a Fortune, and to Tragedy; Suicide Ends the Life of a Wealthy, and Haunted, Man," New York Times, May 8, 1999.

59. Haberman, "J. Anthony Lukas, 64, an Author, Is Dead," *New York Times*, June 7, 1997.

60. Columbia Journalism School, *J. Anthony Lukas Prize Project Awards*.

61. Richard Pollak.com, *Bio*.

Bibliography

Archives

NY Times Records: Daniel Papers = New York Times Company Records, Clifton Daniel Papers, 1955–1979, MssCol 17789, Manuscripts and Archives Division, The New York Public Library.

NY Times Records: Rosenthal Papers = New York Times Company Records: A. M. Rosenthal Papers, 1955–1994, MssCol 17929, Manuscripts and Archives Division, The New York Public Library.

Rosenthal Papers = A. M. Rosenthal Papers, 1959–2004, MssCol 17930, Manuscripts and Archives Division, The New York Public Library.

Sayers Papers = Nora Sayer Papers, 1940–2001, MssCol 4847, Manuscripts and Archives Division, The New York Public Library.

Schiff Papers = Dorothy Schiff Papers, 1904–1989, MssCol l2691, Manuscripts and Archives Division, The New York Public Library.

Interviews

Beker, Brian. Telephone interview with the author, May 11, 2018.

Dorfman, Ron. Interview with the author, August 10, 2012.

Friedman, Robert. Interview with the author, January 17, 2014.

Friedman, Robert. Telephone interview with the author, September 25, 2018.

Frouman, Malcolm. Interview with the author, October 27, 2011.

Jones, Kathy. Interview with the author, November 14, 2011.

Kramer, Michael. Interview with the author, January 23, 2013.

Lukas, J. Anthony, Oral History Memoir. The American Jewish Committee Oral History Collection. Dorot Jewish Division, New York Public Library. Interviewed by Erik Barnouw, June 29–30, 1971. Edited and approved December 23, 1972.

Lusterman, David. Telephone interview with the author, October 31, 2011.

MacDougall, A. Kent. Telephone interview with the author, August 18, 2012.

McBroom, Patricia. Telephone interview with the author, April 30, 2013.

Norman, Marty. Conversation with the author, December 14, 2011.

Norman, Marty. Interview with the author, December 13, 2011.

Bibliography

Pollak, Richard. Interview with the author, September 8, 2011, and February 21, 2012.

Pristin, Terry. Discussion with the author, December 17, 2011.

Robinson, Steve. Telephone interview with the author, October 3, 2018.

Rubin, David M. Interview with the author, October 19, 2011.

Stepno, Bob. Email to the author, June 28, 2012.

Trillin, Calvin. Telephone interview with the author, June 21, 2012.

Published Sources

"The 10 Worst." *(MORE)*: A Journalism Review, May 1974, 16–17.

Accuracy in Media. "Our Mission." https://www.aim.org/about/mission-statement/

Addis, M. "A Study of the Surface Accuracy of *The Columbia Journalism Review* and *MORE*." MA thesis, Central Michigan University, 1974.

Adler, James B. "Under New Management." *More: The Media Magazine*, October 1977, 2.

Advertisement for Liebling III. *(MORE): A Journalism Review*, May 1974, 32.

Advertisement for Liebling IV. *(MORE): A Journalism Review*, April 1975, 11.

Advertisement for Mobil. *(MORE): A Journalism Review*, July 1974, 15.

Advertisement for *(MORE)*. *New York Times Book Review*, May 30, 1971, BR12.

Advertisement for *(MORE)*'s Third A. J. Liebling Counter-Convention. *(MORE): A Journalism Review*, May 1974, 30.

Advertisement for the Fifth A. J. Liebling Counter-Convention. *More: The Media Magazine*, November 1976, 36–37.

"The A. J. Liebling Counter-Convention." *Chicago Journalism Review*, May 1972, 3–6.

Alexander, Katina. "Modern Striking; Spies in the Press." *Chicago Reader*, August 6, 1987. http://www.chicagoreader.com/chicago/modern-striking-spies-in-the-press/Content?oid=870959 (accessed January 22, 2014).

Alterman, Eric. *What Liberal Media? The Truth about Bias and the News*. New York: Basic Books, 2003.

Anderson, C. W. *Rebuilding the News: Metropolitan Journalism in the Digital Age*. Philadelphia: Temple University Press, 2014.

"'Are We Sure They're Just Eating with Their Hands, Bernie?'" The Big Apple. *(MORE): A Journalism Review*, November 1973, 12–13.

Argyris, Chris. *Behind the Front Page: Organizational Self-Renewal in a Metropolitan Newspaper*. San Francisco: Jossey-Bass, 1974.

Aronson, James. "On Assignment with WFBI." *(MORE): A Journalism Review*, February 1972.

———. "On the Banquet Trail of the Failure of American Journalism." *In These Times*, January 5–11, 1977, 23.

"As Soon as You Want Something . . ." *(MORE): A Journalism Review*, June 1972, 4.

Asher, Thomas. "Smoking Out Smokey the Bear." *(MORE): A Journalism Review*, March 1972, 12–14.

Bibliography

Astor, Gerald. "The Gospel According to Mobil." *(MORE): A Journalism Review*, April 1976, 12–15.

Auletta, Ken. "How Carter Plays the Press." *More: The Media Magazine*, October 1976, 12–22.

Bagdikian, Ben H. "The American Newspaper Is Neither Record, Mirror, Journal, Ledger, Bulletin, Telegram, Examiner, Register, Chronicle, Gazette, Observer, Monitor, nor Herald of the Day's Events." *Esquire*, Mar. 1967, 124, 138–42.

———. *The Effete Conspiracy and Other Crimes by the Press*. New York: Harper & Row, 1972.

———. *The Information Machines: Their Impact on Men and the Media*. New York: Harper Colophon, 1971.

———. *The Media Monopoly*. Boston: Beacon Press, 1983.

Balk, Alfred. *A Free and Responsive Press*. New York: Twentieth Century Fund, 1972.

Banning, Stephen A. "The Professionalization of Journalism: A Nineteenth-Century Beginning." *Journalism History* 24, no. 4 (1998): 157–63.

Barhrach, Judy. "Countering: [MORE] than a Convention." *Washington Post*, May 13, 1974, B4.

Barkin, Steve M., and Mark R. Levy. "All the News That's Fit to Correct: Corrections in the *Times* and the *Post*." *Journalism Quarterly* 60, no. 2 (Summer 1983): 218–25.

Barrett, Edward W. "Editorial Notebook: Department of Correction." *Columbia Journalism Review*, Spring 1968, 35.

———. "Self-Coddling on Corrections." *Columbia Journalism Review*, July/August 1972, 47–49.

"Beg Pardon." *Newsweek*, August 28, 1972.

"Best Bets." *New York*, May 24, 1971, 52.

"Best Bets: The Press Gang." Edited by Ellen Stock. *New York*, April 24, 1972, 52.

"Blackout?" Hellbox. *(MORE): A Journalism Review*, January 1973, 18.

"Bloomberg Link: Robert Friedman." http://www.bloomberglink.com/people/robert-friedman/ (accessed January 22, 2014).

Blount, Roy, Jr. "Weathercasters: Getting to Snow You." *More: The Media Magazine*, April 1978, 30–35.

Bradshaw, Jon, and Richard Neville. "Killer Bee Reaches New York: The Sensational History of Rupert Murdoch." *More: The Media Magazine*, February 1977, 12–23.

Branzburg v. Hayes, 408 U.S. 665 (1972).

Braudy, Susan. *This Crazy Thing Called Love: The Golden World and Fatal Marriage of Ann and Billy Woodward*. New York: St. Martin's Paperbacks, 1992.

Brick, Howard. *Age of Contradiction: American Thought and Culture in the 1960s*. Ithaca, NY: Cornell, 1998.

Bridge, Peter J. "In Defense of Newsmen's Rights." *(MORE): A Journalism Review*, November 1972, 3–4

Bibliography

Brown, Lee. *The Reluctant Reformation: On Criticizing the Press in America*. New York: David McKay, 1974.

Brownmiller, Susan. *Against Our Will: Men, Women and Rape*. New York: Simon and Schuster, 1975.

———. "Brownmiller Reviews Mailer . . . Almost." *(MORE): A Journalism Review*, October 1971, 1, 16.

Buck, Rinker. "Can The 'Post' Survive Rupert Murdoch?" *More: The Media Magazine*, November 1977, 11–23.

———. "Watertown, N.Y.: Suitable Grounds for Divorce?" *More: The Media Magazine*, October 1977, 14–20.

Bugeja, Michael. "Making Whole: The Ethics of Correction." *Journal of Mass Media Ethics* 22, no.1 (April 2007): 49–65.

Bugeja, Michael, and Jane Peterson. "How Complete Are Newspaper Corrections? An Analysis of the 2005 'Regret the Error' Compilation." *Media Ethics* 18, no. 2 (Spring 2007). http://www.mediaethicsmagazine.com/index.php?option=com_content&view=article&id=2923347:how-complete-are-newspaper-corrections-an-analysis-of-the-2005-qregret-the-errorq-compilation&catid=138,100&Itemid=486.

Campbell, W. Joseph. "Cronkite 'the most-trusted'? Where's the evidence?" *Media Myth Alert*, June 9, 2012. https://mediamythalert.wordpress.com/2012/06/09/cronkite-the-most-trusted-wheres-the-evidence/.

———. *Getting It Wrong: Ten of the Greatest Misreported Stories in American Journalism*. Berkeley: University of California Press, 2010.

Carey, James W. "Journalism and Criticism: The Case of an Undeveloped Profession." *Review of Politics* 36, no. 2 (1974): 227–49.

Carr David, and Ashley Parker. "House of Cards: What Happens When a Reporter Becomes an Army of One?" *New York Times* Media Decoder blog, February 28, 2013. http://mediadecoder.blogs.nytimes.com/2013/02/28/house-of-cards-what-happens-when-a-reporter-becomes-an-army-of-one/.

"The Case Against the Media, by the Media." *New York*, July 25, 2016. http://nymag.com/intelligencer/2016/07/case-against-media.html?gtm=top.

Cassidy, Robert. "Stripping Out the Facts." *(MORE): A Journalism Review*, April 1972, 3–5.

Cockburn, Alexander. "Death Rampant! Readers Rejoice." *(MORE): A Journalism Review*, December 1973, 1.

———. "Here's to Old Blue Eyes (59)." *(MORE): A Journalism Review*, September 1974, 17.

———. "How to Earn Your Trench Coat." *(MORE): A Journalism Review*, May 1974, 24.

———. "Press Clips." *Village Voice*, May 16, 1974.

Cohen, Claudia. "Top Secret." The Big Apple. *(MORE): A Journalism Review*, October 1973, 12–13.

Collins, Nancy. "*More* Magazine for Sale." *Washington Post*, April 25, 1978, B4.

Columbia Journalism School. *The J. Lukas Prize Project Awards*. https://journalism.columbia.edu/lukas (accessed January 22, 2014).

Bibliography

"Convention Discriminates, NOW Says." *Washington Post*, May 5, 1973, C3.

Cook, John. "'Fox Mole' to Plead Guilty to Misdemeanor Charges over Gawker Posts." Gawker, May 9, 2013. http://gawker.com/fox-mole-to-plead-guilty-to-misdemeanor-charges-over-498575781 (accessed January 22, 2014).

"Correction." *New York Times*, June 2, 1972.

Cottle, Simon. "New(s) Times: Towards a 'Second Wave' of News Ethnography." *Communications* 25, no. 1 (2000): 19–41.

"The Counter-Convention (cont'd)." *(MORE): A Journalism Review*, July 1972, 21.

Cowan, Paul. "Slicking Over the Oil Industry." *(MORE): A Journalism Review*, June 1971, 7–9.

Crouse, Timothy. *The Boys on the Bus*. New York: Random House, 1973.

"Cupid, Changes at Newsday, and That Penthouse Boy." The Big Apple. *(MORE): A Journalism Review*, January 1973, 8–9.

Dabbous, Yasmine Tarek. "'Blessed Be the Critics of Newspapers': Journalistic Criticism of Journalism 1865–1930." PhD diss., Louisiana State University, 2010.

Daly, Christopher B. *Covering America: A Narrative History of a Nation's Journalism*. 2nd ed. Amherst: University of Massachusetts Press, 2018.

"Darts and Laurels." *Columbia Journalism Review*," July/August 1972, 7.

Dennis, Everette E. Review of "*Stop the Presses, I Want to Get Off!*" *Journalism Quarterly* 52, no. 4 (December 1975): 780.

DeZutter, Henry. "The trial: You had to be there." *Chicago Journalism Review*, March 1970, 3.

Diamond, Edwin. "The Cabal at the *New York Times*: Which Way to the Revolution?" *New York*, May 18, 1970, 42–45.

———. "Fishing in Ellsberg's Wake." *(MORE): A Journalism Review*, January 1972, 1, 13–16.

Dicken-Garcia, Hazel. *Journalistic Standards in Nineteenth-Century America*. Madison: University of Wisconsin Press, 1989.

Dorfman, Ron. "Battling the Myths in Chicago." *(MORE): A Journalism Review*, June 1971, 18.

———. "The Journalists' Movement." *Columbia Journalism Review*, July 1973, 5.

———. "Truth, Justice and the American Way." *Revue française d'études américaines* 6 (October 1978): 183–93.

Dougherty, Philip H. "Backer for *More* Sought." *New York Times*, May 8, 1978.

Draper, Robert. *Rolling Stone Magazine: The Uncensored History*. New York: Doubleday, 1990.

Dunbar, Ernest. "Notes from the Belly of the Whale." *(MORE): A Journalism Review*, April 1972, 1.

Durbin, Karen. "Journalists at Play: The *(MORE)* the Merrier?" *Village Voice*, May 19, 1975, 7–9.

Efron, Edith. *The News Twisters*. New York: Nash, 1971.

Emery, Michael, Edwin Emery, and Nancy L. Roberts. *The Press and America: An Interpretive History of the Mass Media*. 9th ed. Boston: Allyn and Bacon, 2000.

"The Enemy Within." *Newsweek*, May 8, 1972, 61–62.

259

Epstein, Joseph. "Furthermore: The Media as Villain." *(MORE): A Journalism Review*, September 1974, 24.

"The First Annual Anchorman Face-Off." *(MORE): A Journalism Review*, April 1976, 16–17.

Fisher, Shelley M. "La Participation." *(MORE): A Journalism Review*, October 1972, 8–11.

Fishkin, Shelley Fisher. *From Fact to Fiction: Journalism & Imaginative Writing in America*. Baltimore: Johns Hopkins University Press, 1985.

Fishman, Mark. *Manufacturing the News*. Austin: University of Texas Press, 1980.

Folsom, Tom. *The Mad Ones: Crazy Joe Gallo and the Revolution at the End of the Underworld*. New York: Weinstein Books, 2010.

"For [MORE] Information . . ." Produced by Anita Frankel. February 1975. Courtesy of the Pacifica Radio Archive.

Fox, Margalit. "Claudia Cohen, 56, Socialite and a Reporter of Gossip, Is Dead." *New York Times*, June 16, 2007. http://www.nytimes.com/2007/06/16/nyregion/16cohen.html (accessed January 22, 2014).

A Free and Responsible Press: A General Report on Mass Communication: Newspapers, Radio, Motion Pictures, Magazines, and Books. Chicago: Commission on Freedom of the Press, 1947.

Freedman, David H. "Survival of the Wrongest." *Columbia Journalism Review*, January/February 2013.

Friedman, Larry. Review of *Stop the Presses, I Want to Get Off! Tales of the News Business from the Pages of (MORE) Magazine*, by Richard Pollak. *Library Journal* 100, no. 10 (May 15, 1975): 979.

"Games *Times*men Play?" The Big Apple. *(MORE): A Journalism Review*, November 1972, 10.

Gans, Herbert. *Deciding What's News: A Study of CBS Evening News, NBC Nightly News, Newsweek, and Time*. Evanston, IL: Northwestern University Press, 2004.

Garfield, Bob. "Regret the Error 2014." *On the Media*, January 8, 2015. http://www.onthemedia.org/story/regret-error-2014/.

Gates, Anita. "Two Artistic Giants, and the Man Who Manipulated Them." *New York Times*, March 12, 2011. http://www.nytimes.com/2011/03/13/nyregion/13theatct.html (accessed January 22, 2014).

Gitlin, Todd. *The Whole World Is Watching: Mass Media in the Making and Unmaking of the New Left*. Berkeley: University of California Press, 2003.

Goldstein, Tom, ed. *Killing the Messenger: 100 Years of Media Criticism*. Rev. ed. New York: Columbia, 2007.

"The Good, the Bad & the Boring." *Village Voice*, May 16, 1974, 25.

"Good News, Bad News." The Big Apple. *(MORE): A Journalism Review*, February 1973, 11.

Goodman, Edwin A. "On 44 Hours in Civil Jail." *(MORE): A Journalism Review*, April 1972, 12–14.

Graham, Fred P. "Will Earl Caldwell Go to Jail?" *(MORE): A Journalism Review*, June 1972, 1, 14–16.

Bibliography

Green, Mark J. "Talking Back to the Hucksters." *(MORE): A Journalism Review*, October 1973, 6–9.

Greenwald, Marilyn. *A Woman of the Times: Journalism, Feminism, and the Career of Charlotte Curtis.* Athens: Ohio University Press, 1999.

Haberman, Clyde. "J. Anthony Lukas, 64, an Author, Is Dead." *New York Times*, June 7, 1997. http://www.nytimes.com/1997/06/07/nyregion/j-anthony-lukas-64-an-author-is-dead.html (accessed January 22, 2014).

Halberstam, David. *The Powers That Be.* New York: Knopf, 1979.

Hale, Grace Elizabeth. *A Nation of Outsiders: How the White Middle Class Fell in Love with Rebellion in Postwar America.* New York: Oxford University Press, 2011.

Hallin, Daniel C. *The Uncensored War: The Media and Vietnam.* Berkeley: University of California Press, 1989.

Harris, Richard. "The Strange Love of Dr. Kissinger." *(MORE): A Journalism Review*, March 1972, 1, 14–16.

Harrison, Stanley L. "'The Wayward Press' Revisited: The Contributions of Robert Benchley." *Journalism History* 19, no. 1 (1993): 19–27.

Haskell, Thomas L. *The Emergence of Professional Social Science.* Baltimore: Johns Hopkins University Press, 2000.

Hayes, Arthur S. *Press Critics Are the Fifth Estate: Media Watchdogs in America.* Westport, CT: Praeger, 2008.

Hellbox. *(MORE): A Journalism Review*, August 1973, 2.

Hellbox item. *(MORE): A Journalism Review,* July 1972, 21.

Hellbox item. *(MORE): A Journalism Review*, June 1971, 2.

Hentoff, Nat. ". . . and on the Printed Page," *(MORE): A Journalism Review*, January 1972, 9–11.

———. "Broyard & *(MORE)*." *The Village Voice*, May 13, 1971, 19–20.

Herman, Edward S., and Noam Chomsky. *Manufacturing Consent: The Political Economy of the Mass Media.* New York: Pantheon, 2002.

Hess, Stephen. "Corrections: When the News Media Make Mistakes." *Harvard International Review of Press/Politics* 3, no. 1 (Winter 1988): 122–25.

Hitchens, Christopher. "Assassination in Nicosia." *More: The Media Magazine*, April 1978, 22–23.

Hofstadter, Richard. *Anti-Intellectualism in American Life.* New York: Vintage, 1963.

Holiday, Ryan. *Conspiracy: Peter Thiel, Hulk Hogan, Gawker, and the Anatomy of Intrigue.* New York: Portfolio/Penguin, 2018.

Horowitz, Julia. "New York Times staffers stage walkout in support of copy editors." CNN Money, June 29, 2017. http://money.cnn.com/2017/06/29/media/new-york-times-copy-editor-walkout/index.html.

Howard, Jane. "No. 3274 Looks Back." *(MORE): A Journalism Review*, January 1973, 4.

———. "'Stay Right Where You Are, Geraldo Is Coming!'" *(MORE): A Journalism Review*, September 1974, 11.

261

Howard, Pamela. "Watch Your Language, Men." *(MORE): A Journalism Review*, February 1972, 3.

Hume, Brit. *Death and the Mines: Rebellion and Murder in the UMW*. New York: Grossman, 1971.

———. *Inside Story*. Garden City, NY: Doubleday, 1974.

———. "The Mayor, *The Times*, and the Lawyers." *(MORE): A Journalism Review*, August 1974, 1, 16–18.

Hynds, Ernest C. *American Newspapers in the 1970s*. New York: Hastings House, 1975.

Ireland, Doug. "Rupert Murdoch Comes to Town." *More: The Media Magazine*, January 1977, 18.

Irwin, Will. *The American Newspaper: A Series First Appearing in* Collier's, *January–July 1911*. Edited by Clifford Weigle and David G. Clark. Ames: Iowa State University Press, 1969.

Isaacs, Norman E. *Untended Gates: The Mismanaged Press*. New York: Columbia University Press, 1986.

Jacqueney, Theodore. "Nibbling at the Bureaucracy." *(MORE): A Journalism Review*, October 1973, 15–17.

Jefferson, Thomas. Letter to John Norvell, June 14, 1807. Document 29 in *The Founders' Constitution*, Vol. 5, *Amendment I (Speech and Press)*, edited by Philip B. Kurland and Ralph Lerner. Chicago: University of Chicago Press. http://press-pubs.uchicago.edu/founders/documents/amendI_speechs29.html

Jones, Alex S. "The Media Business: Media Critics Are Seeking to Turn Talk into Print." *New York Times*, July 2, 1990. http://www.nytimes.com/1990/07/02/business/the-media-business-media-critics-are-seeking-to-turn-talk-into-print.html (accessed March 21, 2013).

"Journalism's Woodstock." *Time*, May 8, 1972, 96.

Kaplan, Jim. "Preserving Dignity on 43rd Street." The Big Apple. *(MORE): A Journalism Review*, December 1973, 12.

Kaplan, Justin. "The 'Literature of Exposure.'" *(MORE): A Journalism Review*, September 1973, 3–6.

Kaplan, Peter. "Baptism." The Big Apple. *(MORE): A Journalism Review*, October 1973, 13.

Keller, Bill. "Is Glenn Greenwald the Future of News?" *New York Times*, October 27, 2013. http://www.nytimes.com/2013/10/28/opinion/a-conversation-in-lieu-of-a-column.html (accessed January 22, 2014).

Kelly, Keith J. "'Death panels' to break pink-slip news to dozens of NY Times copy editors." *New York Post*, July 11, 2017. http://nypost.com/2017/07/11/death-panels-to-break-pink-slip-news-to-dozens-of-ny-times-copy-editors/.

Kempton, Murray. "An Effort to Break with Tradition." *(MORE): A Journalism Review*, April 1972, 6–7, 17–20.

Kilday, Gregg J. "Meet the Press." *Harvard Crimson*, May 4, 1972.

———. "The Short, Unhappy Life of L.A." *(MORE): A Journalism Review*, February 1973, 7–9, 16.

Bibliography

Killen, Andreas. *1973 Nervous Breakdown: Watergate: Warhol, and the Birth of Post-Sixties America*. New York: Bloomsbury, 2006.

Kluger, Richard. *The Paper: The Life and Death of the* New York Herald-Tribune. New York: Knopf, 1986.

Knoll, Erwin. "New Journalists, Old Journalism." *Progressive*, June 1972, 38–39.

Kovach, Bill. "Fighting over Boston's *Phoenix*." *(MORE): A Journalism Review*, July 1972, 8.

Kovach, Bill, and Tom Rosenstiel. *The Elements of Journalism: What Newspeople Should Know and the Public Should Expect*. 3rd ed. New York: Three Rivers, 2014.

Kramer, Larry. "[MORE] Journalism Review Donated to Publisher of Its Rival." *Washington Post*, July 22, 1978, A7.

Kramer, Michael. "The Great New York Newspaper War." *More: The Media Magazine*, January 1977, 12–13.

———. "New Lead." *More: The Media Magazine*, July/August 1976, 2.

Krassner, Paul. *D.C. Gazette*, July 1973, 22.

Kutik, William. "Competition for the Post?" *(MORE): A Journalism Review*, January 1973, 7, 10.

Kuttner, Bob. "The Politics of Leaksmanship." *(MORE)*: A Journalism Review, November 1973, 1, 14–16.

———. "Television Turns on Nixon." *(MORE): A Journalism Review*, December 1973, 5–6.

Landau, Jack S. "Harassing the Press." *(MORE): A Journalism Review*, December 1972, 8–11.

Lerner, Kevin M. "Abe Rosenthal's Project X: The Editorial Process Leading to Publication of the Pentagon Papers." In *Media Nation: The Political History of News in Modern America*, edited by Bruce J. Schulman and Julian E. Zelizer, 144–59. Philadelphia: University of Pennsylvania Press, 2017.

———. "Assessing James W. Carey's Culture of Journalism Criticism Four Decades Later: A Case Study of the *New York Times* Profile of a White Nationalist." Paper presented at the International Association of Literary Journalism Studies, Vienna, May 17, 2018.

———. "*(MORE)* guided journalists during the 1970s media crisis of confidence." *Columbia Journalism Review*, May 10, 2018. https://www.cjr.org/the_profile/more-journalism-review.php.

———. "A System of Self-Correction: A. M. Rosenthal, Daniel Patrick Moynihan, Press Criticism and the Birth of the Contemporary Newspaper Correction in *The New York Times*." *Journalism History* 42, no. 4 (Winter 2017): 191–200.

Levenstein, Alan. "ITT's Big Gamble on a Ten-Year-Old Kid." *More: The Media Magazine*, September 1976, 22.

Lewis, Anthony. "Bad Time for Civil Liberties." *(MORE): A Journalism Review*, December 1972, 8–11.

Lewis, Norman P. "The Myth of Spiro Agnew's 'Nattering Nabobs of Negativism.'" *American Journalism* 27, no. 1 (2010): 89–115.

Liebling, A. J. "The Wayward Press: Do You Belong in Journalism?" *New Yorker*, May 14, 1960, 109.

Lippmann, Walter. *Liberty and the News*. New York: Harcourt, Brace and Howe, 1920.

———. *The Phantom Public*. New York: Macmillan, 1927.

———. *Public Opinion*. New York: Free Press, 1997.

Lippmann, Walter, and Charles Merz. "A Test of the News: An examination of the news reports in the *New York Times* on aspects of the Russian Revolution of special importance to Americans, March 1917–March 1920." Supplement to *The New Republic* 23, no. 296 (August 4, 1920).

"Literati: 'More' Deserves Encore." *Variety*, May 26, 1971, 54.

Long, Charles. "The A. J. Liebling Counter-Convention Colossus." *The Quill*, June 1972, 34.

Lukas, J. Anthony. *The Barnyard Epithet and Other Obscenities: Notes on the Chicago Conspiracy Trial*. New York: Harper and Row, 1970.

———. "Disorder Erupts at Chicago Trial After Judge Jails a Defendant for Using a Vulgarity." *New York Times*, February 5, 1970, 18.

———. "Life in These United States." *(MORE): A Journalism Review*, June 1971, 3–4.

———. "The Limits of Self-Criticism." *(MORE): A Journalism Review*, September 1972, 3, 15, 17.

———. "The Prince of Gonzo." *(MORE): A Journalism Review*, November 1972, 4–7.

———. "Say It Ain't So, Scotty." *(MORE): A Journalism Review*, May 1973, 1, 17–22.

———. "Taking Our Cue from Joe." *(MORE): A Journalism Review*, May 1972, 1.

———. "The Two Worlds of Linda Fitzpatrick." *New York Times*, October 16, 1967.

MacDougall, A. Kent. "Boring from within the Bourgeois Press: Part I." *Monthly Review* 40, no. 6 (November 1988): 13–24.

———. "Boring From Within the Bourgeois Press: Part II." *Monthly Review* 40, no. 8 (December 1988): 10–24.

———. "For Kraft Cheese, How About a Cow?" *(MORE): A Journalism Review*, November 1971, 8–9.

———. "Memoirs of a Radical in the Mainstream Press." *Columbia Journalism Review*, March/April 1989, 36–39.

———. ed. *The Press: A Critical Look from the Inside*. Princeton, NJ: Dow Jones Books, 1966–1972.

———. "Up Against *The Wall Street Journal*." *(MORE): A Journalism Review*, October 1972, 1, 12–18.

MacPherson, Myra. "Meet the Press." *Washington Post*, May 7, 1973, B3.

Maier, Scott R. "Accuracy Matters: A Cross-Market Assessment of Newspaper Error and Credibility." *Journalism and Mass Communication Quarterly* 82, no. 3 (Autumn 2005): 533–51.

———. "Setting the Record Straight: When the Press Errs, Do Corrections Follow?" *Journalism Practice* 1, no. 1 (2007): 33–43.

Bibliography

Mailer, Norman. Letter to the editor. *(MORE): A Journalism Review*, November 1971, 16, 18.

Marzolf, Marion Tuttle. *Civilizing Voices: American Press Criticism 1880–1950.* New York: Longman, 1991.

Masters, T. H. "Media Monopolies: Busting Up a Cozy Marriage." *More: The Media Magazine*, October 1977, 12–13.

McBroom, Patricia. "Seeds of Revolution." *Philadelphia Journalism Review,* June 1972, 3.

McCartney, Laton. "How IBM Spindles the Media." *(MORE): A Journalism Review*, September 1973, 1, 19–21.

McChesney, Robert W., and Ben Scott. Introduction to *The Brass Check: A Study of American Journalism*, by Upton Sinclair, ix–xxxiii. Urbana: University of Illinois Press, 2003.

———. eds. *Our Unfree Press: 100 Years of Radical Media Criticism.* New York: New Press, 2004.

McCormally, John. "Who Cares about the Pulitzer Prize?" *(MORE): A Journalism Review*, May 1972, 9–11.

McIntyre, Mark. "Muting Megaphone Mark." *(MORE): A Journalism Review*, July 1973, 5–6.

McMillian, John. *Smoking Typewriters: The Sixties Underground Press and the Rise of Alternative Media in America.* New York: Oxford, 2011.

"The Media: Promising More." *Newsweek*, June 14, 1971, 64.

Meehan, Thomas. "The Time Renata Adler Didn't Dump Soup on Tom Wolfe's Head." *Saturday Review*, June 3, 1972, 22–24.

Midura, Edmund W. "A. J. Liebling: The Wayward Pressman as Critic." *Journalism Monographs* 33 (April 1974): 8.

Mindich, Daniel T. Z. *Just the Facts: How "Objectivity" Came to Define American Journalism.* New York: New York University, 1998.

"*More* Magazine Ends Publication to Join Journal at Columbia." *New York Times*, July 22, 1978.

"More, the Review of Journalism, Being Sold to Washington Group." *New York Times*, August 30, 1977.

Mott, Frank Luther. *American Journalism.* 3rd ed. New York: Macmillan, 1962.

Moynihan, Daniel P. "The Presidency & the Press." *Commentary*, March 1971, 41–52.

Nachman, Gerald. "Who's Afraid of the Broadway Critic?" *More: The Media Magazine*, July/August 1977, 18–22.

"Nathan's Employes [*sic*] End Their Strike; Agree to Arbitrate." *New York Times*, May 19, 1972, 57.

Navasky, Victor S. "Substantiating the 'Permissible Lie.'" *(MORE): A Journalism Review*, December 1972, 5–7.

"Need Help?" *Chicago Journalism Review*, March 1970, 14.

Nelson, Madeline. "Money Makes the Press Go 'Round." *(MORE): A Journalism Review*, March 1974, 1.

Bibliography

Nemeth, Neil, and Craig Sanders. "Meaningful Discussion of Performance Missing." *Newspaper Research Journal* 22, no. 2 (Winter 2001): 52–64.

Newhouse Faculty: David Rubin. http://newhouse.syr.edu/faculty-staff/david-rubin (accessed January 22, 2014).

"New York City Catches Up: Has a Journalism Review." *Wall Street Journal*, May 19, 1971, 16.

"News-Media Review Begins Publication." *New York Times*, May 19, 1971, 45.

Nobile, Philip. *Intellectual Skywriting: Literary Politics and* The New York Review of Books. New York: Charterhouse, 1974.

Nolan, Martin. "Ron among the Plastic Alligators." *(MORE): A Journalism Review*, September 1972, 11–13.

Northington, Kristie Bunton. "Media Criticism as Professional Self-Regulation: A Study of U.S. Journalism Reviews." PhD diss., Indiana University, 1993.

"Now More has a nose for more than just the news." Advertisement on *More: The Media Magazine*, September 1976, 13.

"NPR Special: Journalistic Lessons of Vietnam War." 2nd Annual A. J. Liebling Counter Convention, May 4, 1973. Accessed via "Vietnam in the Age Of Gonzo Journalism—The AJ Liebling Counter Convention—1973." *Past Daily*. https://pastdaily.com/2014/03/10/vietnam-age-gonzo-journalism-aj-liebling-counter-convention-1973-past-daily-reference-room/.

Pauly, John J. "Finding Ourselves in the New Journalism." In *1968: Year of Media Decision*, edited by Robert Giles and Robert W. Snyder, 133–39. New Brunswick, NJ: Transaction Publishers, 2001.

Peck, Abe. *Uncovering the Sixties: The Life and Times of the Underground Press*. New York: Citadel, 1991.

Perry, James M. "'I See a Big White House . . .'" *(MORE): A Journalism Review*, April 1974, 1.

"*The Phoenix* (cont'd)." Hellbox. *(MORE): A Journalism Review*, August 1972, 2, 16.

Pinsky, Mark. "Riding the Airwaves to Washington." *(MORE): A Journalism Review*, March 1973, 4–6.

Pollak, Richard. "After the Counter-Convention." *(MORE): A Journalism Review*, June 1972, 3.

———. *Bio*. http://www.richardpollak.com/bio.htm (accessed January 22, 2014).

———. "A Case against Press Councils." *(MORE): A Journalism Review*, February 1973, 3.

———. Column Two. *(MORE): A Journalism Review*, June 1973, 2, 14–15.

———. "The Firing of Denny Walsh." Column Two. *(MORE): A Journalism Review*, September 1974, 2.

———. "An Intra-Family Sort of Thing." *(MORE): A Journalism Review*, October 1971, 3.

———. "Liebling IV." *(MORE): A Journalism Review*, July 1975, 14.

———. *Stop the Presses, I Want to Get Off! Tales of the News Business from the Pages of (MORE) Magazine*. New York: Random House, 1975.

Bibliography

———. "Trying to Remember Vietnam." *(MORE): A Journalism Review*, March 1973, 8–9.

Pompeo, Joe. "The Agony and Anxiety of *The New York Times*." *Vanity Fair*, July 24, 2017. https://www.vanityfair.com/news/2017/07/the-agony-and-the-anxiety-of-the-new-york-times.

Porwancher, Andrew. "Objectivity's Prophet: Adolph S. Ochs and the *New York Times*, 1896–1935." *Journalism History* 36, no. 4 (2011): 186–95.

Pöttker, Horst. "News and Its Communicative Quality: The Inverted Pyramid—When and Why Did It Appear?" *Journalism Studies* 4, no. 4 (2003): 501–11.

Potts, Robert. "Surviving the TV Newsroom." *(MORE): A Journalism Review*, March 1972, 6–8.

Povich, Lynn. *The Good Girls Revolt: How the Women of* Newsweek *Sued Their Bosses and Changed the Workplace*. New York: Public Affairs, 2012.

Pressman, Matthew. *On Press: The Liberal Values That Shaped the News*. Cambridge, MA: Harvard University Press, 2018.

Price, Anderson. "How to Become a Reliable Source." *(MORE): A Journalism Review*, May 1973, 11, 14–15.

Pristin, Terry. Column Two. *(MORE): A Journalism Review*, August 1973, 2.

———. "*Esquire*'s Black Pointy-Heads." *(MORE): A Journalism Review*, January 1973, 6–7.

———. "Is Anybody Downtown Listening?" *(MORE): A Journalism Review*, October 1971, 6–8.

———. "Progress Report." The Big Apple. *(MORE): A Journalism Review*, August 1973, 12.

———. "Singles Set." *(MORE): A Journalism Review*, July 1973, 12–13.

———. "Up with People." The Big Apple. *(MORE): A Journalism Review*, August 1973, 13.

"Publisher of *More* Seeking to Sell His Monthly Review of Journalism." *New York Times*, May 24, 1978.

Quinn, Sally. "Countering the Publishers." *Washington Post*, April 24, 1972, B3.

———. "Journalism's New Nation: New Journalism's Counter-Convention; Egos and Insult." *Washington Post*, April 26, 1972, D1–D2.

———. "*(MORE)* Party." *Washington Post*, May 4, 1973, B1.

Rachlin, Allan. *News as Hegemonic Reality: American Political Culture and the Framing of News Accounts*. New York: Praeger, 1988.

Raskin, A. H. "What's Wrong with American Newspapers? A Newsman's Critique of the Press." *New York Times Magazine*, June 11, 1967, 249.

Reedy, George E. "Moynihan's Scholarly Tantrum." *(MORE): A Journalism Review*, June 1971, 7.

Reese, Stephen D. "The News Paradigm and the Ideology of Objectivity: A Socialist at *The Wall Street Journal*." *Critical Studies in Mass Communication* 7, no. 4 (1990): 390–409.

Reese, Stephen D., and Jeremy Cohen. "Educating for Journalism: The Professionalism of Scholarship." *Journalism Studies* 1, no. 2 (2000): 213–27.

Bibliography

"Reflections on Hollywoodstein." *(MORE): A Journalism Review*, April 1976, 7–9.

Reisig, Robin. "The Biggest Freeloaders Around." *(MORE): A Journalism Review*, May 1972, 5–8.

———. "Is Journalism an Air-Brushed Profession?" *Village Voice*, May 16, 1974, 24.

"Review of Press in Bow." *New York Post*, May 18, 1971, 10.

Richardson, Peter. *A Bomb in Every Issue: How the Short, Unruly Life of Ramparts Magazine Changed America*. New York: New Press, 2010.

Ridgeway, James. "Exploits of 'The New Adventurers.'" *(MORE): A Journalism Review*, July 1972, 1, 18–20.

———. "Trying to Catch the Energy Crisis." *(MORE): A Journalism Review*, January 1974, 1.

Rigney, Daniel. "Three Kinds of Anti-Intellectualism: Rethinking Hofstadter." *Sociological Inquiry* 61, no. 4 (1991): 434–51.

Roddy, Joseph. Column Two. *(MORE): A Journalism Review*, October 1973, 2, 20–21.

———. "Judge Tyler's New Mature Courtroom." *(MORE): A Journalism Review*, April 1973, 13–15.

———. "The New Intellectuals." *(MORE): A Journalism Review*, July 1973, 16–17.

———. "Notes from a Bargain Typewriter." *(MORE): A Journalism Review*, November 1971, 3–5.

Rodgers, Daniel T. *Age of Fracture*. Cambridge, MA: Belknap, 2011.

Rubin, David M. "'Behind the Front Page.'" *(MORE): A Journalism Review*, November 1974, 7.

———. "The Perils of Muckraking." *(MORE): A Journalism Review*, September 1974, 5–9.

———. "You Are What You Eat." *(MORE): A Journalism Review*, December 1973, 7–9.

Salcetti, Marianne. "The Emergence of the Reporter: Mechanization and the Devaluation of Editorial Workers." In *News Workers: Toward a History of the Rank and File*, edited by Hanno Hardt and Bonnie Brennen, 48–74. Minneapolis: University of Minnesota Press, 1995.

"Sale of More Magazine Being Negotiated." *New York Times*, March 4, 1976.

Sanders, Keith P. "What Are Daily Newspapers Doing to Be Responsive to Readers' Criticisms? A Survey of U.S. Daily Newspaper Accountability System." In *News Research for Better Newspapers*, Vol. 7, edited by Galen Rarick, 148–51. Washington, DC: American Newspaper Publishers Association Foundation, 1975.

Sandman, Peter M. "Cross-Ownership on the Scales." *More: The Media Magazine*, October 1977, 21–26.

Sayre, Nora. *Sixties Going on Seventies*. New York: Arbor House, 1973.

Sayre, Nora, Richard Reeves, J. Anthony Lukas, David Halberstam, Joe McGinniss, Timothy Crouse, and Roger Wilkins. "Underneath the Nixon Landslide." *(MORE): A Journalism Review*, December 1972, 1, 15–17.

Bibliography

Schickel, Richard. "The Truth Went Thataway." *(MORE): A Journalism Review*, February 1974, 1.

Schmidt, Samantha. "Why hundreds of New York Times employees staged a walk-out." *Washington Post*, June 30, 2017. https://www.washingtonpost.com/news/morning-mix/wp/2017/06/30/the-new-york-times-is-eliminating-its-copy-editing-desk-so-hundreds-of-employees-walked-out/.

Schudson, Michael. *Discovering the News: A Social History of American Newspapers*. New York: Basic Books, 1978.

Schudson, Michael, and Chris Anderson. "Objectivity, Professionalism, and Truth Seeking in Journalism." In *The Handbook of Journalism Studies*, edited by Karin Wahl-Jorgensen and Thomas Hanitzsch, 88–101. New York: Routledge, 2009.

Schulman, Bruce J. *The Seventies: The Great Shift in American Culture, Society and Politics*. New York: DiCapo, 2002.

Schwartz, Tony. "Establishing the Levels of the Game." *More: The Media Magazine*, July/August 1976, 38.

Seldes, George. *Freedom of the Press*. Indianapolis: Bobbs-Merrill Co., 1935.

———. *Lords of the Press*. New York: Julian Messner, 1938.

Shafer, Jack. "The Church of Liebling: The Uncritical Worshippers of America's Best Press Critic." *Slate*, August 25, 2004. http://www.slate.com/id/2105627/.

———. "Move over Bezos, ESPN can do news better than you." *Reuters*, October 23, 2013. http://blogs.reuters.com/jackshafer/2013/10/23/move-over-bezos-espn-can-do-news-better-than-you/ (accessed October 24, 2013).

———. "Our National Pastime: Press Criticism." *Reuters*, April 10, 2013. http://blogs.reuters.com/jackshafer/2013/04/10/our-national-pastime-press-criticism/.

———. "The Rise and Fall of the 'Bus Plunge' Story." *Slate*, November 13, 2006. http://www.slate.com/articles/news_and_politics/press_box/2006/11/the_rise_and_fall_of_the_bus_plunge_story.single.html (accessed August 15, 2013).

Sherman, Scott. "The Long Good-Bye." *Vanity Fair* (web exclusive), November 30, 2012. http://www.vanityfair.com/culture/2012/11/1963-newspaper-strike-bertram-powers.

Sherr, Lynn. "Some *Mad* Predictions." *(MORE): A Journalism Review*, April 1972, 8–9.

Siegal, Allan M. "Introduction." In *Kill Duck before Serving: Red Faces at The New York Times: A Collection of the Newspaper's Most Interesting, Embarrassing and Off-Beat Corrections*, edited by Linda Amster and Dylan Loeb McClain, xi–xvi. New York: St. Martin's Griffin, 2002.

Siegel, Barbara J. "He'll Think You Baked All Day." *(MORE): A Journalism Review*, May 1972, 14.

Sigal, Leon. *Reporters and Officials: The Organization and Politics of Newsmaking*. Washington, DC: Heath, 1973.

Silver, Nate. "The Real Story of 2016: What reporters—and lots of data geeks, too—missed about the election, and what they're still getting wrong." *FiveThirtyEight*, January 19, 2017. https://fivethirtyeight.com/features/the-real-story-of-2016/.

Silverman, Craig. *Regret the Error: How Media Mistakes Pollute the Press and Imperil Free Speech*. New York: Sterling, 2007.

———. "Slate Shuts the Window: A Long-Overdue Corrections Policy Revision." *Columbia Journalism Review*, September 24, 2010. https://archives.cjr.org/behind_the_news/slate_shuts_the_window.php.

Smith, Robert M. "Why So Little Investigative Reporting?" *(MORE): A Journalism Review*, November 1973, 7–9.

Socolow, Michael J. "A Profitable Public Sphere: The Creation of *The New York Times* Op-Ed Page." *Journalism & Mass Communication Quarterly* 87, no. 2 (2010): 281–96.

Sokolov, Raymond. *Wayward Reporter: The Life of A. J. Liebling*. New York: Harper & Row, 1980.

Solomon, William S. "The Site of Newsroom Labor: The Division of Editorial Practices." In *News Workers: Toward a History of the Rank and File*, edited by Hanno Hardt and Bonnie Brennen, 110–34. Minneapolis: University of Minnesota Press, 1995.

Starr, Paul. *The Creation of the Media: Political Origins of Modern Communications*. New York: Basic Books, 2004.

Stephens, Mitchell. *A History of News*. Fort Worth: Harcourt Brace, 1997.

"(Still) Fighting over *The Phoenix*." *(MORE): A Journalism Review*, September 1972, 2.

Stillman, Deanne. "Make Way for the Show Biz Bards." *More: The Media Magazine*, October 1976, 23–31.

Strainchamps, Ethel Reed. "Why We Can't Say B——shit." *(MORE): A Journalism Review*, July 1972, 8.

Talese, Gay. *The Kingdom and the Power: Behind the Scenes at The New York Times: The Institution That Influences the World*. New York: World Publishing Co., 1969. Paperback edition, New York: Random House, 2007.

Tebbel, John. *Open Letter to Newspaper Readers*. New York: Heineman, 1968.

"Things to Do." *D.C. Gazette*, April 25, 1973, 9.

Thompson, Eric. "Lindsay Tosses Aurelio in Ring." *(MORE): A Journalism Review*, February 1972, 12–13.

Tifft, Susan E., and Alex S. Jones. *The Trust: The Private and Powerful Family Behind The New York Times*. New York: Little, Brown and Co., 1999.

"Tom Wolfe and His Dirigible." *(MORE): A Journalism Review*, July 1972, 11, 16.

Trillin, Calvin. "Further More: On Using Newspapers." *(MORE): A Journalism Review*, December 1973, 24, 22.

———. "U.S. Journal: Seattle, Wash.: Alternatives." *New Yorker*, April 10, 1978, 118–25.

———. "A Weekend in a Panel Colony." *(MORE): A Journalism Review*, June 1974, 15.

Tucher, Andie. *Froth and Scum: Truth, Beauty, Goodness, and the Ax Murder in America's First Mass Medium*. Chapel Hill: University of North Carolina, 1994.

Bibliography

Tuchman, Gaye. *Making News: A Study in the Construction of Reality*. New York: Free Press, 1978.

U.S. Bureau of Labor Statistics. *CPI Inflation Calculator*. http://www.bls.gov/data/inflation_calculator.htm.

Usher, Nikki. *Making News at the New York Times*. Ann Arbor: University of Michigan Press, 2014.

Van Gelder, Lindsy. "The Passionate Parvenu: A Guide." *(MORE): A Journalism Review*, October 1971, 5–6.

Volz, Joseph. "Post-Ombudsman." *(MORE): A Journalism Review*, January 1972, 3–5.

von Hoffman, Nicholas. "Pardon . . . Me." *Washington Post*, May 7, 1973, B1.

———. "Where Not to Find Your New Car." *(MORE): A Journalism Review*, November 1971, 1, 14.

Vos, Tim P., and Teri Finneman. "The Early Historical Construction of Journalism's Gatekeeping Role." *Journalism* 18, no. 1 (2017): 265–80.

Washington Journalism Review, December 1981.

WBAI Folio 13, no. 4 (April 1972). Available online at Internet Archive, http://archive.org/details/wbaifolio134wbairich.

"We Remember Dolly." *More: The Media Magazine*, January 1977, 14–17.

Welles, Chris. "Soft Times for Wall Street." *(MORE): A Journalism Review*, December 1971, 1, 10–13.

"What Is Journalism For?" *Columbia Journalism Review*, September/October 2013.

White, Jean M. "*More* Changing Hands and Changing Goals." *Washington Post*, September 1, 1977, B1, B12.

"The White House: Who's Kicking Whom Around?" Produced by Mark Goldberg. June 12, 1973. Courtesy of the Pacifica Radio Archive.

Whitney, D. Charles. "Begging Your Pardon: Corrections and Corrections Policies at Twelve U.S. Newspapers." Research report. New York: Gannett Center for Media Studies, 1986.

Whittemore, L. H. "The Plugging of the President." *(MORE): A Journalism Review*, February 1972, 4–6.

"Why a Counter-Convention." *(MORE): A Journalism Review*, May 1972.

William, Lambert A. *Our Press Gang, or a Complete Exposition of the Corruptions and Crimes of the American Newspapers*. Philadelphia: J. T. Lloyd, 1859.

Willig, Ida. "Newsroom Ethnography in a Field Perspective." *Journalism* 14, no. 3 (2012): 372–87.

Wills, Garry. "What's Wrong with This Magazine?" *(MORE): A Journalism Review*, June 1975, 6–8.

Witcover, Jules. "Media in the Mirror." *The Progressive*, July 1975, 28–29.

Wolfe, Tom. "The Birth of 'The New Journalism'. Eyewitness Report by Tom Wolfe: Participant Reveals Main Factors Leading to Demise of the Novel, Rise of New Style Covering Events." *New York Magazine*, February 14, 1972.

———. *The New Journalism*. New York: Harper & Row, 1973.

Bibliography

Woodward, William. Column Two. *(MORE): A Journalism Review*, March 1973, 2.

Wyatt, Wendy N. *Critical Conversations: A Theory of Press Criticism*. Cresskill, NJ: Hampton Press, 2007.

———. "Press Criticism." In *The International Encyclopedia of Journalism Studies*, edited by Wolfgang Donsbach. New York: John Wiley & Sons, 2018.

Yardley, Jim. "Heir to a Fortune, and to Tragedy; Suicide Ends the Life of a Wealthy, and Haunted, Man." *New York Times*, May 8, 1999. http://www.nytimes.com/1999/05/08/nyregion/heir-fortune-tragedy-suicide-ends-life-wealthy-haunted-man.html?pagewanted=all&src=pm (accessed January 22, 2014).

Zelizer, Barbie. "Journalists as Interpretive Communities." *Critical Studies in Mass Communication* 10, no. 3 (1993): 219–37.

———. "When Facts, Truth, and Reality Are God-Terms: On Journalism's Uneasy Place in Cultural Studies." *Communication and Critical/Cultural Studies* 1, no. 1 (2004): 100–119.

Index

Index

Index